Aging and Menopause
among Indian South African Women

Aging and Menopause
among Indian South African Women

Brian M. du Toit

State University of New York Press

SUNY Series in Medical Anthropology

Setha M. Low, Editor

Published by
State University of New York Press, Albany

For information, address the State University of New York Press,
State University Plaza, Albany, NY 12246

Library of Congress Cataloging-in-Publication Data

Du Toit, Brian M., 1935–
    Aging and menopause among Indian South African women / Brian M.
du Toit.
        p.   cm. — (SUNY series in medical anthropology)
    ISBN 0-7914-0389-0. — ISBN 0-7914-0390-4 (pbk.)
    1. Menopause—Social aspects—South Africa. 2. Aging—Social
aspects—South Africa. 3. Women, Muslim—South Africa. 4. Women,
Hindu—South Africa. I. Title. II. Series.
RG186.D87   1990
612.6′65—dc20

10 9 8 7 6 5 4 3 2 1

This book is lovingly dedicated to the women in my life
Nada, my mother
Sona, my wife
Helene and Desiree, my daughters

Contents

List of Tables

Preface

In their study of aging Karp and Yoels (1982:12) say, "To understand human behavior in terms of the aging process, we must identify the *meanings* attached to chronological age." That is the subject of the present study — an attempt to understand the meaning of the climacteric experience; and more precisely, the meaning of menopause for Indian South African women.

Along the way there have been a number of persons who have assisted knowingly or unknowingly to interpret this meaning. For a number of years Pat Kaufert has shared her insight and also her research devices. We have extrapolated from these in constructing our own research schedules and questionnaires. Others who have been helpful in the planning, execution or write-up of this material include Margaret Lock, Sonya McKinley, Yewoubdar Beyene, Dona Lee Davis, and Anne Voda.

The particulars of research design and approach emerged from hours of brainstorming and systematic planning in which David Suggs and Sharon Anderson shared. In the field, stimulation was engendered by David Suggs, Thea de Wet, and Sona du Toit, who participated in the cross-cultural project while studying women in other ethnic communities.

Formal support and financial assistance came from the Human Sciences Research Council in Pretoria and the University of Florida, which awarded me a sabbatical for study. Julia Lee Dulfer was responsible for editing and Carol Laine typed the manuscript with care and diligence.

In spite of all this planning and support, my greatest gratitude goes to the delightful people in Laudium. Without their acceptance and openness this project would have been doomed. There are a large number of people who assisted in various ways: fifty-six women who made time to share their experiences, hopes, and fears. They are the important people who give *meanings* to chronological age, who interpret their climacteric experiences, and who place menopause in its proper perspective. My hope is that I have been able to present their contributions. All names in the text of the study have been changed; but I must recognize the hospitality and kindness received from the following: Mrs. Choonera, Roshan and Anvir Mohamed, the Thakor and Carrim families (and Nazira who made time to translate), Mrs. Dockrat, Mrs. Kassim, Nurse Desai, and many others. Thank you!

1

ঽ঱

The Cultural Climacteric

Introduction

The aim of this discussion is to introduce the concept of *climacteric* while indicating some of the important studies conducted on this topic. We discuss studies in and contributions by a wide range of disciplines, but this study essentially employs the methods and concepts current in sociocultural anthropology.

Increasingly during the past decade or two, researchers have started to recognize the climacteric as a phase of the life cycle — a period of about 25 years (from 35 to 60 years of age) marked by three phases: premenopausal, perimenopausal and postmenopausal. The climacteric may also be described as spanning the later reproductive and early postreproductive years of a woman's life. The word *climacteric* is derived from the Greek root word *klimax* meaning "ladder" and by extension *klimakterikos* meaning "the rung of a ladder" or "steps of a staircase." It is thus applied to the stages a woman goes through from her later reproductive years, as hormonal and physiological changes occur, until she reaches the postmenopausal phase when menstruation has ceased and a permanent postreproductive phase has been achieved.

It is interesting to note that most researchers also recognize a male climacteric. Though men do not undergo menopause and do not reach a postreproductive stage, changes due to aging do occur in male physiology and lifestyle (see Jaszmann 1978; Featherstone and Hepworth 1985(a), 1985(b)).

Survey of Climacteric Studies

Studies can frequently be classified as having specific disciplinary foci because of the nature of the questions or the methodology employed by the researchers but may also span more than one discipline. The literature surveyed here is presented under subheadings only in an attempt to designate focus, not through a wish to pigeonhole the research or the results. Information dealing with the climacteric is central to all the research, irrespective of focus.

Psychological Perspective

In Neugarten et al. (1963), one finds a plea for more research into the psychology of menopause. That van Keep and Humphrey (1976) echo this call indicates that much remains to be done. Much of what has been done centers on psychologically determined menopausal *symptoms* (Cooke and Greene 1981; Greene 1976; Polit and LaRocco 1980). A great deal of the theoretical work in this area has been done by gynecologists and physicians (e.g., August 1956; Barnacle 1949; Fessler 1950; Ross 1951). Other factors which have received some attention are *personality* characteristics (Stern and Prados 1946; Ballinger 1975; Simon 1968) and *stress/life events* (e.g., Greene and Cooke, 1980; Greene 1980; Malleson 1956). With the exception of Datan et al. (1981); Maoz (1973); and Maoz and Durst (1979), there is virtually no work of a cross-cultural nature.

When approached from a psychoanalytic point of view, menopausal symptoms are said to be a reaction to a loss of femininity. A woman thus experiences a lowering of her self-esteem because, with atrophic vaginitis and related physiological changes due to hormone imbalance she may fear that her libido will weaken and lead to rejection by a sexual partner (Benedek 1950; Fessler 1950). This seems to be prejudiced not only towards the sexual preference of the authors (i.e., heterosexual) but also especially culturally prejudiced.

In a recent paper du Toit and Suggs (1983) discussed this approach. One could hardly have expected traditional women who were "pregnant, lactating, or dead" (Connell 1983) to be very concerned about the cessation of menstruation. These women would not have anticipated it as do modern Western women (Neugarten et al. 1963); to have been concerned about a loss of femininity or youth (Fuchs 1978; McCranie 1974); or to have expected menopause on time (Lennon 1982). In contrast to their modern American counterparts, preindustrial women would have experienced few negative psychological consequences. In fact, many would have welcomed whatever change in status occurred because it brought new roles. Such evaluations, however, would vary both individually and culturally. And we should keep in mind the increased status which follows becoming "like a man" in male-dominated societies — including greater mobility, access to ritual and religious activities, political importance, and greater individual freedom.

Brown and Harris (1978) have developed a model in which a person reacts to a loss event by drawing on internal and external resources. When a woman "develops profound hopelessness because of the feelings of low self-regard [which] she brings to the loss (event)" depression will follow. Self-regard or self-esteem then is the key factor; but we should remember that these evaluations (subjective as they may be) are a product of self-evaluation and other-evaluation. When the members of a society reward the attainment of a new life stage, a climacteric woman will have high self-esteem; when society members look down on such a person, it will result in low self-esteem. Using this model as a point of departure, Kaufert speaks of "a stereotype of menopause." She explains:

> A menopausal stereotype may present either a positive or a negative portrayal of the climacteric experience. If the stereotype is negative, it will pose a threat to the self-esteem of women in that society as they enter the peri-menopause. If the stereotype is positive, the menopause will be rewarding to self image.... A woman whose existing level of self-esteem is high will be less vulnerable to a negative stereotype than a woman whose level of self-esteem is low (1982(a):188).

Self-esteem, as we suggested, is a product of self-evaluation and other-evaluation within the cultural context in which women gain or lose status as they pass through the climacteric years. Almost universally such status derives from the woman's roles as wife and mother within marriage. It is logical, then, that if marriage and family bestow status, it is also in this context that status is lost. Obviously other status markers are present in all societies.

Being a woman, depends on biological and physiological features but is culturally defined and rewarded by members of the society. She grows in status and finally systematically sheds this status as she matures and passes through the climacteric. Derrick Stenning gives a very clear illustration for the Pastoral Fulani of northern Nigeria.

> When her homestead was set up she was given decorated calabashes, which were never used but proudly displayed on ceremonial occasions, symbolizing her milking right in virtue of her status as a mother.... But as her children married her responsibilities for feeding them ended, while her reproductive faculties declined. She gave her own decorated calabashes to her daughters until finally, on the marriage of her last daugh-

ter, her stock of decorated calabashes and her responsibilities as a mother, housewife and dairywoman came to an end (1960:98).

On this basis, we suggest that the menopause in preindustrial or traditional societies is not marked by the last of numerous and regular menstrual periods, but by the cultural definition of having fulfilled the role of wife and mother. The end product may be positively or negatively evaluated, but it is based on a cultural definition rather than a physiological phenomenon.

Life Events Perspective

A growing body of research has recently been given increasing attention in the literature concerning the sociology and psychology of aging. Rather than focusing solely on whether aging occurs within the realm of psycho-social stability or instability, this research strategy, called "life events analysis," regards change as a given, and examines *antecedents* which account for the adjustment...or lack thereof, to aging. Thus, "life events are most commonly defined as those events that create a demand for change in a person's life and that occur over a relatively finite period of time" (Chiriboga 1982: 595). Such an approach has obvious relevance to a study of the climacteric, but presents some methodological problems where the research is of a cross-cultural nature.

Evidence has recently been found which documents increasing psychophysiological changes among women during the climacteric (Moore 1981; Sharma and Saxena 1981; Utian 1980; Cooke and Greene 1981; Greene and Cooke 1980; Neugarten and Kraines 1965). While the bulk of this research has dealt with the causative locus of menopausal symptomatology, very little consensus has yet been achieved on the mechanisms involved. Nevertheless, most writers agree that "such events as the departure of children from home and the illness and death" of loved ones are the crucial events of a psychosocial nature, and that "such events are...effecting a profound change in the social role of women" (Cooke and Greene 1981:5). Furthermore, Utian (1980) notes that alternate roles for women during the climacteric have important effects in terms of decreasing the symptom profile associated with menopause (see also Maoz et al. 1978). However, it warrants mention that demonstrated empirical association between events and distress is currently only marginally established and is framed in terms of Euro-American culture.

One research finding of great importance is that "life stress [is] a more potent factor in influencing the severity of 'menopausal' symptoms at the climacterium than [is] the actual event of menopause" (Cooke and Greene 1981:9). Studies which have centered around the explication of this and related issues have typically utilized the life events approach, sometimes coupled with a measure of total life stress. This is a promising methodology; but it is, as Greene and Cooke (1980:490) note, a paradox that "there is no evidence that such life stress significantly increases at the climacterium." They suggest the general hypothesis that some proportion of women experiencing the climacteric is in a period of transition during which the women are unusually vulnerable to a large amount of normally tolerable, stressful life events. Also important is the discovery by several researchers (Brown et al. 1975; Cobb 1976; Miller and Ingham 1976) that "social support, in the form of friends and confidants, (ameliorates) the event-syndrome link" (Cooke and Greene 1981:10).

Sociologists have recognized that among the aging in Western society, "the number and kind of social contacts decreases; roles are literally lost as retirement, widowhood, the death of friends, and decreasing physical mobility leave the individual increasingly to his own resources. This may be viewed as a shrinkage of roles" (Bengtson 1973:18). While American women thus experience role loss, the literature indicates that women in many African societies experience a positive role expansion at the climacteric which affords them the opportunity of gauging the effects of such role changes in comparative perspective (see discussion under "Psychological," above). And with the proposed focus of this study on the family and kinship context, we have a fruitful arena for examining the impact of differential systems of social support on the experience of climacteric.

However, life-events schedules currently in use are constructed on a social model consistent with experiences of women in Western, industrialized nations. This of course limits their use in cross cultural research or studies in traditional societies without major adaptations. Furthermore, as Chiriboga (1982:595–596) notes, this is not the only problem with 'life-events' research efforts. Any schedule developed suffers from a necessarily narrow and selective range of events. Weighting the various items will be dependent on an initial series of subjective and individual perceptions of chosen events, because the standard weights will have dubious validity in a non-Western, non-industrialized setting. Indeed, Chiriboga questions the validity of the standardized weights for people in industrialized nations. Finally, it has been suggested that life-events may be:

neither as discrete nor temporarily fixed as suggested by adherents of this approach. [Stressful problems] often exist long before they become translated into marker events....[The] event-as-marker explanation points out the limitations of the basic life-events approach. To restrict the definition of social stress to life-events is to ignore a large domain of stress experiences with potential relevance to life course investigations. Examples of such experiences include anticipations of stress, being off-time, nonevents such as not receiving an anticipated promotion or not getting married, and chronic stress conditions...Future studies may do well to attend to the many dimensions of stress that are possible (1982:600).

Sociocultural Perspective

Age at menopause has rarely been studied in relation to social factors of any kind. There are some studies pertaining to variations of *socio-economic* status (Kisch 1928; Kamat and Kamat 1959; MacMahon and Worcester 1966). Works pertaining to the cultural relativity of menopause and menopausal "symptoms" include Flint (1975, 1976); Maoz (1973); and van Keep and Humphrey (1976). Anthropological studies are almost without discussions of menopause in part because of the low life expectancy of traditional peoples, but mostly because male anthropologists have spoken primarily to male informants. Various authors have suggested that one might profitably use ethnographies for understanding the relationship between status and role expectations in given societies and experiences at menopause. As life expectancy increases and as increasing numbers of women enter the infrastructure of developing countries, it is essential that we gain an understanding of the climacteric in cross-cultural perspective. We would emphasize that the life expectancy, health, and living conditions of traditional women make the attainment of biological menopause much less likely than cultural menopause, i.e., having produced and raised a family and reaching the "old woman" status with its positive or negative self-esteem. In a very interesting theoretical and descriptive paper, Skultans reports on her study of the menopause in south Wales: "It became apparent that the concept of the 'menopause' was a cultural rather than a biological one and that the concept was being used to express a cultural or social rather than a biological truth" (1970:640).

Thus, the event of menopause, namely the cessation of the menstrual flow, is a clinical event which may not necessarily coincide with changes in status and role, i.e., with a cultural definition of the change of life or with behavioral variables which Western physicians associate with the menopause. We would suggest that the cessation of menstruation is simply one of the markers of the life change. It may coincide more or less closely with the sociocultural markers which recognize this change.

Some of the earlier surveys of menopause were related to a "menarche and menopause" focus: thus Newcomer (1973) dealt with Micronesia, while Flint (1974) conducted an important study in India among Rajput women. The latter study provided much quantitative data, but it lacked ethnographic descriptive information to accompany the figures. Flint has continued to raise important questions about the menopause and also became involved in the discussion of whether attainment of menopause represented gains or losses, increase or decrease in status (Flint 1975; Kaufert 1982(a)), or possibly that it is viewed in a neutral way and has no significance (du Toit 1986). This may at least have applied to preindustrial traditional societies and may also now apply to postindustrial societies.

Sonja McKinlay conducted one of the early systematic research projects on menopause, first dealing with the age of menopause in London (McKinlay et al. 1972); and later, in Massachusetts, she and John McKinlay conducted "an epidemiological investigation of the menopause" (1985). The latter study involved a survey of eight thousand women who were mailed interviews or contacted by telephone. This work lacks the "hands-on" research methodology normally involving face-to-face interviews and case studies, which marks the studies to be discussed below.

Recently a number of studies have been conducted in which sociocultural variables were the primary bases for interpreting the findings. Over a number of years Pat Kaufert has been involved in a study of Canadian climacteric women. Her findings have been reported (1984) and discussed from different angles (Kaufert and Gilbert 1986). Kaufert (1982(a)) has also been at the forefront of theoretical developments in climacteric studies and was extremely helpful to us in planning the South African research by providing samples of the interview schedules she used in the Manitoba study. The advantage is that some of the same schedules have now been used in two or three cultural settings and are generating comparative data.

Part of the comparative picture is emerging from the work of Margaret Lock — first in a study of women in Montreal (1985) and later in a study of menopause in Japanese women (1986(b)). She comments that a "major problem to date with comparative studies into menopause has been the absence of a standardized approach to the collection of data" (Lock 1986(b):25). However, she used questionnaires originally developed by Kaufert and McKinlay for the Manitoba and Massachusetts studies. These questionnaires pertained to emotional reactions to aging (read menopause) and also to symptoms associated with menopause. The cross-cultural use of the same questions permit comparison of responses and explanations of differences. There are four questions which are reported by Lock that we used as well. Two of these are: (1) Do women worry about losing their minds during menopause? (2) Is a woman only half a woman and thus not a "real" woman after menopause? In the same way, she asked questions about symptoms which will allow comparison of responses. These comparisons and discussion will be treated in a different context. Also in the early 1980s, Marie Haug and her associates at Case Western Reserve University started research on menopause. Yewoubdar Beyene, a doctoral student, conducted a comparative study of Maya women in Chichimila, Mexico, and in Stira, a Greek village on the island of Evia (Beyene 1984; 1986). Once again Dr. Haug was kind enough to share with us the research methodology employed. In the meantime, Dona Lee Davis had concluded her work in a Newfoundland fishing village (1982; 1983). These studies represent the first ethnographies of the menopause.

As one part of the present study, a doctoral dissertation was produced on climacteric women in Botswana (Suggs 1986). Its subject was the coincidence of menopause and old age or at least the knowledge that menopause is a precursor for that life phase. Suggs explains that although not all women experience climacteric symptoms, their concerns regarding menopause "center around (1) their vision of a limited future in which to be productive and independent, and (2) an increased possibility for health-related problems" (1986:183).

A further study which needs to be mentioned is that of Emily Martin (1987), conducted among women in Baltimore, Maryland. Essentially, it is a cultural analysis of reproduction. In spite of the fact that 29 percent of her sample were in "the oldest life stage (menopause and postmenopause)" (1987:8), there is just one short chapter dealing with menopause. This discussion concentrates on hot flashes. Martin asks some critical questions about women's experiences in this context. Is there a correlation between embarrassment and hot flashes?; is there a relationship between embarrassment and social class?; is there a relationship between being anxious and social class? The implication is that the experience of hot flashes may be related to other factors. Although such flashes represent vaso-motor changes, not everybody will be equally conscious of them. If people are not anxious or conscious, would they even designate hot flashes as symptoms? The Japanese do not have a word to describe hot flashes (Lock 1986:33), but urban middle-class Japanese women reported less sweats and flashes than did farming women. Overall, Japanese women report a low incidence of classical menopausal symptoms. Also, the Maya recorded no symptoms except the final cessation of menses (Beyene 1986:58).

Davis, too, looks at factors which influence a woman's experience of "the change." Women in Grey Rock Harbour, Newfoundland, present a number of folk explanations of the role of "blood" and "nerves." Women can have "high or low blood," "thick or thin blood," and "bad or mixed blood." The woman's general health is related to the kind of blood she has. Menstruation results in the loss of blood and has the same function as purging the blood or relieving it of impurities (1983:136). Hot flashes for these women are a relief because they are believed to prevent high blood pressure from developing. Among the Greek women studied by Beyene, hot flashes were also related to blood. They saw the cause as blood boiling in the body (Beyene 1986:63). Because an early menarche meant early menopause and no children suggested a late menopause, the Maya believe that blood is used up in pregnancies and menstrual flow (Beyene 1986:59–60).

The women in Grey Rock Harbour, however, also differentiate between "blood" which refers to bodily processes in contrast to "nerves" which refers to behavior. Individual behavior is due to a person having thick or thin nerves, which are seen as "strings inside the body." A woman who has thick nerves is said to have "good," "more," or "strong" nerves. Thin nerves represent the opposite. Nerves are seen as causally related to menopause.

> Thus menopausal women in Grey Rock Harbour have several means of coping with their real and perceived problems of menopause, including doctors, stoic endurance, sympathetic friends and neighbours, participation in community-wide associations, and not least, an explanatory framework — nerves and blood — that spans all age groups and integrates the biological, psychological and social dimensions of menopause (Davis 1983:156).

In societies where menopause is recognized, it seems to be used as a marker to set aside reproductive versus postreproductive stages of the life cycle; middle age versus old age; or other aspects which are thought to be changed. Lock (1986:40–41) records that Japanese women do recognize the menopause as such a marker and Beyene (1986:64) finds it to be less important among Greek and particularly Maya women. For the American women studied by Martin (1987:176), it served as a milestone for some who could take stock and reach for greater happiness. This "reaching for" implies a positive outlook and, of course, life expectancy reaching beyond the mid-fifties.

Gerontological Perspective

The field of gerontology, like that of climacteric studies, is not a single discipline with a dominant research paradigm. It is interdisciplinary, incorporating the methods and theories of anthropologists, medical scientists, psychologists, and sociologists (Tibbits 1960; Birren 1960). There are a number of source books which include the basic formulations and contributions of researchers in each of these disciplines (e.g., Birren 1960; Birren and Schaie 1977; Binstock and Shanas 1976; Tibbits 1960).

Most of the sociological studies in gerontology deal exclusively with the Western world (e.g., Shanas et al. 1968; Havighurst et al. 1969; Schultz et al. 1968; Rosenmayer 1968; Clarck and Anderson 1967). Similarly, while there are some works pertaining to cross-cultural psychological aspects of aging (e.g., Gutmann 1971, 1977; Cowgill 1971; Briggs 1977), most studies deal with the psychological aspects of aging *in the West* (e.g., Eisdorfer and Wilke 1977; Ryff 1982). Furthermore, studies reviewed as being cross-cultural in nature are very often cross-national, a point which is not unimportant (see below). The disciplines of sociology and psychology meet in a common concern with, and consideration of, "life satisfaction" (e.g., Hoyt et al. 1980; Hoyt and Creech 1983; Liang and Warfel 1983; Usui et al. 1983). The instruments which are used to measure life satisfaction, being based on Western experience, are not designed for cross-cultural investigation. Therefore, this work again is largely limited to the Western world. Further limitations exist, however. The "International Issue" of *The Gerontologist* (Vol. 15, No. 3, 1975) contained not a single contribution on either Africa or women.

Anthropologists studying gerontological issues have, for the most part, emphasized (1) the crucial importance of cross-cultural data for understanding the *process* of human aging, and (2) the differential impact of variant culturo-ideological systems on the *experience* of the elderly.

Prior to 1960, anthropological studies concentrating on aging were very few in number (Fry 1981), the most commonly cited research being that of Simmons (1945) although most ethnographies dealt superficially with the life cycle and older people. The emphasis, however, was on men. The Human Relations Area Files extracted this ethnographic data and it was this material which Simmons used and from which he argued that, in cross-cultural perspective, status varies greatly with regard to age. He also suggested that there was an inverse relationship between the extent of technological development and the status of the aged. Several authors (e.g., Cowgill and Holmes 1972; Cowgill 1971) have since given support to this contention, while others (e.g., Bengston et al. 1975; Palmore and Manton 1974) have argued that the relationship is not so simple. Jack Goody (1976) has provided a more recent survey of the ethnographic data regarding aging in the nonindustrialized world, and Fry (1981) has outlined the major issues in current anthropological studies of aging. These works all indicate areas where cross-cultural data have proven useful in understanding the process of aging. They have given us insights into the position of the elderly and illustrated status and role changes in various social systems. Against this cross-cultural perspective, however, has to be seen the view of Kuhlen who states: "[T]he basic concern of this volume is with the restrictive years, with the years of decline, of loss of significant role, withdrawal from activities..." (1960:862).

Several authors have sought to examine specific cultural regularities in the pattern of treatment of the elderly in the Third World (Benet 1974, 1976; Cox and Mberia 1977; Kertzer and Madison 1981; Myerhoff 1978; Osako 1979; Rogers and Gallion 1978; Shelton 1965, 1968). By and large, such studies have yielded insight into the impact of ideological structures on the experience of the aged.

Finally, Nydegger (1981) and Fry (1981) have produced summary works which point to the role of anthropology in gerontological studies. Far too often, the roles of anthropology (cross-cultural) and comparative sociology (cross-national) have been considered to be equivalent (see, e.g., Maddox and Wiley 1976), and the work of the above four authors is important in implicitly distinguishing these fields of study.

There are three factors which make this gerontological literature of only tangential value to a discussion of the climacteric here proposed: first, except for the anthropological literature, research has been largely confined to the Western, industrialized nations. We hope we need not emphasize the futility of generalizing research findings from these areas to the entire world. Second, there is a clear lack of literature pertaining to *middle-age,* that period coincident with the climacteric. As Dolores Borland says,

> Several researchers...have called attention to [a] void in knowledge about middle age...[and] the over-emphasis on the stage of old age impedes understanding of the aging process (1978:379).

Third, the review indicates, as noted (du Toit and Suggs 1983), anthropology's general neglect of women and women's issues. The work of Sinnott (1977), Kline (1975), and Kertzer and Madison (1981) are exceptions; but only the latter deals with a non-western society. Related to this is the paucity of studies on aging in India or among communities of Indian extraction. Speaking of the need for field research in cross-cultural settings and the collection of data to serve as a base for theory generation, Gutmann has remarked: "Lacking an adequate cross-cultural theory, as well as an extensive body of cross-cultural research, we can only make educated guesses as to the relationship between social phenomena and psychological well-being of older individuals in various societies" (1977:430).

Physiological Perspectives

The literature on physiological factors affecting age at menopause is sparse. *Racial differences* have been noted in age at menopause (Kisch 1928; McMahon and Worcester 1966), but causal mechanisms have yet to be explicated. Much of the literature concerning physiology and menopause reflects the physicians' interests in *endocrinology* (Grodin et al. 1973; Sherman et al. 1976; Vermeulen 1976) and *estrogen replacement* therapy for treatment of symptoms (Lauritzen and van Keep 1978; van Keep and Haspels 1977). Flint (1976) and van Keep and Kellerhals (1974) have noted that the experience of such symptoms varies cross-culturally, and have called for more work in this important area. As van Keep and Humphrey (1976) also note, the nearly complete lack of research incorporating medical histories is a major lacuna in the literature.

Clinical studies, which constitute the bulk of menopausal studies in the U.S. and Western Europe, view the climacteric and the menopause as essentially due to the aging of the ovaries and resultant hormonal changes, especially a deficiency of estrogen. This in turn is associated with depression, irritability, sleeplessness, headaches, and vasomotor changes such as hot flashes, sweating, and atrophic vaginitis (Achte 1970; Ballinger 1975; Barr 1975; Wentz 1976). We already know that some of these do not occur cross-culturally, especially among people in Third World countries, or at least do not occur with the same intensity. This is true where people may even lack a word designating menopause as such, i.e., the cessation of menstruation. This is discussed by Flint (1974) for the Rajput of India and Beyene (1984) for the present-day Maya.

Environmental Perspective

By comparison to studies on menarche, very little has been done concerning the relationship between environmental factors and menopausal age. Exceptions include Cruz-Coke (1967) and Flint (1974) on the effects of altitude and Kisch (1928), Stopes (1936) and Abrahamson et al. (1960) on the effects of climate.

Cross-cultural Perspective

With the exception of Flint and to a lesser degree Datan and Maoz, none of this work has had a truly cross-cultural purpose or design. That is, cultural factors were not the objects of study. That cross-cultural studies on the menopause are needed is clear from the number of authors calling for such research (Dougherty 1978; Flint 1976; The Lancet 1982; van Keep and Humphrey 1976; Utian 1980).

A related problem pertains to the terminology being used to refer to this event. Here, as in other contexts, we find a lack of precision and the confusion of physiological, biological, and sociological terminology, as we read about women who have "passed their climacteric" (Ashton 1967:100), are "past child-bearing" (Lawrence 1957:124), or have "passed the menopause" (Nukunya 1969:153).

The continuing work of Datan and associates (Datan et al. 1970; Datan et al. 1981) has concentrated on differences in the experience of menopause among women in five Israeli subcultures. Many of their conclusions are more psychological than socio-cultural in orientation, but they have shown that the degree of cultural stability/instability (with regard to change) may have important effects on the experience of climacteric.

Summary

It is clear from the above literature that women in various world areas experience menopause differently. Corresponding environmental and physiological variation has been shown to provide *partial* explanation for the differences. But no research has been done which would provide scientists with insight into the degree to which culturally patterned behaviors and attitudes explain this variation. Furthermore, there is a lack of dependable descriptive information on which to base generalizations. Because of the variety of methodological approaches, there is little opportunity for meaningful cultural comparisons. There has been no attempt as yet to generate a standard methodology which would be appropriate for studies of a cross-cultural nature.

The need for a standard methodology is evident not only from a survey of the literature but also from repeated calls for studies in the *cross-cultural realm* — which standardization would make possible. A Consensus Development Conference on Estrogen Use and Postmenopausal Women (N.I.H., September 13–14, 1979) expressed the need for intensive studies of social and cultural factors influencing the menopausal experience. This statement equally implies that such standardization is necessary. An editorial in *The Lancet* (1982) called for studies of the menopause in developing countries and especially for focus on the sociocultural significance of menopausal changes. Flint (1976), Dougherty (1978), Utian (1980), and Kaufert (1982(a)) joined in this call though each singled out specific subjects of focus.

Greene and Cooke (1980:487) also showed the need for a study to include two samples of women: a younger group who are premenopausal and an older group who are postmenopausal. The authors use "preclimacteric" and "postclimacteric," which I feel is not what they had in mind. For the study reported here we learned from earlier researchers and built on their findings. This book reports on Indian South African women, one part of the overall study. A later volume will deal with cross-cultural aspects.

2

๏

The South African Scene

The History of Indian South Africans

The population of southern Africa is marked by diversity of history, origin, ethnic group membership, language, and other cultural factors. Much has been written about the traditional African settlers, the whites who arrived in 1652, the Indian laborers most of whom were brought in after 1860, and the other ethnic groups recognized by the South African racist Population Registration Act (1950). The largest of these groups with the longest residence in southern Africa is the so-called Coloured population group.

This chapter will deal only briefly with the population groups in southern Africa as we outline the backgrounds of the women who are included in the overall study. It should be kept in mind that ethnic, linguistic, and cultural differences are balanced in part by the uniform tradition of a British-type administration, school system, medical model, and other systems. Thus, while Indian and white (Afrikaner) reside in what is today the Republic of South Africa and the Tswana reside in what is today the Republic of Botswana, these groups share a great deal outside of their traditional cultural matrix.

When the discussion turns to that part of the population which is of Indian extraction, three primary differentiating criteria immediately come to mind: caste, language, and religion. Minor criteria like color and economic activity are covered by the history and regions of origin or caste and linguistic groups.

Because of the mix of labor migrants who came to Natal and the conditions under which they lived, caste soon lost its importance. Many had left their mother country without parental blessing or left their home villages without formally taking leave. They could neither return (even if they had the means) nor maintain ties with their traditions. Some groups retained differences because certain family names designated status, and certain groups (such as the Telegu speakers) were rejuvenated by visitors from their home country who reaffirmed their identity. But to a major extent, caste became blurred with (economic) class and being a "good" family. "Good" was derived from linguistic and religious group membership but also from socio-economic status. Even today, the criteria of linguistic group membership and religion are seen as important.

The population of the Indian subcontinent represents two major ethnic categories: the native Dravidian and the Aryan. These groups are represented by differences in phenotype, but it is really in the linguistic groups they represent that the significance lies. The Dravidian peoples occupied most of southern India and are represented by the four major language families: Tamil, Telegu, Malaylam, and Kanarese. Languages associated with the Aryans, who are thought to have crossed the Himalayan mountain range, were originally found in northern India. They are Hindi, Urdu, Gujerati, Memon, and Konkani. Most of these groups were represented by migrants to South Africa.

Religion, however, is superimposed on the linguistic group, which frequently has dialect differences representative of regions or even villages. Indians were originally largely Hindu, but missionaries representing Islam and Christianity made major inroads. The earliest Muslims travelled from Persia and Arabia in the fourteenth century and had a major effect on the belief systems of the northern peoples. This is especially true of the Urdu speakers, some of whom "claimed descent from the Prophet himself" (Meer 1969:16). At a much later time, Christian missionaries entered India. They worked among southern and northern peoples. A small percentage of Indians in general are classified as Christian.

Indian immigration to South Africa really dates to 1860, but "the first Indians to come to South Africa were slaves, brought by Jan van Riebeeck in the 1650s. Over 50 percent of all Cape slaves during the seventeenth and eighteenth centuries were Indian, from Bengal and Southern India" (Meer, ed., 1980:4). The ancestors of persons interviewed for this study came to Natal mostly as indentured laborers, or slightly later, as either free immigrants or passenger Indians. When the Republic of Natalia was annexed by Great Britain in 1843, it became a district of the Cape Colony and thus subject to direct British administration. Most of the Boer frontiersmen left during the following five years, and their places were taken by some five thousand European (mostly British) settlers. Their arrival and subsequent economic initiative, particularly in the expansion of the sugar industry, created a need for laborers, who could not be obtained locally at that time.

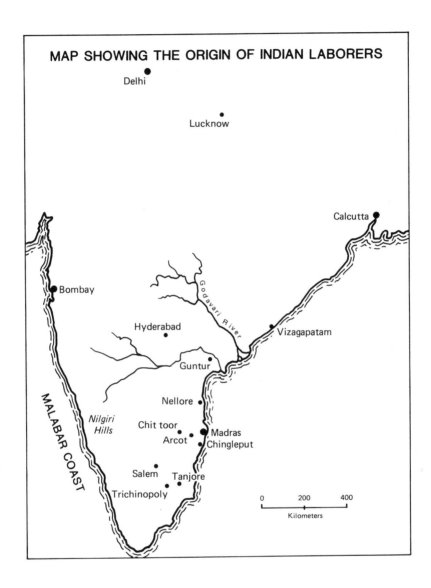

MAP SHOWING THE ORIGIN OF INDIAN LABORERS

Therefore, a public meeting was held in Durban in October 1851 to discuss this most critical need. Various solutions were debated, including the importation of laborers from the East; but no definite steps were taken. In 1855, Sir George Grey, the recently appointed governor of the Cape Colony (and thus high commissioner for Natal), visited that province. The question of labor was brought up during a trip to a sugar estate and Grey expressed his preference for Indian rather than Chinese laborers. Laborers of both nationalities had been used extensively in other areas under British control.

Indians were used as indentured laborers in many sugar producing colonies such as British Guiana, Mauritius, Fiji, and the West Indies, especially Trinidad. With the dissolution of the English East India Company in 1858, the peoples of India came under the direct control of the British government.

Upon Grey's recommendation, the British government, both in England and India, eventually agreed to such a transfer of laborers. Natal Law No. 14, which dealt with the introduction of laborers from India, and Natal Law No. 15, making it possible for persons to import (at their own expense) immigrants from India, were soon promulgated by the Natal government.

In 1860 the Indian Act XXXIII was passed, permitting the emigration of Indian laborers to Natal; and on October 12 of that year the first ship, the Truro, sailed from Madras. Most of the early recruits were from the Madras Presidency and were pariahs. Indian laborers also came from upper Pradesh, Madhya Pradesh, Orissa, Western Bengal, and the northern and northeastern districts. Later migrants, the so-called passenger Indians, came from Kathiawar, Porbandar, and Surat, as well as from Bombay and the northern provinces. Their numbers, however, were relatively small. A few were Muslims although a small number belonged to the Sudra Caste. During the next six years, more than six thousand laborers left Madras and Calcutta. Between 1866 and 1874, emigration was temporarily held up while the living conditions of Indian migrants in Natal were being inspected (Kondapi 1951:21).

Most of the Indian recruits belonged to the agricultural class, for whom the epithet "coolie" in time became a derogatory term used by both English- and Afrikaans-speaking South Africans of different colors. These Indian workers were originally imported to work on sugar plantations, but they usually left at the end of their indentures. They were soon employed in dockyards and railways in Durban, in coal mines further inland, on smallholder gardens, and finally in domestic employment and municipal service. Few ever saw the country of their birth again.

The diversification of life styles which was emerging is clearly described by Chattopadhyaya. Quoting first from the annual report for 1874–75 by the Protector of Immigrants in Natal, Colonel B. P. Lloyd:

While between 7 and 8 thousand (Indians in Natal) are employed on the estates along the coast, the remainder are scattered over the colony in various capacities as domestic servants, traders, storekeepers, market-gardeners, boatmen, fishermen, etc. The Indians still enjoy a monopoly of fishtrade, and a very large proportion of the vegetables and not a little of the fruits, consumed by the Europeans in the towns of Maritzburg and Durban, are grown by them. They are rapidly acquiring land and many are now competing with their masters in agricultural pursuits. I am of the opinion that the coolies hold over 1,000 acres of land in the Manda division alone. They pay on an average of £1 per acre per annum and are most industrious, working morning, noon and night.

The author then continues:

According to the report of the Natal Economic Commission, 1814, 'the indentured Indian of the early days, when his term of service expired, often took up land and grew vegetables, mealies and tobacco. To a certain extent, he reindentured and took service with Europeans, but of late years he has increasingly entered the semi-skilled trades. Today he is engaged in the building trades, printing, boot-repairing, tailoring, painting, mattress-making and other miscellaneous callings of the semi-skilled trades. Many so engaged are Natal-born Indians, and numbers who speak English are employed as cooks, waiters, drivers, vanmen, and in lawyers' offices, as junior clerks and touts' (1970:66).

After the temporary emigration halt of 1866 to 1874, indenturing was resumed and continued until 1911. For some idea of the numbers involved: Kuper (1960) found that from 1883 to 1890, 11,501 persons sailed for Natal from Madras and 4,925 from Calcutta. By 1911, though, the largest proportion of original laborers had left the sugar plantations and had become "free" Indians. Some did return to India under a government sponsored repatriation scheme, which included a cash bonus; but the majority became permanent residents of South Africa.

   In addition to the indentured laborers, a large number of free passenger Indians migrated to Natal. These were persons who came under the ordinary immigration law, paying their own way and enjoying citizenship rights until these were changed (Pachai 1971).

The immigrants were commercially motivated and nearly all went into business in Natal and Transvaal. Such persons were mostly Gujerati-speaking Muslims, Hindus, and some Urdu-speaking Muslims. A smaller group were Parsees from Bombay and were Zoroastrians by religion (Kuper 1960:8).

The Indians who became a permanent part of the South African population were thus composed of the two major ethnic categories, the seven or eight major linguistic groups, and the major religions of India. "There were a conspicuous number of Christians on the Truro, hailing largely from the village of Itchepoorum in the Zillah of Goryam in Malabar" (Meer [ed] 1980:7). No community can remain viable and perpetuate itself if it is not represented by men and women from the same cultural background. The law stipulated that a minimum proportion of every shipload of "recruits" (many of whom had been trapped, cheated or abducted) had to be women. "Ships often waited for days because they did not have the necessary 25 percent (women) of the cargo. The recruiters, in despair then scanned the city and picked up whatever they could" (Meer [ed] 1980:4).

Like Indian immigrant communities the world over, e.g., Fiji (Mayer 1961; Gillion 1962), West Indies (Klass 1961; La Guerre [ed] 1974), and Central Africa (Dotson and Dotson 1968), the South African Indians retained many of their traditions stemming from language and religion and the fact that these two criteria were the major considerations in marriage. Most of the Hindus are nonvegetarian, but do not eat beef (which is prohibited by their religion); Gujerati-speaking Hindus are largely lacto-vegetarians, and Muslims avoid pork (also due to religious prohibitions) (Mistry 1965). Dietary preferences or restrictions have not changed a great deal.

Desai discusses the conditions in South Africa at the beginning of the century when the Indian immigrants, most of whom were Hindus, were experiencing rapid culture change.

> They soon began to adopt the customs and festivals of other religions and to forget their own. These pioneers were illiterate. They did not have any acquaintance with their own culture nor were they sufficiently and firmly rooted in their Hindu faith. Missionaries of other faiths found in them fertile soil for evangelistic work. Indians born here became imitators of the culture and civilization of the West (1960:91).

There was an obvious need for revitalization or for a religious-cultural organization — even with a linguistic group focus — to give them direction and to assist in community-based welfare programs. Thus, the Maha Sabha was formed to serve the needs of the community, and was revived whenever it tended to lapse into a state of somnolence. In time it created a charitable trust which was registered with the provincial administration. As Lalla explains:

> Ever since its formation, the Sabha has been faced with the problem of poverty among the Hindus and the serious consequences flowing from it. It was aware that many Hindu families, unable to survive the battle for bread, had succumbed to the temptation of bartering their faith for food. Moreover, the ugly spectacle of men and women, old and young, in rags and tatters, soliciting alms in the streets, was undignifying to the Hindu community. To these derelicts of human society, Hinduism could have no meaning and to speak of charity as one of the fundamental principles of religion smacked of hypocrisy (1960:110).

Through their languages, taught at a variety of vernacular schools after the regular day school, Indians of different language groups have retained some of the philosophy, ethics, and values of the past. Telegu, for example, was losing ground against other languages, especially English. In 1929, however, Sir Kurma V. Reddi visited South Africa and encouraged the formation of the Andhra Maha Sabha. Today there are about thirty mother-tongue schools and a department of Telegu at the University of Durban/Westville. But it is a losing battle as most persons under twenty-five years of age cannot converse in this language (Naidoo 1979), and increasing numbers use English or Afrikaans as home language. Bekker (1977: 326) reports on a survey by S.A. Naicker of 757 sixth graders in a Durban school. He found that 95 percent spoke English at home. In a survey of high school seniors in Durban, du Toit (1990) recorded 86.2 percent of the students claiming English as their home language. It is interesting that language and religion sometimes separate: we read that the Telugu Baptist Mission has done much for the fostering of the Telugu language (Brochure 1981:8).

Although the Indian laborers had originally been imported to work in the coastal region of Natal, they soon moved into other regions. These include not only towns in the interior part of the same province, but also towns and cities in Transvaal. The latter province contains the second largest concentration of persons of Indian descent, with population concentrations in Johannesburg and Pretoria (see Table 1).

TABLE 1

Population Figures for Asian South Africans

Geographical Category	Census 1985		HSRC Adjusted Total Compensating for Undercount	
	Number	Percentage	Number	Percentage
Natal	659,703	80.3	691,781	80.3
Transvaal	126,201	15.4	132,338	15.4
Cape Province	31,989	3.9	33,544	3.9
Orange Free State	53	–	55	–
Rest of S. A.	3,415	.4	3,582	.4
Total	821,361	100.0	861,300	100.0

Source: Population Census 1985: Geographical distribution of the population with a review for 1960–1985. Report 02–85–01. Pretoria: Government Printer, September 1986.

Before promulgation of the Group Areas Act (No. 41 of 1950), Indians who had trade stores and markets lived in or near them in towns and cities, frequently in the melting pot of a slum where people interacted daily with those of another color, language, religion, and background. Many of the women who form the subject of this study recalled living in Pretoria's slums, but the Group Areas Act forced them into uniform ethnic residential communities or dormitory cities. This has resulted in a whole generation of South African children who have grown up in isolated white, black, or brown neighborhoods. One such artificial residential arrangement is the urban area known as Laudium, just outside Pretoria. Here Indians live and play, but every morning rows of automobiles leave for Pretoria or Johannesburg where these same men and women conduct their national and international business. The dormitory city contains small retail stores, schools, clinics, mosques and temples, a hospital, and a teachers' college — all of which offer limited local employment but do not really integrate with the South African economic infrastructure. For this reason, too, English in Natal and English or Afrikaans in Transvaal is usually the home language of Indians. Many will indicate that their parents spoke Hindi or were from a particular linguistic tradition, but increasingly the official languages of South Africa are becoming the home languages of the educated Indian.

The Position of Indian South Africans

As happens frequently in migration patterns, specific groups or particular categories of persons might preponderate in one locale as compared with another. This was true in South Africa as Indians migrated inland, being excluded by law from residence in the Orange Free State but settling in Transvaal. As Mistry (1965:693) points out, it is generally accepted that the Transvaal Indians, when compared to their cousins in Natal, are more westernized and urbanized, economically more advanced and better off, and include greater proportions of Muslims and Gujarati speakers. This material is presented in Table 2.

In selecting the research sample from the Indian community, attention had to be paid to the linguistic and religious-group membership of the women. Mistry (1965:694) presents a useful summary

TABLE 2

Home Language of Asian South Africans

Predominant Language Used	Transvaal		Natal		South Africa	
	Number	Percentage	Number	Percentage	Number	Percentage
Afrikaans	3,951	3.4	883	0.1	10,010	1.2
English	78,789	68.0	588,009	89.0	691,495	84.5
Gujerati-Memon	15,725	13.6	8,047	1.2	24,788	3.1
Hindi	713	0.6	20,252	3.1	22,020	2.7
Tamil	568	0.5	20,253	3.1	21,125	2.6
Telegu	49	–	2,921	0.4	3,009	0.3
Urdu	2,018	1.7	9,622	1.4	11,982	1.4
Other & Mixed Asian languages	14,095	12.2	11,182	1.7	34,773	4.2
TOTAL	115,908	100.0	661,169	100.0	819,202	100.0

Source: Population Census 1980. Home language by statistical region and district. Report No. 02–80–10. Pretoria: Government Printer, January 1985.

TABLE 3

Religion of Asian South Africans

Religious Group Membership	Transvaal		Natal		South Africa	
	Number	Percentage	Number	Percentage	Number	Percentage
Hindu	37,249	32.1	475,268	71.9	524,913	64.1
Muslim	58,459	50.4	92,513	14.0	165,842	20.2
Christian	12,937	11.2	76,271	11.5	100,973	12.3
Other (Buddhism, Confucianism, etc.) and no religion	7,263	6.3	17,117	2.6	27,474	3.4
TOTALS	115,908	100.0	661,169	100.0	819,202	100.0

Source: Population Census 1980. Home language by statistical region and district. Report No. 02–80–10. Pretoria: Government Printer, January 1985.

of Indians who immigrated to South Africa from India. They belonged to the following groups:

A. Dravidians
   a. Hindus:
      i. Tamil-speaking
      ii. Telegu-speaking
   b. Christians
B. Aryans
   a. Hindus
      i. Hindi-speaking
      ii. Gujarati-speaking
   b. Muslims
      i. Urdu-speaking
      ii. Gujarati- and Memon-speaking
      iii. Konkani-speaking

All of these linguistic groups are well known, except the Memons. They derive originally from the Kathiawad peninsula and were early converts to Islam — in fact, a Believer was a Momeen. Like the Kathiawadi Hindus, the Memons are known for their keen business sagacity. It was reported "that 10 Kutchee Memons and 1,225 Kathi-awadi Memons had settled in the Transvaal" (Mayat 1981:82). No dates are given. This business acumen is also recognized farther afield. Dotson and Dotson (1968:140) mention that in the Zambia-Malawi area "they have a stereotyped reputation for great shrewd-ness." They quote a higher caste member that a "Memon can leave India with only a penny in his pocket and go anywhere in the world and eventually become a millionaire." A major characteristic we found was great pride in being Memon.

Brief mention needs to be made of two major ethnographic sources which supply comparative and background information on Indian South Africans. Fatima Meer, a member of this community, was born and grew up in Natal. For the past three decades, she has written about her people, offering valuable insights. *A Portrait of Indian South Africans* (1969) presents not only a thorough overview of Indian culture but also rare insights in the form of vignettes of daily life. Her study of suicides in South Africa is a masterly treatment of crisis behavior as it relates to racism. Academically of equal importance is the work of Hilda Kuper who, while she taught at the University of Natal, made a thorough study of the local Indian — particularly Hindu — community. She also worked with Leo Kuper, her husband, on studies of race and color in Durban and South Africa generally. *Indian People in Natal* (1960) is monumental for its historical depth and ethnographic thoroughness. Together, Meer and Kuper present a balanced and empathetic understanding of Indian South Africans, their cultural traditions, and their lives during the 1950s and 1960s.

With this background knowledge about the population groups and the census data presented in Table 1, we aimed at selecting study participants who would be representative of this sample population.

Studying Indian South African Women

During a sabbatical year in 1984–85, I directed an extensive research project titled, "The Climacteric in Cross-cultural Perspec-tive." Done in southern Africa, this study included contempora-neous comparative studies of five population groups: urban Indian, urban black, rural black (Botswana), urban white, and rural white.

Methodology included selection of the subjects according to clearly defined criteria and the subsequent gathering of quantitative and qualitative responses over a twelve-month period. The aims

were: 1) to reach an in-depth understanding of aging and the menopause among women representing each sample population; 2) to
gather comparative data by using the same questions in all cases;
3) by the use of standardized research devices, to arrive at information which could be compared within each population sample,
between the populations in this project, and between different populations where the climacteric has been studied.

A question which might well be asked is why, in a study of the
climacteric with a focus on the menopause, we did not include a
perimenopausal sample of women. In our original research design,
we had, in fact, included such a third category; and it would have
permitted certain conclusions about the event itself. The decision to
omit it was made, however, as we progressed in the preparation of
the interview schedules. We arrived at an ideal research sample
which would permit statistical analysis, and a decision was made.
We would be hard-pressed to complete all four interview schedules
with sixty women; it would have been impossible to do so with
ninety. Since we wanted to contrast pre- and postmenopause, get
recall of perimenopause and get anticipation from the premenopausal women, the decision was a practical one. Rather a complete
and elaborate study of sixty women than a survey of ninety. Using
two cohort groups who were distinct enough in age and experience
would also satisfy the suggestion by Greene and Cooke (1980) for a
study of the before and after view of menopause and simultaneously allow us a generational contrast.

According to the research design, each population sample
needed thirty premenopausal women, about thirty-five to forty-five
years old. We also needed thirty postmenopausal women, about
fifty-five to sixty-five years old. The former category were all married
and menstruating regularly, though many indicated that they hoped
their childbearing role was completed. All of the postmenopausal
women were, or had been, married and had reached their condition
due to natural aging and ovarian failure rather than from surgery.
Unless a woman had had a double oophorectomy, however, she
would still go through menopause, and the critical criterion was that
she retained at least one ovary. A postmenopausal woman is defined
as one who has not menstruated for at least twelve months.

Because the complexity of laws has created a segregated society
in South Africa, ethnic groups occupy different residential areas. To
the west of Pretoria are two large such areas, one for blacks (Atteridgeville) and another for Indians (Laudium). It is with the people
in Laudium that we dealt primarily.

Shortly after arriving, we visited the Laudium Hospital where I was introduced to a young Indian social worker. She offered her assistance and during the first weeks of the study we visited homes. She introduced me to a woman she knew both socially and professionally, and we got the research launched. On a number of occasions I joined the hospital staff for tea and discussed the research with some very interested and informed members of the staff. Among the women who wanted to participate in the project was the matron of the hospital. Within days the superintendent, an Afrikaner, ordered the staff not to cooperate with "the American." As a result, the matron withdrew as one of our research subjects, and the social worker was fired. The project continued with the enthusiastic support of the women in Laudium and the medical personnel associated with the clinic.

To find research subjects, I used the friendship networks of persons already cooperating. However, variables of religious, linguistic, and socioeconomic group membership were deciding factors. After meeting a prospective subject and explaining in some detail the research aims and methods, it was always necessary to go through three steps: making sure that she was premenopausal and menstruating regularly; or that she was postmenopausal (having reached that condition naturally); and noting finally her religion, language, and economic status. Because we were interested in contrasting and comparing the two menopausal samples in the study, quantitative data is always presented separately for each category.

Using these criteria, the sixty subjects were selected. During the year's research, we returned at least four times to each for lengthy interviews. A number of subjects dropped out, leaving a final sample of twenty-nine pre- and twenty-seven postmenopausal subjects. Of these fifty-six women, forty-two were married, thirteen widowed, and one divorced. The mean age of the premenopausal women was 41.8 and the median forty-three. For the postmenopausal women, the mean age was sixty and the median sixty-one. With early marriage and motherhood stated ideals among Indians we can thus postulate these women as truly representing two generations. Table 4 shows their subgroup membership as regards language and religion.

The project under discussion attempted to move away from the biomedical model in the clinical setting to a cultural-behavioral model in the home and social setting. The project further envisioned comparing data from Third World situations while contrasting such variables as rural-urban, religion, and language. It had recently been

TABLE 4

Home Language and Religious-Group Membership
of Women in the Indian Sample

Home Language	
Tamil	13
Gujarati	11
English	11
Memon	10
Afrikaans	8
Hindi	3
Total	56

Religious-Group Membership	
Hindu	26
Muslim	25
Christian	5
Total	56

emphasized that "information from developing countries in particular is scanty; there are virtually no data on such basic matters as the age distribution of the menopause; and little is known about the socio-cultural significance of the menopause in different settings" (The Lancet 1982). In a different context, Utian points out that "the response to menopause is modified by many factors, one important one being the socio-cultural environment....Certainly, far more attention needs to be directed at the socio-cultural aspects of menopause and much more recognition given to its role in the overall mechanism of symptom production" (1980:114-115). In preparation for the study and as part of the research design, I met every morning for months for about an hour with graduate students David Suggs and Sharon Anderson. In the beginning, we used these sessions to brainstorm the kind of questions we would ideally like to ask. At a later stage, we searched the literature for questions which would add to or replace ones we had already formulated. We received some interview schedules that Pat Kaufert had used, and we incorporated some of those questions. As a dry run, Suggs and I administered an adaptation of the Neugarten et al. (1963) attitude index to women in an American city and included the adapted list of items in our cross-cultural interview schedule. This was phase two of the preparation.

We now started to organize the hundreds of questions resulting from the brainstorming sessions. Could we organize them according to topic or theme, arrive at a topic per interview, or organize a couple of topics per interview?

At the last stage, we arrived at not only a final set of questions but also additional devices, e.g., a set of nonverbal tests that could be applied across linguistic and cultural lines and a nutritional survey. The latter was not completed for lack of time. The interview schedules which resulted from these planning sessions were organized into four lengthy schedules, each covering a number of topics. Each topic was covered by an extensive array of questions, both quantitative and qualitative, thus permitting more extensive questions and answers. It is possible that other researchers might notice a question or approach of theirs in our data without having received credit. If so, I say thank you for making it available. The reason you are not listed is certainly not a conscious omission — it is simply that all the information out there has been tapped and incorporated. We attempted a saturation approach to this topic. We did not achieve it but do feel that the four interview schedules, which require a total of at least ten hours each to complete, provide the data we need.

It is also necessary to say something about the writing style employed in this study. With a few exceptions I have employed the editorial "we." This does not reflect on the research. Every interview was conducted by me personally and I did all the data gathering. To be grammatically correct, therefore, "we" is "I."

During the four visits with each research subject, interview schedules were used which systematically dealt first with personal background; family and kinship; and socialization. The next visit discussed "being a woman" (both role and image); support groups and networks; coping behavior; and information flow — including information about menopause. I returned a third time to discuss life style and life course (past and present). By this time I had known each woman at least nine months, had been in and about the community, and had visited each house at least three times — though by this time social visits were increasing. I now turned to the most personal and confidential topics of the research. In a lengthy fourth visit, we explored medical history (including general health); family history; menstrual history; and reproductive health. I then turned to climacteric beliefs (physiological, cognitive, and behavioral); menopausal symptoms (expected and experienced); sexuality (including reproductive sex, variations and expression); and finally personal sexual experiences.

Interviews were always conducted in private with the subject alone. In most cases, the interviews were conducted in the living room or at the dining room table. But a researcher must accommodate the needs of those being interviewed. One lengthy interview was conducted while Mrs. Naidoo, a seamstress, was completing a wedding dress on assignment. I was asked to hold, measure and baste while she did the finer more important work. Arriving at Mrs.

SOUTHERN AFRICA:

Indians reside essentially in Natal and Transvaal

Ebrahim's home on Thursday , I found her feverishly cleaning the kitchen for the weekend. Since Mrs. Ebrahim was no taller than four-feet-ten inches, she could not reach the top shelves to clean off bottles of jam, home canned fruits, atjar, and chutneys. And so, between bottles and plates and dust cloths the interview progressed. The most enjoyable interview, however, was definitely done while "we" prepared, made, and fried a large batch of samoosas. The curry-aroma that hung in the kitchen is still very clearly imprinted... as is the flavor on my taste buds.

3

꽃

Population Description

Introduction

The aim of this study was meeting the Indian woman in her home and family. Since this is the normal and expected milieu for these women, we focused on this natural setting. An Indian woman is a member of a kinship group, and she achieves her current status as housewife through socialization and acceptance of roles envisaged by her parents. The most important role is that of mother; but she must also administer a household to the satisfaction of her husband.

For each of these two roles there is a culturally sanctioned ideal— a proper way. Such ideals result in patterned forms of behavior, in actions and choices which are rewarded; in short, in expressions of culture which differ from one society to another, exacting rewards for adults who perform the roles correctly and praise for young persons who follow them as blueprints for behavior.

Population Profile

The original selection of participants produced thirty women in each category; but for a variety of reasons, the final sample contained twenty-nine pre- and twenty-seven postmenopausal women.

A brief explanatory note on the age of these women seems appropriate. We planned to have two contrasting cohort groups, one representing a premenopausal status and aged between thirty-five and forty-five; the other representing a postmenopausal status and aged between fifty-five and sixty-five. These are ideal and relative age categories. When we got into the field and found persons who satisfied all criteria of menopausal status and linguistic and religious group but were somewhat below or above the strict (but relative) age criterion, the latter was overlooked. After all, the criterion was pre- versus postmenopausal status, and that requirement was met.

Premenopausal. Of this sample, twenty-eight were married at the time of the study and only one widowed. (The spouse of a second woman died of a heart attack just before we completed the study.) The population of Transvaal originally derived from the settlers in Natal, and while they had close family ties in Natal, the Cape Province, Maputo, and even India, the local group had significant time depth. Thus eighteen (62.1%) had been born in Transvaal, eight in Natal, one in the Cape, and two in India. The oldest woman in this category was forty-eight, the youngest thirty-four. The mean age was 41.8 and the median was forty-three. When discussing the educational background of the research participants, we touch on an interesting and contrasting subject. The younger women as a whole have had a much better opportunity to attend school than their mothers. Among this premenopausal category, all had some schooling and five had more than twelve years. Thus, the sample included college lecturers, teachers, registered nurses, homemakers, and workers.

Postmenopausal. The twenty-seven women in this category had all been married, but one was divorced and twelve were widowed. It is quite unusual to find a divorced woman, particularly one representing the older generation. In this case the man had simply walked out after the birth of their son and never returned. The woman worked at any and all jobs she could get and raised the son, who qualified as a teacher shortly before we completed the research. Most of these women, namely twenty-one (77.7%), had been born in Transvaal and two each had been born in Natal, the Cape, and India. The women in the younger category who had been born in India were, in fact, born of South African mothers who returned to India for parturition. In the older age category, the women had come to join husbands but were born of Indian nationals (see Table 5). In this category there is quite a range of age. The oldest woman was seventy-five and the youngest forty-two. The mean age was sixty; the median was sixty-one. Living conditions were different for the older generation. Women recounted the domestic conditions encountered while living in a slum or in the same building as a trade store. They also spoke of the attitude of conservative fathers. After experiencing menarche, girls were not permitted to remain in school, especially if it was coeducational. Some of the strongest feelings of resentment were expressed when the women told of how much they loved school, how well they did, what ideals they had, what a positive role model a teacher was... "but my father was old fashioned and strict." The result frequently was that a thirteen-year-

TABLE 5

Place of Birth of Women in the Indian Sample

Place of Birth	Premenopausal	Postmenopausal
Transvaal	18 (62.1)	21 (77.7)
Natal	8 (27.6)	2 (7.4)
Cape	1 (3.4)	2 (7.4)
India	2 (6.9)	2 (7.4)
Total	29	27

old girl had to stay home to cook, assist her mother, or serve behind the counter in a trade store. Among the women in the older category, only one (3.7%) had more than twelve years of schooling and seven (26.0%) had no schooling whatsoever. The one woman who had advanced training is unique. She broke out of the mold, being permitted by a widowed mother (with financial support from an uncle) to improve herself. She ultimately became the first registered Indian nurse in Transvaal and the first Indian matron of a hospital. Today this sweet little old lady cares for her grandchildren as it becomes any "decent" (Indian) grandmother.

Age of menopause. One would not expect a great deal of empirical knowledge in a folk community, particularly on a subject about which specialists may disagree. It is important to state that participants in this study were interested in the material because, as a number of them pointed out, it was not a subject which they discussed or thought about on a regular basis. When a woman reached menopause, she might discuss changes she noticed with a friend; she might visit a physician to be reassured that she was not pregnant. She did not then dwell on her condition or the subject. As will be the case in most folk communities regarding empirical information, we found a range of impressions and attitudes based essentially on personal experience or what could be recalled about such experiences. What is interesting is that when the women were asked about the age of menopause, the two groups did not differ significantly. In fact seventeen (58.8%) premenopausal and nineteen (70.3%) postmenopausal women gave an age range of forty-five to fifty. (See Table 6.) This no doubt is based on personal experiences or the experiences of relatives and friends. However, I was told repeatedly that women do not discuss menopause or changes which accompany it. They certainly do not anticipate the cessation of men-

TABLE 6

Expected Age of Menopause

Age	Premenopausal	Postmenopausal
0–39	1 (3.4)	2 (7.4)
40–44	9 (31.0)	2 (7.4)
45–49	10 (34.4)	14 (51.8)
50	7 (24.1)	5 (18.5)
51–54	1 (3.4)	2 (3.7)
55–+	1 (3.4)	2 (3.7)

struation, nor do they consider its likely effects, physically or mentally.

There is no terminological change designating a postmenopausal woman because the knowledge of menstruation is a very private affair. Life-cycle changes and particular status change due to family composition and the birth of offspring may be recognized terminologically and interactionally, but these are not marked by menopause. One woman explained, "nobody knew about menstruation except the woman and maybe her husband."

Social Organization

Indian South Africans have retained some important features of the traditional social organization from which they derive. They, in many cases, have adapted and changed to fit in with a new setting. The roles of religion, language, and family have retained their importance as organizing forces, but the caste organization and structural isolation have largely disappeared. Kuper states it quite succinctly: "Coming as labourers, not lords nor even traders, the indentured Indians could not impose (or even maintain) their traditional values and social structure. Caste developed in a pre-industrial social system encircled by village boundaries and supported by a peasant agricultural economy; it inevitably declined when the boundaries were globally shifted by migration, and when home crafts were replaced by the technological developments of modern industry" (1960:20).

The Kutum and Joint Family

Perhaps the single most important social group in the Indian community is the patrilineal core of a familial and residential group known as *kudumbam* or *kudumor* amongst Tamil and Telegu speakers, and as *kul* or *kutum* amongst Urdu, Hindi, and Gujerati speakers. Kutum was the original Sanskrit term used in classical Hindu law. In time it became generally known and will be used in the context of this discussion. Jithoo (1970) speaks of the kutum as the joint family; Kuper (1960) uses the term to describe the extended family, and Meer (1969:64) states that the term defines "a kinship system of several nuclear families hierarchically arranged by male seniority."

If we look in more detail at the compositions of this group, we find a number of extensions which will effect descent members and spouses. Following Kolenda (1968) and Shah (1974), Jithoo (1978) deals in more detail than the other authors with the composition of the joint family. She distinguishes four aspects (which we will refer to in a number of contexts in the body of this study) of the joint (extended) family. These are the genealogical aspect, the fact of co-residence, the commensal aspect, and the common or coparcenary aspect.

The primary aspect which marks the *kutum* is that it is a genealogical group. This has prompted Mayer (1960:169) to speak of it as a "unilineal descent group of up to three generations," while also allowing for the term to refer to a group "whose members recognize agnatic ties in some circumstances and uterine links in others" (1960:170). Gupta (1974:47) speaks of "the kindred group or kutumb which embraces agnates and cognates," while Shah (1974:116-121), basing his approach on Hindu law and jurisprudence, also arrives at a wider, more embracing definition. The most important concept relating to this aspect of the kutum is the structural one which implies the joining together of virilocal patrilineal joint families in such a way that a number of nuclear families are joined into a larger group by the patrilineal ties which bind the male heads of these families. But the structural linkage, though necessary, is only part of the overall characteristic.

The nuclear families must reside together. Gupta (1974:47), states that the kutum shares "a common dwelling," while Ishwaran (1974:164) says the joint family members "reside in the same dwelling." The normal pattern, to be elaborated on in our discussion of marriage, is for adult sons to reside with their parents, and as they marry, to bring their wives "under the same roof." This may be a temporary condition lasting a number of years while they await independent housing.

A third aspect marking the kutum is that members will all eat food "cooked at one hearth" (Shah (1974:113); that they all "share a common...cooking hearth" (Gupta 1947:74; Ishwaran 1974:164). While the same hearth may be used and is frequently presided over by the mother of the sons or by the wife of the eldest brother, it does not require that all the members eat together. The men of the joint family may eat alone, the women and children in a separate group. This is particularly true in traditional families where women are housebound and their husbands are employed outside.

A fourth aspect marking the kutum is that of being *coparcenary*. This term derives from Hindu law. "Membership of the coparcenary is confined to the male descendants in the male line from a common male ancestor up to four degrees inclusive" (Derrett 1963:249). The implication is that members of the family own property in common, frequently a family estate inherited from the father, which later may be partitioned between the sons or grandsons. Gupta (1974:47) says they "pool their incomes and property, [and] spend jointly for all purposes." Ishwaran (1974:164) also states that they "own property in common." Although it is true that only men are coparceners, "the wife, widowed mother, and widowed daughter-in-law have the right to maintenance, and even to a share in property according to the shastric texts and modern statutes...." (Shah 1974:118)

The kutum, joint and extended family as it is, is flexible because it permits a certain degree of leeway for interpretation. Women may be excluded or included; they may be isolated or incorporated; they may be given little respect or bestowed honored status. Kapadia states this very nicely when he explains: "A joint-family of a man, his wife and children, his parents, his dependent brothers and sisters, is founded on emotional intensity: it is sustained by moral obligation and is backed up by public opinion" (1966:307).

It is interesting that the kutum, with its structural aspects just outlined, has persisted among Indian South Africans. In the first decades after settling in Natal, individual families occupied what space was available to them. In time, as their economic conditions improved, some large families could afford quite sizeable homes which permitted the coresidence of joint family members. When the Group Areas Act (1950) forced Indians into separate residential areas, it had one advantageous effect. People were moved from existing single-family style dwellings or squatter quarters to separate areas where the government had built uniform single-family homes or apartments or — and this is important — allowed owner designed/owner built homes. The result is that in Laudium (as is the case in Durban/Westville or Lenasia near Johannesburg), some impressive mansions have been erected. Repeatedly one hears it said among whites that the Indians have too much money, or don't know what to do with their wealth and, therefore, build elaborate structures for display. It is only in getting to know the families involved that you find many of these residences are in fact "the big house" — the residence of the joint family. In many cases, the father heads a major business and the sons are involved in the same concern. Thus, as they marry, the sons bring their wives into this large home. When the father dies, the eldest son normally continues to reside there, though younger brothers may move out as their families grow.

The inhabitants of a number of these separate residences, some smaller or larger but spatially separated, form a kutum. Each group of "house people," having a separate residence, recognizes the most senior male as "house head." But, over and above this is the kutum head. Many younger and less traditional Indians no longer recognize the kutum and its role.

Speaking of Indian South Africans, specifically those living in Natal, Fatima Meer points out that the kutum is actually like a large family whose members have obligations and privileges. It could, for some people, be the core of their social universe; a core within which they visit, perform ceremonies, have social interaction, and relax.

> Irrespective of the composition of his immediate household (nuclear or otherwise), the average Indian is firmly rooted to his *kutum*. His *kutum* consists of all those with whom he can trace consanguinity through a common paternal grandfather or grandfather's brother. The average size of the Indian nuclear family has been variously stated to be between 6.1 and 8.8 persons. These are the essential members who must attend all informal occasions, ranging from picnic parties to the more exclusive ceremonies which precede formal engagements, weddings and prayers. The *kutum* is a restricted kinship group tracing descent through a male head, in which the classificatory principle defines relations between members. Members of a *kutum* are in similar relation to each other as members in an immediate family.... (Meer 1969:66)

Their immediate reference and interactional group is the family, especially members of the nuclear family.

The Family of Orientation

The domestic group. In spite of some important changes due to secularization, education, and economic conditions, the Indian family contrasts sharply with the family among other ethnic groups.

We have already discussed the joint family through which more than one nuclear family constitute a household. Traditionally, Indian marriages were arranged or involved infant betrothal and some of the postmenopausal women fell in this category. Indian families are also marked by the small number of widowed, separated, or deserted women who live alone or with minor children.

Within the family there is a delicate balance between sex, age, and kin relationship. Males always take precedence over females, even among children; seniority always is primary, as in the kutum; and consanguineal ties are always more important than affinal ones. The use of "always" in the previous sentence implies ideal and expected behavior; exceptions are present but extremely rare. Thus in the family, both Hindu and Muslim, the patriarch or senior male had complete authority. He not only controlled the family income and expenditure but always decided upon actions by family members such as marriage proposals or negotiations. Mothers had authority over children, male and female, but an adult son might have certain rights which contradict this statement. However, respect relationships avoided confrontation. Marriages resulted in a rotation of women; daughters left and daughters-in-law joined the family. A mother who controls the household and supervises a daughter and a daughter-in-law will invariably give preference to the former as she assigns duties for cleaning, caring, and cooking.

The women in our study sample indicated that they spent their childhood years predominantly in families of the nuclear or extended type. Thus twenty-seven (93.1%) of the premenopausal and twenty-one (77.8%) of the postmenopausal women grew up in homes with both parents or such homes where grandparents were also present. The latter category might have involved the child and her parents still living with the grandparents in a joint-family arrangement. The second most frequent residential category was that in which either the father or mother was deceased.

These families of orientation were frequently added to as grandparents or uncles and aunts visited. Not infrequently these relatives were from India. Among the postmenopausal women there were thirteen (48.2%) who had one or more grandparent who either resided in India or who had come from India. If the visiting relatives resided in India, the parental couple had either gone to South Africa or one of the pair had immigrated. Grandparents were dearly remembered. "My father's father was the head of the family and very strict," one woman remembered; another explained, "My father's mother was partly a substitute mother after my mother died." This role was frequently filled by brothers and sisters of the parents. It was particularly a younger aunt who may have been a confidante, giving advice about morals and sex or explaining the occurrence of menarche.

Of the premenopausal women, nine (31.0%) stated that at least one grandparent came from or lived in India. While some of these women indicate that the grandmothers spoiled them, about the same number speak of a distance between them caused by discipline or because the father's mother did not like her daughter-in-law. One explained, "There were bad relations between mother and all of my father's family because mother only had daughters." Once again we find that female siblings of either parent often became very close "on girl things" and supplied information about menarche. Important in the context of the Indian family, they also "warned us about boys." The context is one in which girls were never allowed to be alone with boys, and from puberty this was very strictly enforced. An aunt might serve as a chaperon on excursions, and if she herself were young, she might be slightly more permissive than a parent would. Such allowances are not forgotten.

The ultimate responsibility for child rearing obviously rested with the parents. It seems that strict discipline and supervision were as much aimed at moral protection as safeguarding the family name. The father and mother were the persons with most at stake. Generally speaking, those families that were socioeconomically most secure, in part because of original caste status, having gone to South Africa as passenger migrants rather than as indentured laborers, and/or because of coparcenary commercial enterprises, could insist more on the maintenance of tradition in terms of mate selection, supervision of children, and continuity of traditional family patterns. The members of a single nuclear family who were also poor and lacked kin support were more likely to disperse.

The parental homes of the women who participated in this research, were quite uniform. In most cases the mother was a homemaker, administering the cooking, cleaning, and child care. If she had a daughter-in-law, that facilitated matters; but frequently she was solely responsible. In fact, twenty-three (79.3%) of the premenopausal women and sixteen (64.0%) of the postmenopausal women grew up in homes where their mothers were involved full time. Most of the rest, six (20.7%) of the pre- and eight (32.0%) of the postmenopausal women had mothers who were self-employed. Among the latter are some interesting cases. Mrs. Munsamy tells of her mother, a short heavy-set woman who always wore her traditional sari and earned money by selling curry and rice. She and her husband, a tall gentleman who was born in India and migrated to South Africa, decided after thirty years to return to India for a visit. The husband remained there while the wife, Mrs. Munsamy's mother, return to South Africa because "she could not do farming and preferred life in South Africa."

Mrs. Kassim's mother was also forced to earn money as a hawker assisting her husband. As a teenager he had run away from home in an Indian village and migrated to South Africa, "a place where money grew on trees." Arriving in South Africa he was taught to wear boots (no boots, no pay!), to wear pants instead of the traditional dhoti (a long loincloth worn by Hindu men). Although the dhoti can be gathered between the thighs, Mrs. Kassim remembers her father complaining bitterly about the icy cold mornings in Transvaal; but he refused the discomfort of pants.

The strangest case was that of Mrs. Joosub. Her mother was Afrikaans-speaking because her parents had "given" her to a white family when she was six or seven years old. "I was like a child in the white family," she said, "and we were like grandchildren. They really loved us. You know, the old white Afrikaners loved us more than they loved the English." Thus, even after her Muslim marriage to a tailor out of Kashmir, Mrs. Joosub's mother had to visit the white family every few weeks. The tailor, however, suffered from diabetes. As his health deteriorated, he decided to return to India, leaving his wife and children. Mrs. Joosub remembers her mother making ends meet by dress making and selling cakes that she baked.

The premenopausal women whose mothers had worked included three Hindu and three Muslims, none of whose husbands came from India. For recent migrants not having had kutum support was influential in forcing the older generation's women into the market place; this factor did not concern the younger women. Two of the six women were forced to become self-employed because their husbands were alcoholics (both Hindus) and two because their husbands just could not earn enough as part-time wage laborers. A fifth worked in her husband's business and was extremely active outside the home. Mrs. Mohammed was the daughter of a Muslim father who was remembered as being very sociable and generous. However, his wife (Mrs. Mohammed's mother) had only daughters. As she failed to produce a male child, her mother-in-law urged her son, under Islamic law, to marry another woman. This especially affected the domestic relationship when his second wife had two sons. In time he went to live with his second wife at the insistence of her father's mother. Mrs. Mohammed's mother became withdrawn and less sociable. She had to start a sewing and dress-making business to provide for the needs of herself and her daughters.

If we focus on the fathers of our research sample, we find that only eight (27.6%) and six (23.1%) respectively among the pre- and postmenopausal women, were regularly employed for wages. Most were self-employed. Among the premenopausal category twenty (69.0%) and among the postmenopausal group, nineteen (73.1%) were self-employed. They owned a store, a butchery, a taxi, a wholesale business, and a variety of other economic ventures which guaranteed financial independence.

Indian families were generally large. This guaranteed that children grew up with siblings; that the older ones soon learned to care for younger ones; that cousins in an extended family always had age mates; and that a support group developed early. These advantages carried over into adulthood when kinship ties and bonds of amity served individuals beyond the household.

Age and sex are important factors influencing relationships in the domestic situation. Boys are favored, in part because they satisfy the mother-in-law and other affines who want an heir but also because, in the economic sense, they ultimately represent a partner for the father and security in old age for the mother. Thus boys receive special favors, they are permitted free time, and are not required to do household chores. They are also favored in educational opportunities.

Brothers are soon taught to look after their sisters and to protect them if it is required. Older brothers may escort sisters outside the home; they may take them to the movies or accompany them to a party. They have surrogate authority and may assume legal authority should parents decease. "Among the Gujerati-speaking Hindus the bond between brother and sister is given expression in an old custom known as Rakshabandan, a festival when the sister ties a yellow string on the wrist of her brother and in return he gives her gifts" (Jithoo 1970:90). With a blessing from the priest this relationship is given a sense of permanence even after the marriage of one or both.

Among siblings of the same sex, seniority regulates the relationship. The status of eldest, however, is not one to be misused but one which requires giving assistance and support. The bonds between brothers carry over into adulthood, particularly within the kutum or when there is a coparcenary commercial enterprise at stake. There is, of course, the possibility of rivalry, jealousy, or quarrels. Sometimes a man may break with the family and go it alone. Such friction is particularly possible after the death of the father, who held the kutum together.

The relationship between sisters is less formal and tends to wane as they marry and move away. It should be kept in mind that girls used to marry at an early age and to establish ties in their new homes. Among Hindi speakers it was quite common for two sisters to marry two brothers or for sister-brother exchange marriages to occur. Tamil-speaking sisters often encouraged marriage between their children. In fact, one of the Tamilian women in the postmeno-pausal sample had received a marriage proposal from her mother's sister on behalf of her son.

The role of religious group membership cannot be over empha-sized because children are educated, formally and informally, within a certain moral and philosophical code.

Socialization. Talcott Parsons (1965) remarked that the family has two basic functions, one dealing with the socialization of the child, the other in providing security for the normal adult. In the Indian context, these functions are really only two sides of the same coin. They are interrelated because the child who has been social-ized within the values, behavior patterns, and expectations of a linguistic and socioreligious tradition and who is expected to marry a person essentially from the same background, should develop into a secure, normal adult. It is only when this pattern is interrupted, e.g., by education of women, that new expectations are awakened or new consciousness regarding their status is brought home to them.

Decision making. Given the structure of the Indian family and its residential arrangement, it is not strange to discover the domi-nant domestic role of the mother. She is the first person to interact with a child and she is always available. Even in the case of servants who take care of and feed the child, as is increasingly the case in the higher socioeconomic class, the mother is normally close. She is also the person to whom a young girl goes if she wants anything. While some of the fathers of the women in this study were seen as "push-overs," they normally were stricter, more distant, and generally unavailable because they worked outside the home. Most of the women in both research categories indicated that when they needed special permission, they turned to their mothers. In some cases this was true because the mother had authority in the home, in others because she was willing to approach her husband, and in still others because of the nature of the mother-daughter relationship. Two responses from the older category of respondents are clear. "She was the one I could confide in," stated one woman. Another said, "Mother always listened and had plenty of time for us. She was my only best friend." This statement is important because most of the older women described strict parents, restricted mobility, few close outside friends, domestic responsibilities at an early age, and usually early marriages. The aim of socialization, particularly among these conservative people was best expressed by one woman who said, "Mother wanted to bring up reputable girls." This theme is present throughout. Don't do anything that will shame your family. For this reason, it was better to let the parental generation make important decisions — even about marriage — because they know best. Children should always consider their families; they should make decisions and take actions which would not reflect negatively on the family and (especially women) should remember this throughout their lives. This made the female universe somewhat more restricted and monotonous with somewhat fewer choices available.

In those cases where a mother was deceased or was forced to work outside, leaving the children at home, we found that kinswomen or kinsmen took over the role of supervision. These persons in order of frequency are brother's wife, mother's mother, elder sister, and elder brother.

We should keep in mind that the Indian male is the undisputed household head; that this status position is sanctioned by both the Hindu and Islamic faiths; and that it is anchored in the family structure. The father, then, makes the final decisions about most matters pertaining to wife and children. Comments frequently heard: "Father was the strict disciplinarian; we feared him." "Father laid down the rules. Very simply, don't go out with boys and there would be a good mood at home." "Father was altogether too strict. We were not allowed to talk to boys. We were not allowed to dress the way we pleased."

Discipline. Discipline took a variety of forms, from direct corporal punishment to grounding and forced prayer. Some fathers (and mothers) used a variety of forms of physical punishment such as a strap used sparingly, a belt or "a rolling pin on our legs" or, in another case, "over the knuckles." In one case, the father was strict but fair. When one of the three children caused trouble, all of the siblings were beaten. This resulted in their watching over each other. Other parents simply used their hands to administer a few slaps. Normally this form of punishment was restricted to pre-teenage children, but one woman is still very resentful about a remembered incident. "Father slapped me," she said. "I was about fifteen and had been out with a girlfriend. We happened to meet a boy I liked and we came home late. He asked where I'd been. I said, 'I'm a big girl now,' and he slapped me. I was fifteen." "Tamilians are strict," one woman stated, and to illustrate she explained, "I was about nineteen or twenty. We were in our room laughing out loud. Father came in and hit me with a stick, saying girls must not laugh aloud and people in the street must not hear."

A variety of withholding punishments were as frequent as the physical punishment. Mother might, for example refuse to give a girl a new dress for some ceremony or she might be grounded and not permitted previous excursions such as Saturday afternoon "bioscope" (movies). The withholding of spending money was the most common punishment of this type.

In a number of cases, Muslim fathers forced their children to pray. "He would make us pray, even in the middle of the night." one woman explained. Another was sent to her room for long periods of time and told to pray.

The most common form of punishment was scolding. But one woman explained that her father never "punished" the children. He made them sit down right in front of him and talk it out. It seems that all forms of punishment achieve their desired aim — normally, obedience. "Dad only once gave me a spanking — after that he would just widen his eyes, raising his eyebrows, and we'd sit still." Boys received more physical punishment than girls, but girls were kept more strictly in line. Girls got punished for petty things that boys would not be punished for.

As the mother was most frequently approached for special permission, she was also most frequently employed as mediator. When some special permission was needed, the mother was asked to intercede with the father. In a few cases though, where there was a strict mother, the reverse was true. Others frequently approached were an older sibling, a sibling's spouse, or a grandmother (either maternal or paternal). Most women looked back on their childhood with a chuckle — no doubt seeing matters in perspective since they now occupy the parental role.

Role models. It is normal for people to have role models who are close to them as youngsters. These may be parental figures, grandparents, or other kinsfolk. They may also be people outside the home environment. There are a variety of reasons why someone is remembered, often depending on the personality and experience of the child, herself, but such an impression may last a lifetime.

Almost uniformly, the persons who were best remembered were those who affirmed these young Indian girls who, though loved by their parents and kinsmen, were almost all denied intellectual growth. Almost all were restricted in their movements and social life and prepared solely for life as a wife-mother-homemaker. Not all of them resent it, but some did.

What are the reasons that these Indian women, after forty years or more, still remember certain people? The people were from different ethnic backgrounds and included a "Tamil lady"; "Miss Manley, our English teacher"; "Mr. Noble, he was a Coloured"; and a number of teachers in the *madressa* (vernacular school meeting in the afternoon). Most frequently such people were teachers who: taught what was right; treated the youngsters with respect; encouraged students and made them feel wanted in class; taught positive values; gave advice on how young girls should behave. These are the same issues which concerned the parents, especially the fathers; but they were better reinforced by extrafamilial role models. Other parents who were involved were in a religious context, e.g., the *molisab* (leader at the madressa) or a priest who gave good advice — one woman said, "He drew me out because I was very shy and interested me in community oriented work." Of a teacher another older woman explained, "...she gave her love, we are still friends after forty years."

In the younger category of women, almost every person who was remembered was a teacher. (It will be recalled that the premenopausal category had better opportunities to attend school and have a higher level of education.) Some of those who were remembered were a white school principal who took one afternoon a week to teach crocheting; a Hindi teacher who taught more than just the language; an Indian male teacher who made a girl aware of her worth as a girl/woman, hygiene, menstruation, etc., and a number of teachers of different genders and ethnic backgrounds who praised, reinforced, encouraged, and showed interest in their students. It was also interesting to find out what kind of person these women admired, i.e., those not associated with them but whom they looked up to, admired, or emulated. As one can imagine, there was the usual group of movie actors, actresses, and singers, including those in British/American movies and Indian movies in which the name of an actor, Kumar, appears frequently. However, when we exclude those, there is a interesting array of names. The person mentioned most frequently was Mahatma Gandhi (twelve times), admired for his honesty, his philosophy of life, the simple truths he espoused. Next in order were the Queen Mother (six times); John F. Kennedy (four times); the Prophet (Mohammed) (twice); and Jawral Nehru (twice). Queen Elizabeth, Queen Victoria, Prime Minister Banderanaika (of Ceylon), Jackie (Kennedy) Onasis, Madame Curie, Helen Keller, Florence Nightingale, and Dr. Jana Aswat (an exiled South African Indian living in London), who took a stand against discrimination, were also mentioned. Interesting that General Smuts (a former prime minister) was also listed, as was President Paul Kruger. In each case, we asked for the choice to be justified and positive bases for selection given such as Helen Keller for her perseverance in overcoming obstacles. One woman who mentioned the Prophet (Mohammed) explained, "He had a simple life and was fair. He solved practical problems. The more you read about him, the more you find that he had the answer for practical everyday problems. If we could follow his example we would have few problems in everyday life."

In some cases, of course, names were remembered because of personal or family experiences. Such events remain indelibly etched on the memory. When Queen Mary visited Durban in 1934, one woman explained that "she gave my mother a red carnation when they met. I wanted to meet her — or just look in her face." A Tamil woman told me, "When Mahatma Gandhi came to Johannesburg, my mother met him. He later gave her a photo of himself, as a young man in which he was standing next to his seated mother. It still hangs in her living room." Another related how her parents had gone to jail with Gandhi during his defiance campaign. She said, "We don't carry passes because of him!" Still another woman told how "my mother played in Paul Kruger's backyard down on Church Street. He was not color oriented." And from another in a slightly different vein, "My mother was a street vendor and always sold bananas to Paul Kruger. One day he didn't have change and promised my mother he would give it to her the next day. He never did and the war broke out. They still owe us fifteen cents," she said with a chuckle.

It is significant that these women who, with few exceptions, have a very low level of education and who are essentially homemakers, have such a wide perspective on persons they admired when they were growing up. As important, though this can be expected, are the reasons why they looked up to them. Many are associated with example, positive philosophy, or are people one would emulate (one lady even mentioned an air hostess because of her freedom). One case however, stands out for the pathos it invokes. An elderly Hindu woman had two porcelain plates hanging on her dining room wall. They show an artist's rendition of Florence Nightingale and are dated "November 1906." She explained, "I always told my father, if you put me in school I will be a nurse, a good nurse like Florence Nightingale. I still have her picture (pointing to the two plates) after all these years. She was the first nurse and I admired her. But father never sent me to school, and even today I cannot read or write."

Education. Education for the South African Indian population has a twofold meaning: on the one hand it refers to public education, which is academic in nature. On the other, it refers to vernacular and religious education, which has components of cultural traditions, home language, and the nonsecular.

Large numbers of Indian children return home from public school (government-run), have lunch, change into traditional dress, and are off to a vernacular school or an Islamic school. At the former, they learn an Indian language and also receive training in cultural and Hindu philosophical issues. At the Islamic or Koranic school, children learn Arabic, enabling them to read the Koran.

Tradition is reinforced at the vernacular schools. These are distributed throughout Indian communities and cater specifically to Hindi-, Tamil-, Gujerati-, and Telegu-speaking children. Students study the language of their ancestors (mainly through religious texts and books) and are instructed in proper behavior. The Gujerati speakers are most insistent that their children attend vernacular school. Telegu gradually lost ground as its role among South African Indians decreased. However, the creation in October 1954, of the linguistic state of Andhra Pradesh in the eastern part of India gave great pride to those belonging to this linguistic group. It also caused an awakening in South Africa, where the language was introduced both at vernacular schools and the university.

Concerning secular education, Meer has summarized the South African situation: "Only the select few reach university, the vast majority dropping out even before they complete primary school. Girls become useful at home and wait to be married. Boys take their places in the job-hunting queue and far too often become absorbed into a life where work is intermittent, and the long gaps between jobs become filled with idling, gambling and cinema-going. In that situation their horizons contract by the day, and their expectations, lower by the month" (1969:99).

In the early days of settlement, there were no state schools which Indian children could attend. The European private schools for the children of English settlers admitted only Indians who conformed in dress and habit to European standards. In time, a number of schools were opened by missionary groups, and Indian children gradually started to attend other schools available. However, the roots of segregation were already present. The result is that boys (in 1899) and girls (in 1905) of Indian parentage were denied admission to European (read white) schools. From that date, Indian schools were essentially financed by the Indian community. Teachers were poorly qualified and underpaid.

The Indian community rallied by using its own resources and personnel. In 1928 Sastri College, a secondary school for Indian was opened in Durban. Large numbers of pupils simply could not gain admission to any school because of racial segregation and lack of facilities.

> By 1959 [that] number had been reduced to under 4,000 through the concerted efforts of the Natal Indian Teachers' Society (whose members are contributing a self-imposed levy for school buildings), the Indian public (through donations) and the Natal Provincial Administration (which contributes on a pound for pound basis) and it is possible that in a few years every Indian child will be able to enter a primary school (Kuper 1960:66fn).

These were the years when most of the women in our study were of school-going age, i.e., the 1940s and 1950s. Even at this stage of our discussion it needs to be pointed out that for girls, the availability of facilities was not always the deciding fact — especially once they had reached menarche. It should also be emphasized that rural versus urban living produced a different milieu. Among urbanites, the position of women was different from that of their rural cousins. Generally speaking, urban girls and women had greater independence and mobility before and after marriage. This was true to an even greater extent if the parents also had been educated. Though he is speaking of India, Kapadia states the situation succinctly:

> Education has brought women out of the confines of the house and put them into contact with the philosophy of liberalism

and the democratic traditions of the West. It has deferred the age of marriage and enabled women to exercise her choice in the selection of a partner. It has brought about a new relationship between husband and wife (1966:268).

The South African educational system is based on the British system. Accordingly, and particularly as pertaining to the years when the women in this study sample were in school, there were a number of important phases of schooling.

The first two years, referred to as grades A and B or grades one and two, taught a child very little more than elementary reading, some writing, and arithmetic. Most children go to school first at age six or sometimes a year later. The next logical break-off is the end of standard two, i.e., after four years of schooling. Standard six completed junior school and frequently involved going to another school — which may have created problems for persons in rural areas. Standard six normally involved children of about ages thirteen to fourteen. The next logical break is at the end of standard eight, or Junior Certificate. This required a public examination; and with "JC", a person could get a job, or in some cases, qualify for professional training. Indians and Africans could qualify as junior school teachers. This is no longer the case. Most students aspire for standard ten, Matriculation, which gave a school-leaving certificate and also university entrance. The important points at which one would expect students to leave school, matched with their likely ages (provided they were not required to repeat a particular standard), are thus as follows:

Standard Two: four years schooling, age nine or ten
Standard Six: eight years schooling, age thirteen or fourteen
Standard Eight: ten years schooling, age fifteen or sixteen
Standard Ten: twelve years schooling, age seventeen or eighteen

We note in Table 8 that there are, in fact, major dropouts after standard six. As a cumulative percentage of the total number of women, we find that 48.3% of the premenopausal category and 60.0% of the postmenopausal category (keep in mind that seven women had no education whatsoever) did not continue schooling. The reason, I would suggest, should be sought not in the level of education but in the physiological change they had undergone. The average age of menarche for women in the premenopausal category was just over age thirteen, for the postmenopausal women, it was about fourteen.

TABLE 7

Years of Schooling of Women in the Indian Sample

Years	Premenopausal #	Premenopausal %	Postmenopausal #	Postmenopausal %
0	–	–	7	(25.9)
3	–	–	2	(7.4)
4	1	(3.4)	1	(3.7)
5	1	(3.4)	3	(11.1)
6	3	(10.3)	1	(3.7)
7	2	(6.9)	2	(7.4)
8	7	(24.1)	3	(11.1)
9	1	(3.4)	4	(14.8)
10	4	(13.8)	3	(11.1)
11	–	–	–	–
12	5	(17.2)	1	(3.7)
13	–	–		
14	1	(3.4)		
15	1	(3.4)		
16	1	(3.4)		
17	–	–		
18	1	(3.4)		
19	1	(3.4)		

It is well documented that fathers did not want their daughters, once they had become "young women," i.e., once they started menstruating, to be around boys and that included coeducational schools. The young women were then supposed to help around the house or store, be under the watchful eye of a parent, and prepare for marriage.

Sexuality. Sexual morality is one of the most important and most emphasized issues in socialization. Children, particularly girls, are told early on to avoid physical closeness. They play the normal games of "house-house" where they copy domestic role and routine, but sexual connotations should be avoided.

Older women suggested that there was less sexual activity among the young when they were growing up. Not a single postmenopausal woman and only one premenopausal woman admitted to sexual involvement before marriage. We should keep in mind that marriage was usually at an early age, frequently fourteen or fifteen for girls, and thus fairly close to the age of menarche. Illegitimacy

TABLE 8

School Grade or Standard Achieved by Women in the Indian Sample

	Years	Age	Premenopausal	Postmenopausal
No schooling	0	–	– –	7 (25.9)
Grade 1–2	2	7/8	– –	– –
Standard 1–2	4	9/10	1 (3.4)	3 (11.1)
Standard 6	8	13/14	13 (44.7)	9 (33.3)
Standard 8	10	15/16	5 (17.2)	7 (25.9)
Standard 10	12	17/18	5 (17.2)	1 (3.7)
B.A.	15		5 (17.2)	0

was always relatively low among South African Indians, but its occurrence was one of the major causes of suicide among young women (Meer 1976).

Courtship. Strict control by parents and the relative house-bound life of young girls, are additional reasons for early marriage without ever having dated. When they did have the opportunity of going out with a boy or young man, it often was in the company of mothers, elder sisters or some other relatives. One reason for these restrictions was that fathers were protective of the family name and feared that an impressionable young girl might get involved with an older and more experienced boy. They also were very conscious of "what the neighbors would say."

Most of the examples of punishment which women remember, concerned their actions in this regard. Going to the bioscope with a girlfriend resulted in a hiding with a strap for one twelve-year-old; accompanying a friend on an errand without permission resulted in grounding; leaving the house to visit her auntie close by caused a scolding for another teenager. In some cases, children were expected to remain essentially in the family. One woman told us that when she was about twelve or thirteen and there was a knock at the front door, she had to go to her room and remain there till the visitor left. In other, more common cases, the daughter was supposed to be in the kitchen when a visitor arrived and had to serve tea. In many cases, this also turned out to be the first view a young woman would get of a suitor or future husband. But there were a number of ways to meet prospective girlfriends or boyfriends.

One Durban newspaper which circulates predominantly among Indian readers contains a section entitled, "The Lonesome

Corner," in which Gori Bibi receives letters and discusses problems of the lonely. De Kock (1977(a):1-2) analyzed letters of the lonesome over a period of a couple of months. There were 144 notes, of which 119 were seeking boyfriends or girlfriends. Of these, 80 required age compatibility, 73 religion, 45 language, and 17 education. A typical note by these more independent young people is the following: "HEART FREE AQUARIUS — I am a respected Tamil-speaking female from a decent and respectable family seeking the friendship of decent Tamil-speaking gentlemen of between 35–40 years who possess sober habits. I prefer simple things in life" (*The Leader,* July 9, 1976).

The most common way of contracting marriage was for the families to decide on likely matches. Infant betrothal, though present in South Africa, especially among persons of South Indian origin, was not very common and was not involved in the marriages of any of the women who cooperated with us in this study. Most marriages, especially but not exclusively, among the older category of women were arranged. This involved various degrees of influence over the selection of a marriage partner — anywhere from a long-term "brainwashing" to condition the girl to the "correct" decision, to consulting her.

> Romantic love is idealized in Hindu classics known in South Africa, but is not accepted as a sound basis for marriage: 'Love should come after marriage, not before.' The circle of potential mates is defined by race, ethnic group, religion, caste and kinship, and within this circle a balance is sought between the individual qualities of the boy and girl by reference to character, reputation, education, health, and physical appearance. The investigations are extremely painstaking — and among the orthodox the final verdict rests with the *panchangum* (almanac) to see if the stars of birth match (action described in Tamil as *porthum parthal,* compatible seeing); if not, the whole matter is dropped by mutual consent. It is generally considered easier to marry off a son than a daughter (Kuper 1960:162).

The last sentence indicates why parents are almost paranoid over the actions of their daughters, especially the postmenarcheal daughters. Over and over, in one form or another, the older women told me that the couple "must learn to love each other;" the most important point is to find the right person. "Look at me and my husband, here we have been married almost fifty years and I had never seen him before my marriage," said one woman. The role of the kutum had something to do with it, but more important was the fact that there was no alternative. Divorce is a novel alternative in Indian marriages.

Indian women correlate having had boyfriends not with a long pattern of dating and going out, but with proposals for marriage. In other words, they may not have had the opportunity of going out or getting to know men in a social and even sexual context, but the families of men were interested in them as prospective marriage partners. Influencing factors were language and religious group membership; but equally important was their family background and the absence of negative information about the girls or their families. Two statements are typical (both by women in the younger age category): "I had no boyfriends, but received a couple of proposals," said one. Another stated, "I was admired by many boys and had about twenty-one proposals." The typical response to this question regarding boyfriends was an explanation about how strict the parents (especially father) were; that they were not allowed boyfriends (one woman called it "Memon law"); or that they met secretly at the store, at school, or on the street corner. One woman told of her mother entreating her, "Don't cut my nose," (i.e., don't cause me shame) by having an affair or getting involved with a man with whom she was not matched. A number of cases, among the younger women only, involved the friends of brothers who were allowed to visit the home or a really "modern" father who said that he would rather have them visiting at home than meeting in secret on the street corner.

Of course, among girls who went to high school or beyond, matters would be different and dating might be more permissible. We should keep in mind, though, that during those years, in contrast with modern-day school, most secondary schools (these are schools that would be attended by postmenarcheal girls) were for boys or girls only.

It is important to keep this situation in mind because it means that girls from age fourteen who get married enter into a relationship which they have never experienced. They will be expected to be good wives and remain married even though they may be ill-equipped for an intimate relationship. In many cases, betrothal involved a man much older than the girl. The combination of male status in Indian society and her own inadequacy at a relationship, plus possibly residence with a mother-in-law, caused untold pain, heartache, and loneliness for the young bride.

Independence. This subtitle may be a misnomer because in most cases, a young woman was never independent. However, at this stage of her life, she will be leaving her family of orientation and moving beyond it, either for marriage or for a job. The latter is the exception because girls normally remain in the parental home until marriage even if they do work. The only exceptions in this context are women who became professionally qualified — a nurse, a college lecturer, or a teacher. If they did not move into professional appointments which took them to another town, or if they did not get married, women remained in the family. Single women did not have rooms, flats, or houses by themselves or with other girls.

Table 9 lists the ages at which the women in our study sample left home. In almost every case, the reason for leaving the parental home was to get married. One woman among the postmenopausal group left for nurse's training. She is the single exception to the rule. Of the younger women, Mrs. Pillay had left home as a twelve-year-

TABLE 9

Age at Which Women in Indian Sample Left Their Natal Families

Age	Premenopausal	Postmenopausal
12	1 (3.6)	
14	–	1 (3.7)
15	–	3 (11.1)
16	1 (3.6)	5 (18.5)
17	2 (7.1)	5 (18.5)
18	4 (14.3)	3 (11.1)
19	6 (21.4)	1 (3.7)
20	3 (10.7)	1 (3.7)
21	6 (21.4)	4 (14.8)
22	3 (10.7)	–
23	–	–
24	–	1 (3.7)
25	1 (3.6)	–
26	1 (3.6)	1 (3.7)
27	–	–
28	–	–
29	–	–
30	–	1 (3.7)
31	–	1 (3.7)
Total	28 (100.0)	27 (99.9)
Missing	1 –	–

old to go to a convent. Even though her parents were Tamilians by tradition, they spoke English in the home and had converted to Catholicism. She spent a number of years in the convent, finally returning home to get married. In the younger age category were women who had had better opportunities and who had access to tertiary education or nurse's training. These women had a greater likelihood of being involved in heterosexual social groups and in relationships of that nature. The result was that previous ideas or arrangements by parents about likely matches for their daughters simply could not be executed. One young woman, who had a university degree, explained that a long-time relationship gradually lost its intensity and finally ceased because she was too educated. There was a fear that she might dominate the in-laws.

The family of procreation. Infant betrothal, once common especially among immigrants from South India, was normally used to cement friendships or bonds between the parents and has all but disappeared. However, the role of parents in selecting (or minimally in influencing selection of) a marriage partner is still extremely strong. Between marriage partners, status and economic security are second only to religion and linguistic-group membership. But here is the paradox: the higher the socioeconomic status of the family, the greater its prestige and the more important for the father (and mother) to influence mate selection in order to maintain the family's status. Yet these families are also those most likely to have children who are at college or are professionals who have moved beyond the family realm — or at least insisted on personal choices.

The father (and later the husband) is treated with great respect and has complete authority over the household. Oosthuizen explains that the father may be greeted "in the same manner as a deity" (1975:51). Karsten, writing about Indians in Surinam says the "father is like a god to his wife and children" (1930:16). The woman dominates the kitchen and domestic domain, but she always remains under male control. As a child, her father controlled her; as a married woman, she is under her husband's control; and in old age, her son will take over that authority. But the woman who remains patient, self-controlled, chaste, and loving will be called a good wife and mother. "A wife gains respect when she bears a child, particularly a son" (Hiebert 1981:224). This makes her acceptable in the eyes of her in-laws because it assures an heir. We should keep in mind in this context that in the traditional joint-family with its viri-local residence, much valued and desired by families in the higher socioeconomic group, the young bride was placed among strangers and forced into an apprenticeship, totally dominated by her mother-in-law. Only as she matured and gained her own children was there a possibility of persuading her husband to establish an independent household. A husband may divide his loyalty between his mother and his wife, but a wife is expected to be totally dedicated to him. Kuper says: "The domestic role of women — the care of the home, bearing and rearing of children, preparing the food — is recognized as the foundation of family life" (1960:118). Being a companion and being a homemaker are the ideal roles for a woman. In time she will find fulfillment in her own home, be provided for by a husband, and hope for a family of her own.

Marriage. Marriage among Indian South Africans followed closely on religious and language group affiliation. Because of the role of parents in arranging unions or family and social pressures, marriage mates tend to belong to the same religious group. Thus, de Kock 1977(a):5 found that 96.4% of marriages he recorded were between members of the same religion. Rajah (1980:126) also states that there are few unions between persons of different religious and language groups.

Lately, secularization has become more common as education has increased. In part this is due to romantic love becoming a basis for marriage. Older informants echoed the views of Ramasar (1966:25) that parents took all things into consideration when they arranged unions which were compatible as to status, economic and social group, religious and linguistic group membership, and for which the young people had the backing and support of the family. They learned to love each other. That came later rather than being the first consideration. A study of more than a thousand Indian marriages between 1923 and 1973 found that in 50.9% of cases the parents alone decided who should get married. In a further 28.2%, the bride was at least consulted, but the parents still made the decision. Thus, in about 80% of all marriages, the parents made the basic decisions about who should marry their daughter (de Kock 1977(b):2–3). When the parents are not involved or do not have the primary influence, one finds that marriage partners frequently are older or are out of the core of family support and protection. These individuals frequently resemble whites in lifestyle and individualism.

Hindu. In the orthodox Hindu family, the parents have a major voice in the decision, even at the outset, by restricting the visitation of a prospective husband or his representatives. Slightly different patterns of visitation and gift-giving prevail among the different sociolinguistic groups.

Kuper points out that among the Hindi, the parents of either girl or boy may take the initiative. They seek the assistance (unpaid) if necessary of a matchmaker (*agwa*), a person of wide contacts and good reputation. Among the Tamil, the girl's parents must wait for suitors and hope to receive indirect help from various kin, more especially the mother's brothers who should be willing to give their own sons as husbands (1960:162). Fully half the women in our sample are Muslims, and accounts of their betrothals follow a wide range from orthodox to modern procedures.

It seems that the number of proposals a girl receives is something to be proud of. It also seems that parents frequently did not respond immediately to a proposal, even one they liked, because they did not want to appear too relieved or eager to marry off their daughter. Nevertheless, for parents to receive a proposal for a daughter, particularly one from a family they value, is the ideal. It may also happen — and here is a delicate balance for a father's idealism — that a girl receives only one proposal. A woman told us that her father was very proud and refused the first proposal she received, but after ten months finally consented. Her two sisters never married (which means they never received an acceptable proposal). Another said, "The mother of my future husband came to talk to father. She left a proposal. Then she came back a second and a third time. Father didn't want to give them the idea that a daughter is not worth much and was easy to get. After the fourth visit, father consented."

The prospective groom's mother plays a very important role in opening discussions, but the bride's father will evaluate the proposal and make the decision. In more modern families, the father will discuss proposals with the girl. One woman explained, "Father evaluated the proposals and the worthy ones he discussed with me." This is true more for the younger women than for the postmenopausal group. From one of the latter we learned of the boy's parents bringing sweetmeats which her family enjoyed while discussing the impending union of their children. She was in the kitchen and only served the tea. Other older women said they were *told* they were getting married or that they never saw their husbands before the marriage ritual. One woman spoke of being in the kitchen when the prospective husband and parents arrived. She was later told to bring tea, at which time she would be looked over in every detail of carriage, comportment, manners, health, and others matters. From her side, she should steal a glance or two at the young man because, if her evaluation is invited, she should at least know what he looked like. Mrs. Joosub, a Memon woman, told of her early years, attending " white school" (academic) all day, *madressa* in the afternoon to learn Arabic, and Gujerati school in the evening. She met and fell in love with a boy, but they kept it a secret. "Our father got me and my sister both engaged to men from India," she said. "I was engaged to my mother's sister's son (the elder of two), my sister was engaged to the other." The latter was still in India. She broke the engagement and remains single to this day. A typical comment was, "I married the man my family brought but it didn't last....I didn't even stay with him...I was scared."

Consider two very interesting examples of the persistence of cultural tradition. The first involves a Hindu woman from a Tamilian family tradition. She graduated from college and while a student knew a number of boys; but she was considered a snob because she didn't spend time with the group, who were loud and who drank. While she was teaching in her first job, a young man whom she had known well as a student came to visit her and proposed. She refused and told him that he had to use the proper channels. He did and they were married six months later.

Another teacher, currently a college lecturer, tells how as a postgraduate teaching intern she always had tea with the other female teachers. For about six months, a male teacher came to have tea with them during break. Then around November they started to date and dated for three years. When their relationship became serious, she said that he personally asked his father's sister to approach his girlfriend's eldest sister (because his parents were deceased as was her father. Her mother was totally against it). Eventually they (also her mother) agreed because she wanted it.

Marriage proposals and negotiations are all preparatory to the actual marriage ceremony. The series of investigations and visits between the two groups may finally lead to a formal proposal of marriage which, if acceptable, is publicized in an engagement-cum-betrothal (*nitchium* in Tamil; *chekai* in Hindi). Mutual vows and gifts are exchanged between the future fathers-in-law, and the "promise" is consecrated by a priest reciting appropriate mantra. Among the Tamil, the gifts are brought to the bride's home by the groom's kin; among the Hindi it is the reverse (Kuper 1960:163). An auspicious day for the ceremony may be decided upon after consultation with a priest, and this may even be narrowed down to an hour of the day depending on the time and date of birth of the couple who are to be wed. The horoscope is central to the ritual calendar used by orthodox Hindu. Among Gujerati-speaking Hindu, red is considered an auspicious color that brings luck to newlyweds. Before the actual wedding, the bride-to-be visits her in-laws' home after smearing her feet with a red powder (*kumkum*). She walks into the house leaving red footprints symbolic of the luck and happiness she will bring. On the day of the wedding she simply walks in. She is cared for by *Butchmee* (or Lakshmi), the wife of Vishnu, goddess of prosperity and happiness, whose lamp burns in most Hindu homes and who represents the life and prosperity of the home.

Because it is outside the focus of the current study, I will not attempt here to cover the details of the marriage ceremony. For descriptions of South African Hindu marriages the reader is referred to Hilda Kuper (1956(a), 1956(b), 1957, 1960); Rambiritch (nd.); and Meer (1969), who deal separately with Hindi and Tamil-speakers' traditions. The respect given to the bride and the lip service afforded the equal partnership of the two sexes belie, somewhat, the experience of many a bride. She is now moved to the in-laws' home, where the husband, caught between being loyal to his mother and honoring his wife, may not recognize the vows he made.

In spite of the somewhat negative image of the mother-in-law, there are cases where this relationship can be a warm one. The Catholic woman who was the oldest, at thirty-four, when she got married had had an affair with a man who was her junior by five years. She explained, "Indians wear a *tali* — a yellow-colored string with a medallion on it. Tamilians have signs on the medallion, we wear the same with a (Christian) cross. Usually the mother of the husband ties the *tali* around the neck of the bride when they get married. Since I was pregnant, my future mother-in-law tied the *tali* for me even though my husband's divorce did not go through for another two years." In the Hindu marriage ceremony, the Tamil groom ties a *tali*, a marriage necklace, around the neck of his wife. This necklace is a cord treated with turmeric to give it the yellow color. With a red powder a Hindi groom marks two spots on the forehead of his wife. One is at the parting of the hair (*sindhoor*), the other in the middle of the forehead (*tika*). The Tamil *tali* and the Hindi *tika* are only permanently removed when death separates wife and husband. At this time, the Hindi wife can wash or permanently remove the red spot, while the Tamil widow has the tali cut and either washes it in milk, which makes it into just a cord again, or she places it in the coffin of her deceased husband.

Muslim. Muslim marriages produce greater uniformity and follow a more rigidly defined code but give less recognition to the woman. As in the case of the Hindu, marriage is a process rather than an event. It starts with the negotiations and proposal and is not really fulfilled until the birth of the first child. Muslim law has its roots in the traditions of Saudi Arabian culture and is specifically based on pronouncements of Muhammad uttered as he was giving order to the new kind of community which took shape in Mecca and later in Medina. Koranic laws which were laid down in those years "were revealed which replaced or revised old tribal customs with new rules.... Some of the most important and fundamental reforms of customary law were made by the Quran in order to improve the status of women and strengthen the family in Muslim society" (Esposito 1982:3–4).

But the Muslim marriage is not religious and is, thus, not a sacrament. Even though it may take place in a mosque, strictly speaking, it is a civil contract between two people and has two objectives: procreation and the promotion of "culture and civilization" (Mandudi 1974:83). However, the bride is not present. Her willingness to marry is conveyed by her maternal and/or paternal uncles who serve as witnesses. The marriage is first recorded in a marriage register held by a priest and then sealed in a ritual called the *Nikah* ceremony, the part that takes place either in the mosque or a private home. In any case, the bride is not present because, following the ceremony, the husband will go to her home to formally greet and give thanks to his mother-in-law and to greet members of her kutum. At this time, the bride is preparing to accompany him and his family.

Whereas the Hindu marriage ritual gives respect to the bride, emphasizing her equality with the groom, Islamic patriarchal prejudice and law condemn her to second-class citizenship. "Legal and social inferiority in any sphere of life can harm sexual relationship and impede the development of love based on the spouses' respect for each other as equals" (Minai 1981:158). This status derives not only from her absence at the marriage ritual, but also from verses in the Koran, e.g., sura IV, verse 34: "Men are in charge of women, because Allah hath made the one to excel the other...." Women are also instructed about being veiled, modest, secluded, and of course, part of a polygynous set-up. Sura IV, verse 3, limits the number of wives a man may have to four. The wife may have only one husband. Islamic scholars are quick to point out how much higher the status of Islamic women are when compared to pre-Islamic Arab women (Soffan 1980:16 and Esposito 1982:16). It should also be kept in mind that under Hanafi law, a Muslim man could marry a Christian, Jewish, or Muslim woman, but a Muslim woman could marry only a Muslim man. Given the key role of the woman — not merely as wife but more important as mother — and Islamic emphasis on the child and society, the choice of mates seems strange.

While Nikah is a legal ceremony performed within Islamic law (and religion), the Hindu marriage is a sacrament establishing a moral bond between bride and groom, but it had no legality. Hindu women in both age categories of our study elaborated on this. Said one, "The parents of Hindu girls found that in some cases the couple would get married in Hindu rites and then the boy would disappear. And so, if they're suspicious they may require a court marriage even before the Hindu wedding." Explained another, "My parents insisted on a court marriage with the Hindu rites. A common-law wife may sue for maintenance if she has children. A civil marriage results in a legal wife who has claims on support and maintenance."

Safeguarding a marriage by adding a legal magistrate's court contract in terms of South African law has become more common. In the sample of marriages we studied, about twice as many Hindu marriages as Muslim marriages included the court contract.

Most of the marriages are lasting because divorce is extremely complex in both the Hindu context and in Koranic law. Kuper states: "Marriage is a sacred, not simply a civil, union, and divorce is not recognized by orthodox South African Hindu" (1960:116). Secular law does of course allow for annulment or the dissolution of a marriage on grounds of adultery or desertion. Divorces among Hindus are rare. In the previous discussion, mention was made of Mrs. Joosub, a Memon woman whose parents married her to a son of her mother's sister. She states that the man was twenty-five (she was only eighteen) and lived a wild life. The marriage was never consummated and after six weeks it was over. At age twenty-six, she married her "love choice" (he was twenty-seven) against the wishes of her father, who subsequently cut her out of his will. She is happily married.

Under Koranic law, Muslims find it very hard to divorce, but it is still easier for men than for women. In a number of cases, women felt that they simply did not receive attention from the husband and that he was seeing another woman. However, these women felt that as uneducated persons they would have a hard time making a living alone, even if they were granted a divorce. "While the Quran granted her some judicial relief from undesirable unions, the strong influence of social customs, especially in the Hanafi school of law, succeeded in limiting that relief to very narrow grounds" (Esposito 1982:30). In contrast, the husband can terminate a marriage simply by making a pronouncement that he divorces his wife, "...if the husband uses the formula of repudiation in jest, in drunkenness, or even under compulsion, it is still considered to be valid and effective" (Esposito 1982:30).

Ideally, then, marriage is of lifetime duration. Should an unmarried Hindu woman die, a symbolic marriage is performed by a priest in which he ties a tali to the corpse as it is prepared for burial. This is done to assure that supernatural punishment for shirking her duty in this life will be warded off in the next life. The home which suffered a death is "in darkness" for a year. A photograph of the deceased woman is placed, with bowls of rice sacrifices, at the sacred lamp in the living room. This practice is common in Transvaal where our research was conducted, but in Natal the photo is put away after the funeral.

Women may inherit from a deceased husband. Koranic law also allows a Muslim wife to inherit from a deceased husband. This is true even in the case of divorce that is revocable. However, in the case of irrevocable divorce, all rights of inheritance terminate.

Marriage, then, is intended to work. A woman is supposed to make it work or to accept it whether she had much to say about the choice of a spouse or not. Blessings await those who have long marriages.

Residence. Following marriage, the normal pattern was for the bride and groom to move in with his parents or joint family. Where such residential arrangements were not possible, they frequently rented a room, flat, or house.

One Tamil woman explained how the groom's parents had come to propose: "I was out at the time but was told about it. I was so scared because his family had many daughters. I was afraid of living with the in-laws because the girls were fairly small and lived at home. Girls can be very nasty, expecting the daughter-in-law to do everything."

Table 10 indicates that 65.5% of the premenopausal women and 51.9% of the postmenopausal women had moved in with the in-laws after marriage. Given the generational difference, one might have expected these percentages to be reversed; i.e., that the kutum and the joint family would have found stronger expression among the older generation. But there are circumstances which explain why these figures form the pattern they do. It will be recalled that the Group Areas Act (1950) forced Indian South Africans into areas where they were residentially segregated from other ethnic-color groups, but had greater freedom to select residential style and size.

TABLE 10

Postmarital Residence of Women in Indian Sample

Postmarital Residence	Premenopausal	Postmenopausal
1. With parents	2 (6.9)	3 (11.1)
2. With relatives	–	1 (3.7)
3. With in-laws	19 (65.5)	14 (51.9)
4. Private room	3 (10.3)	1 (3.7)
5. Flat	3 (10.3)	1 (3.7)
6. Hostel	–	–
7. Own house	2 (6.9)	7 (25.9)
Total	29 (100.0)	27 (100.0)

Separate residential areas had a number of detrimental influences, but one positive effect is that Indians could design their own homes. There was, in fact, a resurgence of the joint-extended family. Women who were married after 1950, and that includes all the women in the premenopausal category, therefore lived in segregated neighborhoods. It is also interesting that a larger percentage of them lived with the in-laws than is the case with the older category of women. In the postmenopausal category, we find a larger percentage who had their own homes, frequently shacks, in urban slums.

Household. Because parents wanted their daughters married and education for girls was not valued in the past, we find that the women in our sample were married at a relatively early age. Among the premenopausal category, twelve (41.3%) were married by age nineteen, while eighteen (66.6%) of the postmenopausal women were married by that age. The latter figure includes one married at fourteen and four who were married at fifteen. In contrast to the women, we find that their spouses were markedly older. In the premenopausal category, there were only two (6.9%) men who were nineteen years of age or younger at the time of marriage; and in the postmenopausal category, there was only one (3.7%) man of that age.

The men, being the breadwinners and the dominant figures in these families, were consequently significantly older than the women. At the time of marriage, only six (20.5%) of the women in the younger category were aged twenty-five or older while eleven (37.9%) of the husbands were in that age bracket. The age difference was much more pronounced among the older women. In the postmenopausal category, only four (14.8%) women were over age twenty-five at the time of their first marriage, but seventeen (63.0%) of the husbands of women in this category were over twenty-five. The age difference between wife and husband in the younger category of women was quite marked, but for the older women it was impressive.

We will return to the importance of children in the family, so it will suffice here simply to point out that no family is complete without children. In the same way, a woman is not complete unless she has given birth, producing an heir. The nuclear household among South African Indians will thus consist of wife, husband, and children; but usually two other categories must be included on a daily basis; namely, the extended family and an African servant(s).

Domestic roles. In few other times has there been a sharper contrast between the ideal compared to the actual. Young people grow up with movies which portray loving relationships, caring and understanding husbands, wives in well-financed homes smiling at husbands and children. Every girl dreams of the role she will play; how lucky and happy she will be; what a good marriage partner she will select and the long, happy, trusting, relationship they will have. Every girl believes and hopes. In retrospect women often realize that they emphasized the wrong values or that matters started slipping without their realizing what was happening. Marriage, in different dialects and cultural idioms, is " 'til death do us part." It is interesting for women to look back on their ideals. When the women in this study were asked whether their feelings about what characterized an ideal husband had changed in the past ten years, eleven (37.9%) of the premenopausal and eleven (40.7%) of the postmenopausal category stated "yes". This can be ascribed to a number of factors, but mostly it represents a coming to grips with reality, human nature, and role performance sanctioned within cultural contexts. There are, of course, those women who indicated that since their marriages were arranged, they never had much to say about the mate selection.

It is also interesting to look at how women view ideal characteristics for wife and husband. It should be kept in mind that the characteristics of the ideal husband, as well as the feminine ideal they expect to be held by men, were both presented by the women in our study sample.

Characteristics of the ideal wife. What do women think men expect in an ideal wife? What priorities do they think men have? Obviously much of their knowledge is based on what they have been told. The woman who emerges as a composite of these valued attributes was actually summarized by one of the older women in the study sample. According to her, "A man wants a good wife who is honest, sincere, clean, and who can care for his house and children, help him in his work and social life, and who is not too free with other men — she must be sociable but not flirtish."

The characteristics of the ideal wife fall into a number of general areas. In order of the frequency with which these are mentioned, they are:

Beauty and physical attraction. The Indian woman should not be very dark, not fat, but have a good figure and know how to walk. She must be clean and neat and dress smartly. Any "proper" Indian woman will have long hair. This is a composite of physical attributes most frequently mentioned. The simple criterion of "beauty" was mentioned most frequently by both categories of women in the research sample.

Good housekeeper/wife. A man marries a woman essentially to run his household and raise his children. For these reasons it is important that she take care of his food and has decent clothes. She should manage the domestic routine properly; she must be at home, be a good cook, and make sure that he gets his tea or supper when he gets home. The good wife will adapt to his routine, will be the "slave of his home," giving him simultaneously domestic security and a shoulder to lean on. It is equally important for her to socialize and raise his children, creating the right atmosphere by getting them dressed and fed and off to school and madressa or vernacular school. In short, a good wife sacrifices herself, first for her husband and later for her children.

Companionship. Part of the sacrifice is in seeing that the husband is happy. To a woman, being a companion means "partaking of his world," sharing his problems and his interests, allowing him to confide in her and always being there, a partner for life who will stick it out. This is best achieved by being understanding and sociable. Men all have professional, business, and family networks of people who must be entertained or visited. An ideal wife will entertain his friends and family and get along with and respect her in-laws. A number of women singled out respecting his mother, or looking after her.

Personality. It does, however, require a certain type of person to satisfy the Indian husband. An ideal wife is patient (she doesn't nag); she is submissive (and obeys the husband); she is humble and loyal and shows respect for him. Good wives do not have "big mouths," do not "back chat," and do not "speak out of turn." They are happy persons who "smile when he walks in the house," who "make him proud to go out with them," and who "don't bother him with their problems." Ideal wives, moreover, come from a respectable background, are decent women, reasonably educated but smart, are hard working, religious, able to live within a budget, and on top of everything tolerant of their husbands. Strangely, the whole aspect of sexuality was under emphasized. It was pointed out by a few that a wife must be a good lover, or a sex partner. More frequent mention was made of the requirement that she had to be loving. In the context of the extended family and traditional male line, it was mentioned that she should not be barren but be able to bear children, or produce an heir. In this same context fidelity and faithfulness were mentioned. As one woman explained, "Being faithful is necessary first, trust comes in time."

The other side of the coin concerns those characteristics which describe the ideal husband. Here women were asked to project their values and priorities regarding a husband. Immediately following their response they were asked whether their criteria had changed after ten years of marriage. Two of the older women stated that they would not marry if they had to do it all over. "Too much trouble," they said.

Characteristics of the ideal husband. A common response when women spoke about the ideal husband was that they used to prefer good-looking men but now would be much more interested in other qualities. The two qualities singled out overwhelmingly were understanding/companionship and financial security.

Understanding/companionship. Talking with the South African Indian women in this sample created a very clear impression of lonely, somewhat ignored women. They were finding expression in their children, not in their own lives or in the relationship with a spouse. What were the components of this criterion?

Most sought and valued was a man who was loving (you must see the love in his eyes) and through commitment provides a good home. This implies understanding — a man who responds to the needs of his wife, who communicates with her, and encourages her with understanding. This also implies empathy: a husband who listens; a husband who needs her.

All of this suggests appreciation for the person who is his wife. A man must respect his wife, show her affection, have a nice way of speaking to her and be friendly. "A smile can do so much," said one.

Respect also implies trying to make her happy, looking after her when she is ill; sharing time with her; permitting give and take on an equal footing because he is trying to be compatible. This is best achieved by a husband who is gentle and soft-spoken and who treats his wife as a partner. As a life's companion they have things in common, share joys, problems, and experiences. In short, a wife needs emotional security and moral support.

The ideal husband is kind, good, considerate and has a sense of humor. He is sober in his habits and well behaved. He does not abuse his wife emotionally or physically. He is polite, well mannered, good natured, gentle — in short, he is a decent man, a nice person.

Financial security. This is clearly the second most frequently mentioned criterion. It implies that the husband should be a hard working, dependable provider, have a good job or be well-established. In such a case, he will be able to provide his wife and family with a home and the security that comes with it, something so well said by one of the postmenopausal women: "Give me a home and I'll be the queen!" Security in a material sense implies responsibility, caring for a family, and providing their immediate needs.

Other valued criteria. Appearance was singled out by an equal number of younger and older women. A husband should be good-looking: this implies being tall, not too fat, handsome and attractive. Associated with this is dress, which is neat and proud. The ideal husband is able to father a child; for without a child, a woman is not complete and a home has no permanence. Furthermore, he loves children and is a good father, giving and earning respect. A husband is intelligent and educated, not narrow-minded but modern in outlook. (The same older woman who mentioned education also set as a requirement that the husband must be "our caste.") A number of women valued a husband who is outgoing and sociable. Two stated that their husbands must take them out because they never had that as girls.

The ideal husband shows respect for his wife's family and friends and respects her mother. He should be religious, from a good family background, and "domesticated."

One criterion, mentioned by only a single younger woman but by ten older women, is that of faithfulness — fidelity and dependability in the marriage context. The older women stated quite clearly that husbands should not run after women. One older woman summed it up. She thought for a while before describing the ideal husband, then said, "I think it is somebody who is understanding and sympathetic and who cares for his family."

Characteristics of the ideal mother. Those features which make for a good wife almost certainly influence the kind of mother a woman will be. Both roles are performed in relationship with others and both roles are domestic.

The consensus was first and foremost that a mother loves her children sincerely. That implies quality love characterized by kindness, help, and understanding which always seeks what is best for the children. She is devoted to them, listens to their problems, reasons with them, which implies talking and listening. This communication assures that she will learn their viewpoint because she must aim at becoming their best friend, having their confidence.

A second very important role is that of helping her children with their education. Basically this involves getting them ready for school, getting them there, and supporting school activities. She must care for them by giving her time to them, and obviously, this means staying home — not working. One woman said, "A good mother dedicates her life to her home and children." In addition to day school, it is incumbent upon her to see that her children have cultural roots by sending them to vernacular school or madressa. A related responsibility is giving spiritual guidance (religion), or attending temple with the children. Combined with the latter is her responsibility to teach children respect for elders and how to be well-behaved. She must supply moral guidance. As one woman explained, "She must teach children the values of life and humanity — be good human beings; be honest. Don't hurt, don't steal, and be good to all people."

Related to these two roles are a number of specific characteristics of a good mother. She runs a well-kept home that is neat, clean, and on time. She may not be involved in divorce because it would ruin the child's security; thus, she must be a good wife to her husband. She must also mediate between her husband or eldest son and the other children. In this context it was stated that she must get along with the in-laws and be available to help if her husband or his relatives were in need. As mother, she must learn the delicate balance between keeping the children home and giving them freedom — but in the case of girls not too much freedom. She must know where they are and see that they have the right friends. And the secret: she must not nag her children; she must not be cheeky or rude with them. She must be authoritative but not authoritarian.

One aspect emphasized quite heavily by the postmenopausal women (perhaps because they also were grandmothers) is that a good mother does her own cooking — prepares nice things, and always has something sweet for the children to eat when they get home.

Grandmothers are not very much different from mothers except that they spoil the grandchildren — they are expected to do so. They do tend to favor the sons' children, especially the first born. Said a Muslim woman, "Your son is milk, but the child of your son is like the cream on the milk...cream is sweeter than milk." Grandmothers are supposed to give moral and religious guidance. Grandmothers used to seem old due to living conditions, ill health, and shorter life expectancy. But one woman explained, "A change between earlier years and today — Ayas used to look old early, now they stay young!"

Decision making. Given the changes that are taking place in the Indian South African family and the status of women, one might well ask about who makes decisions. Is it the man/husband or the woman/wife? On what basis is this justified?

In response to the statement: "It is the man who should decide the important matters for the family." twenty (69.0%) of the pre-menopausal and twenty-five (92.6%) of the postmenopausal women agreed. There obviously is a generational difference here, with the younger, better educated women more often disagreeing with the statement. But what justification is given by those who agree with the idea of male dominance? Two basic reasons appear: his status as household head and his status as provider.

The status of the Indian South African man as household head is in keeping with his general status of authority. In all situations, it is incumbent on his wife and children to show him respect, even reverence. His word is seldom questioned, especially by the children. He makes all major decisions regarding home and family.

In her study of the Hindu joint family in Durban, Jithoo explains:

The devotion of a wife is depicted beautifully in myths and legends contained in the sacred Hindu texts, the Mahabharath and Ramayana. Every Hindu knows the story of the devoted and faithful Sita who did not succumb to the advances of the lecherous Rawana who was king of the demons. Every woman

is expected to have the fine virtues of Sita. One of the heads of
a household in this study returned home after a long absence
and was greeted by his wife who held a brass tray at the door
with a lighted camphor and circled it round the head of her
husband. This is the method of worship of Hindus towards
their deities (1970:104).

The respect situation is much the same among Indians who are
Muslims.

Ascribing decision-making to the husband is found equally in
both categories of research subjects. Most women simply stated that
the man is the head of the house or the head of the family. A Hindu
explains that when the tali is tied, a woman takes a vow to recognize
the position of her husband. "Tamils respect their husbands and say
they are godlike." Another explained, "He is lord and master: a
woman cannot take over the reins." One woman gave a twitch of the
shoulder and said, "Well, that is Indian tradition. If he is wrong,
you just tell him he is right, because he has all the rights." Indian
girls are brought up in homes where the father is the dominant
figure and (partly to assure a good marriage) girls are taught from
childhood to respect men. "We take our husbands like a boss in the
house; women live under the man." A Muslim woman is in the
same position; the man is the head and she must obey. Volunteered
one woman, "The Koran says, 'After Allah, the next person you can
prostrate yourself before is your husband.'" A Memon Muslim
woman explained, "The Islamic religion says man and woman are
equal. However, Indian men do not accept everything in the Koran
because they are afraid and want to dominate women. They must
make the final decision and can act independently, but women
cannot and must ask permission for any action." So a combination
of traditional socialization and religious reinforcement place the
male, especially the older male, in a dominant and domineering
position.

A second basic justification for his status, his role as provider,
is really forced on the domesticated Indian woman. This is the
simple reason given. Indian South African women, especially those
in the older category, simply are not economically independent.
There is a Memon idiom stating, "The man is the roof of your
house." This is true in a number of ways and economic security is
one of them.

In the younger age category, there were a number of women
who disagreed about the status of men. A number of young women

felt that they were thinking individuals who could see problems in a different light. As women they had their opinions. Others suggested that women have greater foresight and insight. They are logical, cold and calculating and can separate fact and emotion. They added that a woman's strength is her sensitivity and emotions. After all, the man is not always right.

In spite of education and a degree of economic independence through earning capacity, the younger Indian woman is caught in a dilemma. If she insists on her new independence, she threatens her relations with her in-laws, the extended family, and possibly her husband. If she remains in the traditional relationship, she is also subject to many of the old traditional prejudices in that relationship. One younger woman explained, "Men are supposed to be the dominant sex; we are the weaker sex. Indians believe men are superior ...especially the in-laws."

Men make all the decisions on business matters and financial ventures. They decide about buying a home, a car, acquiring furniture, or any other major expense. Important decisions about the children are almost always made by the father. This leaves a very limited sphere of decision making for the wife/mother. She has full authority about what food to prepare, the day-to-day running of the household, and her own clothing. In some cases, the husband shops on his way home from work; in others, the wife may go shopping or send a servant. Decision-making on a day-to-day basis is essentially the husband's, in some cases shared with the wife or clearly apportioned on the basis of domestic expedience. Two women were quite bitter. Said one, "My husband makes ALL decisions. I must even get permission to go see my own mother here in town." The other explained, "If I have a lady friend and my husband doesn't like her, I must avoid her."

Male authority. Male authority extends beyond decision-making into other areas of the marriage relationship and the domestic routine. The husband's decision is supposed to be accepted, yet twenty-seven (93.1% of the younger and twenty-three (85.2%) of the older category of women said a wife may disagree with her husband. However, such disagreement may be restricted by topic and location. One of the younger women explains, "...she is not supposed to (disagree). She must be a very gullible character. She has no voice in finances but may disagree on children. Never in public (only in the bedroom), otherwise mother-in-law or some other relative will be there." This pretty much defines the limits. Women may disagree with their husbands about matters concerning the children, running the household, spending money unnecessarily, getting drunk, wasting money or being "too sexy" or "having girlfriends." In doing so, however, the wife must give reasons for the disagreement; it must be done in the privacy of the home, preferably the bedroom. "A good wife doesn't put her husband in the public eye!"

Some of the younger women stated that they may disagree in public but suggested that they sort it out at home. One young woman said, "Yes, I'll disagree with him in close company or in private. I'll say you're wrong and then explain what is right." Women realize that public disagreement including in front of their children, ultimately cause stress, may bring the in-laws into it, and may be useless because ultimately the man gets his way. There is a Memon idiom *Mooth band rakh* (keep your fist closed). Quoted in this context the implication is that a married couple must iron out their personal problems within the family instead of (opening the fist and) sharing their problems with neighbors and relatives. The women also had an impression that Koranic law decrees "What he says is right, what I say is wrong."

Does the husband then have authority over the wife's movements — visiting friends, coming and going? Most women, of course do not seriously question that they do because they grew up that way. They found it interesting to ponder the question of whether a husband can insist on knowing at all times where his wife is, and its converse, does she have the right to know where he is. In response to the first question, we notice quite a clear-cut generational difference: twenty-one (72.4%) of the premenopausal and twenty-six (96.3%) of the postmenopausal women felt that a wife must get permission (or at least inform her husband) if she leave the home. Some justified it on the basis of Indian custom, others that it was only right or a good practical measure in case of emergency. It was also felt that it was better for the marriage that the husband know rather than be told that his wife was seen about town. The one older woman who disagreed stated simply, "If he has a good wife he needn't ask." but she is obviously in the minority on this issue.

When the tables were turned and women were asked whether they had a right to know where their husbands are, matters changed. For the younger women, the numbers are almost the same: twenty (69.0%) felt that the wife also needs to know, in case of emergency, where the husband was. Others justified it on the grounds of courtesy or trust because they were equals. However, many who suggested that this was proper were quick to add. "He should...(but) my husband certainly doesn't." A number of the women were resentful that a wife could not go anywhere without her husband's permission or presence, but men, by nature gregarious, could come and go without explanation or anyone's permission. They may visit relatives or friends. They are free and have all the power. By day they are at work and "working late" can be a cover for a multitude of extra-domestic and extra-marital activities. Said one woman, "...even when he's been to the girlfriend he says he's worked late." One of the older women, with the wisdom of tradition and experience said, "...but the husband must be allowed to tell you where he was, rather than put him on the spot." In her view, then, it is the husband's privilege, not the wife's right. It was retroactive and most likely selective.

If men are the authority figures who dominate the household and make the important decisions, are they also given priority in their wive's attention? Does a wife consider the husband's needs before her own and those of the children? When it is only the wife and husband, before the birth of children, he has priority and his every whim is catered to. This is, of course, during the first years of marriage — when the wife frequently is experiencing her first independence and the new relationship is at a peak, emotionally and sexually. Even when moderation is required because of residence in the husband's joint family, novelty mitigates against boredom.

In later years, once the children have gone to school or have become teenagers, marriage settles into a routine. Most women continue to place the needs of their children before their own, even as the children grow up. Children may be given priority when they are infants, but the husband regains his preferential status when they become relatively independent.

The premenopausal women did not all place their children's needs before their own. A number of them explained that they had their lives and their professions which required attention. The postmenopausal women all said that they placed their children first. This may be due to the fact that fewer of them had professions and that they were more home and family centered. It may also be that, in retrospect, they liked to remember it that way, particularly since most of them now are grandmothers.

About an equal number of premenopausal women stated that they considered the needs of the children first or the needs of the husband first. The latter group of fifteen (51.7%) was bigger than the corresponding group of postmenopausal women, only ten (37.0%) of whom stated that they considered the husband's needs first.

Good mothers naturally give priority to the needs of their children. "The child did not ask to be born, we wanted a child and must take care of her first." Every one of the postmenopausal women stated that they always saw to the needs of their children first even if this implied a sacrifice on their part. Explained one, "We look after the husband and kids first; we tend to neglect ourselves." With one (3.7%) exception, they also thought most women of their generation expressed similar priorities in behavior. As if this were a universal, a woman stated, "Indian women are dedicated to their children." The premenopausal women had better living conditions, and a larger number were either professionals or involved in extra-domestic roles. Among these younger women, two (6.9%) stated that they did not necessarily give priority to the needs of their children. Six (20.7%) of them thought that Indian South African women of their generation would not automatically do so. One of these women explained, "I make them comfortable but won't neglect myself." Others qualified their answers with "mostly" and "within reason." The situation was summarized by Mrs. Alli, a mother of four. "Indian women don't have much career orientation and spend all their time caring for their kids. Once career enters, things might change."

Children. The arrival of the firstborn is a relief to the mother, a symbol of security to the father, and a bond between parents. Indian South African children, on the whole, are pampered. From a very early age, children spend more time with the mother in the domestic situation. Girls are protected, restricted, and taught the role of wife. Boys are spoiled. They will carry on the father's name; be a security to aged parents; and especially, take care of the mother. The mother-son relationship is one which is nurtured throughout life.

The mother/wife must perform the delicate feat of balancing her love and attention between children and husband. One woman explained, "I told my husband, 'I *saw* you coming but I *felt* my child coming.'" She must give her time and attention to the children as behooves a good mother, but she must show interest and give attention to the husband because Indian men, I was told, are only "partially domesticated." Explained one of the postmenopausal women, from her retrospective position, "In certain instances, the husband must get the priority to have a happy home. Indian men are funny; if the kids get all the attention, the husbands go astray for sex and companionship. If they don't find it at home, they'll find it elsewhere. It was true of the old generation and it still is today."

As members of the family, children are expected to play their part, but role differentiation places greater responsibility on girls than on boys. Girls are minimally expected to clean their rooms and make up their beds. In some cases their chores may extend to other parts of the home, especially to kitchen activities. Boys have few if any domestic chores and may be expected to run errands or do things outside the home. In general, they are freer to select their own activities.

Servants. When one woman was asked about the chores of her children, she responded, "...they have chores but they don't do them. This is one of the disadvantages of a servant society." Other women indicated that the children had chores on weekends only if the servants were off.

The Indian community of Laudium is located immediately west of the urban center, Pretoria. Adjacent to it, but separated by a low hill, is the black residential community of Atteridgeville. Blacks have a short way to walk from their homes, across the hill, into Laudium, or they may take a bus, which is more comfortable but takes a longer route. As is the case in a very large percentage of white homes, Indians also employ blacks as domestics and for yard care.

In our two samples of women there is a slight difference in the pattern of servant employment. Among the younger women, there were thirteen (44.8%) who had full-time live-in servants and thirteen (44.8%) who had part-time servants. These include black women who come in on a daily basis, two or three times a week, or every week to do the laundry. There were only three (10.3%) of the families who did not employ a domestic servant.

Among the older women there are twelve (44.4%) who had full-time live-in servants; seven (25.9%) who had part-time servants; and eight (29.6%) who did not employ a domestic servant. In each of the categories, there was one family who employed two live-in domestic servants. Servants may be required to do just about any job in the home as well as accompany small children to school or to the vernacular school or madressa. They may be sent on errands or to do shopping. There are two activities that may be restricted. Some women told me that they made their own beds, either because husbands preferred it or because they felt that it was close to the very core of the conjugal relationship. Cooking was almost universally done solely by the wife/mother. When a single nuclear family resides in a home or flat, the wife will perform the cooking; in a joint family household the mother-in-law may oversee it. In both cases, daughters may help, but it is the wife/mother/mother-in-law who measures the condiments, says when and how long foods should cook, and actually becomes a director of kitchen activities. A servant may be asked to peel or prepare vegetables but hardly ever to cook the food.

Running a home. The previous discussion offered a glimpse of the Indian home in which every member of the household has certain roles. We have also seen that the home is the woman's realm. where she makes decisions and where the fluidity of routine is a good measure of her ability.

The question arises whether women are satisfied with this arrangement. It implies that they have full authority but also full responsibility. They see to it that everything is done or do it themselves. Should men (husbands/fathers) leave the housework and domestic activities to the women or should they help? The younger women were evenly split, with fifteen 51.7%) stating that men should stay out of the kitchen and essentially leave the domestic realm to the women. The house is the "responsibility of the woman," and since "the man goes out to work," he should not be expected to work at home. Others blamed it on "Indian custom" or "Muslim belief" (one explained, "the man in the house is like a god"). One woman offered a very practical consideration, "In our community the husband's mother would react...it would be degrading to me." But the fourteen (48.3%) who felt that the husband should help at home had equally justifiable reasons. "If the wife works, the husband should give a hand." "The man should help, then the wife feels happy, like a partner." One young woman was quite adamant, "There are certain things that the husband can do — sons are spoiled and make slaves out of their wives."

Of the older (postmenopausal) women, twenty (74.1%) felt that men should stay clear of the kitchen. They saw "no dignity in a man standing around washing dishes or cooking" because it is "that way in our Indian culture." One woman had a much more practical reason, "If he stays out of the kitchen we don't step on each other's toes." For the seven (25.9%) who felt that the husband should help, the most common occasions were when the wife was ill or working. One elderly woman who had worked as a hawker all her life and had permanently deformed arms from carrying her large basket from dawn to dark every day, said that her husband helped to prepare food and watch the kids while she lugged the basket. Somehow a role reversal would have been preferable! One older man is a caterer at a large hospital, and he occasionally bakes bread or cake or makes dessert. Younger husbands are more likely to assist with "peeling the veggies," washing up, or even using the vacuum cleaner, but these activities may be restricted to when she's ill or he's in the mood.

Domestic routine or running a home requires some clear conceptualization of the partners' duties which should not be arbitrary. Duties clearly stake out realms of responsibility and predictability of performance by the marriage partners. A husband can be expected, minimally, to be a provider who sees to the everyday material needs of his family. This is the first and most frequently stated prerequisite for husbands because it is the basis on which a household functions.

With fairly clearly demarcated realms for husband and wife, whose work or role is more important? Perhaps because of the emphasis on the material needs and financial requirements for existence, only six (20.7%) of the younger women and seven (26.9%) of the older women felt that their roles were most important. However, twelve (41.4%) premenopausal and sixteen (61.5%) postmenopausal women believed that the husband's role was most important. The rest stated that they really didn't know or thought that their roles were complimentary and they contributed equally. It is obvious that if the husband is the sole provider, he works and brings home the pay. Not so, said one woman. "All he does is go to work and sit there all day, I work all day, then must be ready to serve him when he gets home; and during the evening I must supervise the children." The third position says that the two roles are really equal: "His is measured in monetary terms; mine in terms of the house and children." The three positions were all well-justified and illustrated.

But it is in the home and in matters concerning the home that a woman finds fulfillment. Since there are relatively few women who work, or who have professional or career interests, a woman's universe revolves around her children, her home, and her husband. For most, having a child is the one single event that stands out as the happiest of their lives. When asked what gives meaning to their lives, an overwhelming number of younger women stated first their children and second their husbands or marriage. All of the older women mentioned having children or grandchildren and a much smaller number said husbands. We should, of course, keep in mind that a number of these women were widowed. The third topic of meaning for their lives, mentioned by both categories of women, was their beliefs or religion. One younger woman stated it succinctly,

"Being healthy; blessed that I can accept most things as they come; having kids who are respectful; and having a husband who appreciates what I do for him." The Indian South African woman's universe evolves around her home and family and matters which are associated with these. Fatima Meer, contrasting the expectations for women with that of men, says:

> Women must remain virtuous, protected within the domestic confines, and in turn, through their isolated and narrow orientation to life, protect the conventions of those confines. Thus, if there is a family scandal, an unregulated love affair, an unmarried pregnancy, the women are blamed. Popular Indian films never fail to depict heroines as virtuous, patient, suffering, and completely faithful in marriage. The wickedness of female villains never goes beyond malicious gossip or attempted, but never successful, seduction of heroes (1969:71).

Reproductive profile. No marriage is complete without children; no house is a home if there are no children; a female is not a woman unless she has had a child; marriages without children are not secure.

Matters dealing with sexuality are to be discussed in Chapter VI but need to be mentioned here. Indian South African women recognize the connection between sexual intercourse and pregnancy even though there may be a lack of clarity about the mechanics of fertilization. Most women, 93.1% of the younger group and 80.8% of the older group, stated that a single act of sexual intercourse was sufficient to cause pregnancy. The rest said that multiple acts were necessary. There was a postmenopausal woman who suggested that women didn't become pregnant as easily when she was young. This suggests, possibly, improvements in hygiene, health and nutrition.

Questions concerning fecundity and fertility refer to biological determinants, but these are influenced by a variety of cultural and psychological factors. Specifically, fecundity is a woman's physiological ability to reproduce, fertility is the realization of that potential. Fecundity (potentiation) will be measured by the actual number of pregnancies, fertility by the actual number of live births a woman has had during her reproductive years. This number may be influenced by genetic or hereditary factors; general health or the frequency of sexually transmitted diseases; nutrition which will affect the health and vitality of mother and fetus; age of the woman in terms of adolescent subfecundity and climacteric ovarian slowdown;

psychological problems; menstrual and ovulatory cycles; the number of pregnancies and possible duration of lactation. A woman who experiences pregnancies but does not give birth would be fecund but not fertile. Essentially both concepts, for practical reasons, are measured by the number of offspring. However, it is essential to keep in mind that while we speak of and measure a woman's fertility, we must also consider the fecundity of the male. In reality, we are speaking of the fecundity of a couple.

Menarche is accepted as defining puberty and thus allowing the potential for pregnancies. Although conception is possible at this time, healthy eggs may not develop regularly until some years later. Cultural factors enter here, both morality and familial restrictions as well as the age of marriage. In the case of these South African Indians, we found relatively early marriage and first pregnancies ranging from age sixteen to thirty-seven for the younger women; between fifteen and thirty-four for the older cohorts. The mean age of first pregnancy is 23.0 for the premenopausal and 20.4 for the postmenopausal women.

Childbearing years differ from culture to culture. Realistically, they are from twelve to fifty (i.e., average ages of menarche and menopause), but a variety of cultural and technological factors may influence this. When we speak of completed family size, we also might have to differentiate between the number of children per woman, per wife, or per mother. Among black South Africans a young woman is usually expected to prove her fertility before a man will start negotiations about bride wealth. The result is that there are many mothers who are not wives. Among Indian South Africans, due to religious and cultural norms, mothers in almost all cases are wives; and since there is such a premium placed on marriage, almost all women are wives. Looking back over the women's reproductive years, we find that the last pregnancy for the younger ones was between ages twenty-eight and forty, with a mean of 33.3; for the older women the range of last pregnancy was twenty-one to forty-two, with a mean of 32.1.

Overall there is a lowering of the birthrate among Indian South Africans. This may be explained in part by birth control, the emancipation and education of women, and family planning in general. It is also due, however, to the age of marriage and the percentage of women in a particular age category who are married (in contrast to widowed, divorced, or single). Unfortunately, we do not have recent figures, but data presented by Mostert (see Table 11) show a gradual decrease of the total percentage of women in each age category who are married. This also reflects on the age of marriage.

TABLE 11

Percentage of Indian South African Women Aged 15–49
Who Were Married

Ages	1936	1946	1951	1960	1970
15–19	38.7	23.1	18.2	11.7	9.9
20–24	80.2	70.2	63.2	50.9	51.3
25–29	90.7	87.2	83.6	76.2	74.2
30–34	91.7	89.5	88.1	83.4	80.0
35–39	89.0	86.2	86.7	86.5	82.0
40–44	82.2	79.9	80.0	81.5	80.1
45–49	74.5	71.9	71.4	74.1	75.1
15–49	73.6	66.6	63.5	57.3	56.5

The number of pregnancies for the younger women ranged from one to nine, the mean being 4.2; among the older women, the number of children ranged from one to seventeen with a mean of 6.3. Of course, not all pregnancies resulted in live births. Fifteen (51.7%) of the pre- and fifteen (55.6%) of the postmenopausal women had one or more miscarriages or stillbirths. (Only one of the younger women had an abortion.) The largest number of live births for the younger women was seven, the mean being 3.4; for the older women, the largest number was fifteen, the mean 5.1. It is important to keep in mind that while the older women have all completed their reproductive careers and, because of menopause could no longer experience a pregnancy, this was not true for the younger women. Most of them stated emphatically, though, that they did not wish to become pregnant again — but there was the possibility; and for this reason, their reproductive careers must be seen as incomplete.

Medical facilities in South Africa have been adequate for decades, but home-birthing was prized among Indian South Africans. Cost certainly was a factor. Of greater importance was the familiarity of the setting and the support a woman, in many cases a very young woman, would receive from her mother, aunt, or elder sister. Related to this is the seriousness with which birth is viewed and the inherent danger of producing a new life. A doctor, nurse, or midwife will always be in attendance for the delivery or for the immediate postpartum period. Among the younger women, 65.5% stated that they did not have any children born at home, but only 14.8% of the

TABLE 12

Infant Mortality Figures for Indian South Africans
According to Gender, 1940–1971

Time Period	Males	Females
1940–44	96.8	84.3
1945–49	81.7	70.9
1950–54	70.7	48.1
1955–59	69.7	60.0
1960–64	64.9	51.2
1965–69	51.0	41.6
1970–71	39.6	32.2

Source: Lotter and van Tonder (1975(a):11).

older women did not have home births. Relatively few delivered at a clinic. Although only 37.9% of the younger women did not have a child delivered in a hospital, 81.5% of the older women did not. We notice here a major shift in one generation from home delivery to hospital confinement. This also involved changes in attendants. In home deliveries, 24.1% of the younger women were attended by a midwife and 41.4% by a physician. Among the older women, 55.6% were assisted by a midwife and only 7.4% by a physician. Nurses were present for about one-third of the cases in each age category. The midwife, *dhayi* in Hindi, *murtavachi* in Tamil, was both a link with the cultural tradition, thus psychologically reassuring, and also well versed and experienced in folk remedies. As women became better educated and housing arrangements changed, the midwife gradually lost her appeal. If she is present at an urban birth these days, it is because a traditional grandmother or mother insisted.

With better medical care, pre- and postnatally, infant mortality has decreased drastically. Lotter and van Tonder (see Table 12) discuss infant (including neonatal and post-neonatal) morality among Indian South Africans.

Our figures, though on a small sample, allow some interesting calculations. Table 13 presents the number of pregnancies — obviously the postmenopausal women have already completed their reproductive lives — and the number of live births. It also shows the number of pregnancies which miscarried and the number of infants who died before their second year. Infant mortality figures calculated as twenty per one thousand births among the younger, and

TABLE 13

Reproduction and Infant Mortality Among Indian South Africans

Category of Women	No. of Pregnancies	No. of Miscarriages/ Still Births	No. of Live Births	No. of Infantile Deaths	Infant Mortality
Premenopausal	123	23	100	2	20
Postmenopausal	169	32	137	4	29

twenty-nine per one thousand births among the older women, suggests a population that is urban and better-off than the rest of the Indian South African population.

Aging

In preparation for a workshop on aging organized by the Behavioral Sciences Research program in the National Institute on Aging in 1981, Matilda Riley enunciated four principles as general guidelines. These have applicability for the anthropological study of aging.

— Aging can be understood only in dynamic terms. The aging process cannot be separated from the social, cultural, and historical changes that surround it. People do not grow up and grow old in laboratories. Therefore, we must learn how different cohorts age and how society itself is changed by these differences.
— Aging can be understood only from the perspective of its socioculturally patterned variability, both within a single society and across societies.
— Aging can be understood only within the framework of the total life course. People do not begin to age at any specific point in life. Rather, aging occurs from birth (or earlier) up until death. And within the total society, people of all ages are interdependent.
— Individual aging, wherever and whenever it occurs, consists of a complex interplay among biological aging, psychological aging, and interactions with the changing social and cultural environment (Riley 1984:8).

We have discussed the families in which women grow up and within which they grow old. Indian South Africans have an expectation of marriage. They grow up in a family where some of the first things women can remember is being told the roles of (Tamil or any other specific group's) girls. They were socialized into expecting and accepting marriage (usually without a major role in the choice of a partner). Upon reaching menarche, "big girls" had to avoid boys; behave in certain ways; frequently drop out of (co-educational) school; and in many cases start preparing for marriage. In extended families and joint households, these girls grew up with a parental generation and frequently members of the grandparental generation. Except when financial considerations necessitated their absence, mothers and especially grandmothers were in the home. This presence is described as the ideal role, and ideal role performance takes place in the domestic setting. Aging, as it is perceived, learned, and experienced, is generational. A mother is a woman who has had a child, and a grandmother is one whose child has had a child. Grandmothers, irrespective of age or menopausal status, are expected to perform similar roles. They obviously differ in age but not in status or role expectation.

People are always somewhere in a continuum. They are no longer children, but they are not yet old; they may be old but they are still alive. Hammel speaks of this as secular age, stating that the "tune scale on which age is measured goes from zero to some maximum but does not repeat again from zero for the same unit" (1984: 142). He contrasts this with cyclical aging, as "in the repetitive renewal of households" (1984:142), and refers to the work of Meyer Fortes in this context. The household is, of course, no more cyclical than the life sequence of the individual. In fact, Fortes spells it out quite clearly in terms of three main stages, the third being that of replacement "which ends with the death of the parents" (1966:4–5). What takes its place is a new family or domestic group which in turn will run its course of three stages (or whatever number we designate).

Individual aging is, as Riley points out, an interplay of biological, psychological, and sociocultural factors (1984:8). For this reason, no two persons experience life the same way, nor do two persons age the same way. It is the responsibility of researchers to record details, note uniformities, and designate categories within which patterns of aging can be studied. One way of approaching this is through the relative age of research subjects. The age-stratification system consists of a series of age strata, each associated with a bundle of roles and statuses, and a series of cohorts passing through each stratum at different points in historical time. From the

TABLE 14

Ages Designated as "Middle Age" for Women

Age	Premenopausal		Postmenopausal	
	Middle Age Starts	Middle Age Ends	Middle Age Starts	Middle Age Ends
30	1 (3.4)			
35	6 (20.7)			
40	10 (34.5)	3 (10.7)	9 (33.3)	
45	5 (17.2)	2 (7.1)	4 (14.8)	
50	6 (20.7)	8 (28.6)	12 (44.4)	8 (32.0)
55	1 (3.4)	1 (3.6)	– –	6 (24.0)
60		13 (46.4)	2 (7.4)	7 (28.0)
65		1 (3.6)		2 (8.0)
70				2 (8.0)
Total	29 (99.9)	28 (100.0)	27 (99.9)	25 (100.0)
Missing		(1) –		(2) –

societal perspective, age serves as one mechanism (others are sex and social class) which structures roles and allocates individuals to these roles (Keith and Kertzer 1984:31). In this case, one studies cohorts and contrasts them with another category of cohorts. Such cohorts might be premenopausal versus postmenopausal women or smaller categories within these groups could be designated.

When the Indian South African women in this study were asked at what age a woman reached 'middle-age' and at what age that designation ended — the start of 'old-age' — they were quite explicit. Table 14 shows that there is a clear difference between the younger and the older women. There is always a range within each cohort, but each expects middle-age to last a number of years. The premenopausal women see middle-age as lasting from an average of 42.1 years until an average of 51.6 years of age. The postmenopausal group see a middle-aged woman on the average between 46.6 and 56.4 years of age. It is interesting that there is a difference between when the two cohorts think a person is middle-aged, and thus, by extension, when a woman is old. (On the average, men were seen as about five years older when designated middle-aged and when past middle-age.)

Many women found it difficult to place an age designation on a life stage. After all, a woman's status is dependent on the condition of her family and her grandchildren. Silverman (1975:313) points out that in "Colleverde," in central Italy, the designation "old woman" begins when "the daughter-in-law assumes charge of the household, or when the woman is considered old." Much the same role related criteria are employed in many other societies. Once again, it seems, whether a woman is menstruating or has reached menopause has little to do with her designation.

Among Tswana, Suggs (1987:116) points out that a woman relinquishes the role of an adult woman gradually, thus assuming the role of an old woman as she loses her capacity to perform as an adult woman. Age is very relative. What Riley (1984:8) referred to as an interplay of different kinds of aging was also recognized by Birren, who stated that there is biological, psychological, and social age. The latter "has the additional criterion of the extent to which the individual has acquired or performs various social roles which his society and his immediate social group expect of a person of his age" (1960:19). The problem may be that age may only refer to relative stages and thus be defined by the role performed rather than vice versa.

Some illustrative examples will clarify. The end of the child-bearing years do not necessarily agree with clinical menopause. Most researchers now agree that the age of menopause, around fifty, has not changed significantly in centuries. When we read that a woman's status changes after she has completed her childbearing years, we are usually dealing not with menopause but with a socio-cultural (and environmental) influence which causes a woman to have her last child between the ages of thirty and forty-five. Usually, having completed this phase of her life, she is considered an old woman. Roberts and Sinclair, discussing the menstrual cycle among women in Jamaica, explain that it terminates at ages over forty-five, "that is, after the completion of their childbearing period" (1978: 92–93). Also in Colombia (Reichel-Dolmatoff 1966:335), old age is transferred to the period of the forties, and relatively few people reach old age in Peru (Stein 1961:164).

Age thirty-five in women seems to have been considered a critical transitional age. Speaking of the Bontoc Igorot of the Philippines, Jenks states that by thirty a woman is getting old (1905:44). For the Waropen of New Guinea, Held sees thirty-five as the critical age (1957:38; see also Viljoen 1936:71). Data for some of the American Indians mention the same ages. "A woman is old on the plains at the age of 35 years, and seldom healthy" says Denig and the reproductive age was from eighteen to thirty-five (Denig 1930:513, see related ages given by Dorsey 1884:267–268). This also pertained to the Inuit in the Canadian Arctic (McElroy 1975:668).

African ethnographies suggest much the same picture in terms of statuses that are recognized. The Nyamwezi recognize the female life cycle as consisting of baby, young girl, young woman, and old woman (Abrahams 1967:67). The status "old woman" among the Dorobo is achieved "when they begin to look old" (Huntingford 1969:62). None of these authors refer to the cessation of menstruation nor do any of the ethnographers who use the term "menopause." By the use of this term they refer to a woman who is old, who no longer experiences pregnancies, or who no longer has sexual intercourse (Wagner 1960:42; Winter n.d.: 174; Schapera 1941: 194). In fact, women of this age are frequently expected to refrain from sexual intercourse. Such women may be grandmothers, women whose children have reached marriageable age, a woman whose eldest child is circumcised (at puberty) and so forth (see discussion by Ware 1979). Women past childbearing age could no longer pollute hunters of their gear (Amoss 1981:231). But these references should not suggest that such conditions are restricted to traditional societies. During the 1930s French doctors advised that postmenopausal women abstain from sexual activity and this was also true in Germany (Stearns 1976:106, 141).

Research among Indian South Africans has failed to produce a culturally recognized status of the postmenopausal woman. Thus, the woman who is released from *purdah* in Indian society or the woman who is terminologically recognized as having entered the status of older woman may or may not menstruate — it is beside the point. Tamil-speaking informants recognize the *peri pombla* or "big woman" in her forties and fifties (usually a young grandmother) in contrast to the *kalevi* or "old woman." If these people are related to the speaker, they might be addressed an *ama* (mother) or *aya* (grandmother) respectively. Gujerati-speakers use *dosima* or "old lady" based on age only. All of these categories of women are expected to be past the age of sexual involvement. In research, discussion of a possible pregnancy at age forty-three is invariably met with dismay and the statement that it would cause great embarrassment. Part of this derives from a woman having grown children, especially sons, because her status is enhanced by having a daughter-in-law. Such a senior woman should not be sexually active especially facing the possibility of pregnancy.

Not being sexually active assures that there will be no pregnancies. When this is associated with early anovulation, the status change from "woman" to "neutral" is recognized early. Khmer women at this stage crop their hair close to the scalp showing that they renounce worldly concerns — and it also "neutralizes their sex" (Ebihara 1968:501). At this stage women are said to be without sexual allure (Crapanzano 1980:31); or may be said to look like men (Warner 1958:132); or are often called men (Kidd 1904:239). Women who were beyond the childbearing age were said to be ritually neutral and could thus participate in religious and ritual activities. Not only did their status change but also their role in society.

Most societies in the world mark the attainment of menarche with some ritual accentuating a girl's potential for childbearing. Keith and Kertzer point out that "Anthropologists have burned the life-course candle at both ends. Until recently the only life stages examined thoroughly in terms of human development, norms and transitions were those at the youthful end" (1984:24). Having completed the childbearing stage of their lives, these same women return to a liberated state in which they may once again enter the cattle byre, appear in public without a veil, or sit in the company of men.

Black Carib women in their mid-forties have "borne their last children and at about this age they begin to take more active part in the ritual affairs. They enjoy greater freedom of movement, association, and activity as fertility declines and they pass the age of childbearing" (Kerns 1983:191). In Algeria, also, the childbearing years are correlated with the sexually active years when women are secluded. Those who have passed the childbearing years are seen on streets without veils (Walpole et al. 1965:128). This is essentially the same for Pakistani women, for whom there is a relaxation of the constraints of *purdah* (Pastner 978:445). The same freeing from restrictions and freedom of movement is also found in Taiwan (Gallin 1966:215), Korea (Osgood 1951:114), and Yugoslavia (McDonald et al. 1973:127).

Expansion of status and role. Freedom from restrictions, social as well as ritual, is not necessarily equivalent to an increase in status and access to new spheres of authority. The latter features are, however, found in association with the climacteric in numerous societies. By graduating from sex and childbearing a woman also graduates from the restrictions of the female role. In a legal sense she becomes a 'man.' In patriarchal societies, such a designation or ascription of status is seen as a gain.

This expansion of roles is clear among the Mundurucu. In the meetings of men, which are usually closed to adult women, men will make room for such a liberated woman to sit among them

(Murphy and Murphy 1974:105–106). The liberated Zapotec woman may go anywhere alone and attend fiestas (Chinas 1973:60). For the first time since menarche, a Gypsy woman is not subject to the strict *modaki* regulations (Trigg 1973:54–55). In Ethiopia, a woman may mark her attainment of venerated elder status with a rite of *Kasa*, for it is assumed such an elder, man or woman, is "too old to sin any longer" (Gamst 1969:111). Speaking of a Serbian community, Halpern (1958:203) points out that women of forty have reached the status of respected elder, which also gives them prestige and authority. Much the same status change is found among Puerto Rican women (Steward, Manners et al. 1956:223), and Iteso women (Lawrence 1957:124) past the childbearing age; among Sotho women who have passed the climacteric (Ashton 1967:100); and among postmenopausal women in Central America (Cosminsky and Scrimshaw 1982:44). Such older women may in fact become involved in cults and secret societies "in search of a new sphere of authority" (Lewis 1974:99). In an overall sense, it could be suggested that as the economic or reproductive roles of men or women decrease, so the ritual roles and access to supernatural forces will increase. In most societies, the respect with which the aged are treated is a direct result of this shift of power.

The useful new role. It is uncommon for women who are no longer childbearers to lose their domestic roles. They usually continue to serve as baby sitters for grandchildren and still do light household chores. They are usually seen as experienced or even experts at child rearing; as having the wisdom of age combined with the practical experience; and as having more time and patience.

Amoss and Harrell (1981:8–9) point out that because of this role continuity, women in many societies managed to weather the aging process better than men. The senior citizens, as we like to call them, are not isolated from their families but continue to be a vital part, giving and receiving support. In Malaysia women in this new status are treated with polite deference (Maday 1965:150), as are women in Burma (Henderson et al. 1971:74–75), Poland (Benet 1951:228), and the Andean region of South America (Bourque and Warren 1981: 105). In Thailand we find much the same situation as postmenopausal women retire from active household management but spend their time caring for grandchildren and helping with general chores such as cooking. At this age they are freer in their behavior and manner, breaking many taboos and prohibitions (Blanchard 1958: 437; De Young 1955:66–67).

Rituals are frequently part and parcel of status acquisition. There is not necessarily a ritual to mark the beginning and the end of a particular status. Marriage is marked by a ritual; its termination normally is not. Becoming a student is not ritually marked; graduation has all the trappings of ritual. The interesting fact is that while the attainment of the reproductive phase of life and the status associated with it is commonly marked by ritual, its termination is not. In Van Gennep's terminology, the attainment of fertility is a *rite de passage*. Hardly anywhere in the world is the menopause marked by such a ritual. The single example which we have come across pertains to the Meo of Northern Thailand.

> Each village has what is called a playground where the younger people assemble after a hard day's work in the field and pair off. Sex is available and happy. They also have a menopause ceremony for the older women. When a woman goes through the menopause she has a celebration if she can afford it. It is the only culture which I know of which celebrates the menopause in a positive manner. The woman gains some of the social attributes of a man. For instance, she is allowed to plant the first rice in the fields, which previously only men could do. This ceremony is a great celebration for all the family and the whole village is invited to it; it involves killing a good many ducks and pigs and is obviously expensive. Also, caution has to be exercised. One woman went through this ceremony and then her husband died — she remarried which manifestly proved that she was a woman again. This meant the new husband had to pay back her original family for all the animals that had been killed for the ceremony. Another woman had a child after the ceremony and she had to repay many ducks and pigs! (Potts 1979:162).

Interesting as this example may seem, it is obvious that we are once again dealing with the inaccurate use of the term 'menopause.' If a woman had in fact gone through the menopause, we would not expect either a renewed menses or a pregnancy. We would suggest that this refers to the termination of reproduction, i.e., the achieving of 'old woman' status, rather than clinical menopause.

These comments bring us to the ritual and religious realm. Hardly anywhere is this better expressed than in those communities where Muslims dominate.

The Middle Eastern or more specifically Islamic societies, are particularly conservative. Female religious activities mostly take place at home while men practice public worship. The latter activity is shared by postmenopausal women (Saunders 1980:64). In daily life, women are strictly controlled, first by their fathers and brothers and later by their husbands. But once they have passed the child-bearing years, they are considered to be without sexual allure and are permitted greater freedom (Crapanzano 1980:31; see also Maher 1978). Speaking of Iranian nomads, Nancy Tapper states: "For women, leadership is only possible after menopause, when their status approximates that of men. This happens both because of the old woman's presumed loss of sexuality and because of her freedom from many of her former domestic responsibilities, including child-bearing" (1978:377). Although her status may improve outside the home, she dreads the loss of the wife-and-mother role in the home. "Out of panic, they sometimes try to have just one more child, who will rejuvenate them in their husbands' eyes more effectively than a face lift" (Minai 1981:194–195). The Egyptian sociologist Hamed Ammar documents the freedom which an old woman enjoys and the fact that she may pass a group of men without covering her face (1954:49–50). These restrictions and their relaxation are based squarely on injunctions found in the Koran. Women who are menstruating are not pure (*tahir*) and may not enter the mosque or handle the sacred writings. Certain fasting periods are also affected as is the pilgrimage to Mecca. Those who are pregnant or postmenopausal may participate in these rituals. Saudi Arabia has a question on their official immigration forms asking whether an applicant has reached the menopause or not.

Women as mothers. Almost universally, we find reference to old age coinciding with changes in the mother role and the cessation of sexual activity. These two, are, of course, separable. One of the best examples in this connection is the so-called ghost marriage among the Nuer, a pastoral people in the Sudan. In this case, an influential older woman who has no children or who wishes to have an heir may marry a girl. The older woman finances the marriage trans-action, complete with bride-wealth, as if she were a man. The young woman may be visited by lovers and bear children. These serve to establish the older woman as their 'father' for purposes of inheri-tance and social status (Evans-Pritchard 1951). It is important to recognize that we are dealing here with the social recognition of a certain status. Gender is incidental to the role played (and ritual

performed) and the status thus achieved. As an old woman, classified as sexless, may adopt a child, so an older woman can "generate" a child without sexual involvement.

Negative views. Less common is the tendency to view the later
climacteric years in a negative way. This may be related to the Western European syndrome associated with fear of the loss of youth
and the loss of status attached to it. Grunberger (1971:262) and
Schalk (1971:314) respectively comment on the "twilight of eugenic
superfluity" and the "fortyish matron" when writing about the
German woman. In the United States and some other Western European countries we also find the fear of status loss which accom-
panies the maturing of the family, the 'empty nest syndrome,' and
tensions created by a role change forced on women in the absence of
the extended family.

Pauline Bart, in a number of very stimulating studies has
addressed this issue (1969, 1970, 1972, 1976, 1977). She suggests that
the presumed causal relationship between menopause and mental
depression is spurious. Rather, depression results from a situation in
which a woman either cannot continue rewarding roles or her role
receives negative value. For example, her changed role after the children leave home — men experience the same depression when after
retirement there is no role continuity. Bart, speaking of the United
States, says: "Black women had a lower rate of depression than
white women. The patterns of black female-role behavior rarely
result in depression in middle-age. Often, the 'granny' or 'aunty'
lives with the family and cares for the children while the children's
mother works; thus, the older woman suffers no maternal role loss"
1972:140). Much the same positive experience due to generational
interchange is reported in Italy (Silverman 1975:313–314).

A question that has not yet been studied is the total constellation of women's roles, i.e., what components other than mother and
sex partner are of critical importance in different cultures. Dougherty raises a very important question when she asks: "What transitions occur cross-culturally for childless women (customarily 10–20%
of women and a higher proportion in some groups) and women
who have no children that survive to adulthood?" (1982:149). What
happens to women who adopt children? Is adoption equal to natural
parentage and does adoption substitute in cases where parents do
not have naturally born offspring? Counts points out that adoption
is quite common and widespread in the Pacific; in West New Britain,
people continue adopting children into their seventies (1982:149).

Does the social and legal role of parenthood substitute for the biological one? Our own research among New Guinea highlanders
(du Toit 1974) and currently among urban Indians in South Africa
tends to offer a positive reply. In the case of childlessness, adoption
is repeatedly mentioned as a viable alternative — one which would
satisfy a very critical and demanding mother-in-law.

It is quite common in traditional societies to find a great deal of
ritual and status associated with motherhood. This is related no
doubt to the need for offspring to strengthen the kin group numeri-
cally, to generate bride-wealth, and to give continuity to the family.
Thus, premarital women among the Homa nomadic pastoralists care
for the cattle, a role which is also assigned to spinsters and divorcees. The postmenopausal woman, however, does not resume these
duties, even though she has lost her reproductive functions, because
she gains new authority free from ritual restrictions (Elam 1973:219).
She is also freed from restrictions which mark women who are married and can have children. "Having a child...changes the status of
a woman in all classes of Indian society," says Manischa Roy (1975:
125). She goes on to discuss the Bengali woman in her middle-age
but ties it directly to the aspect of motherhood and childbearing.
Large families are common, but urban and better-educated women
valued having fewer children.

> Women may stop reproducing before she is even close to the
> age of menopause. But after her last child she is made to
> believe by society that she is entering the time of waning sexual
> and reproductive capacity, even though in reality she may not
> be. If she has her last child in her mid-thirties, she may only
> remain absorbed in rearing it till she is forty. In this respect,
> the Bengali proverb, 'A woman is old by the time she is twenty,'
> has some truth in it (1975:128).

Indian South African women also recognize major changes
occurring around middle age. The single most frequently mentioned
change is menstruation stopping. One woman volunteered, "Indians
say after forty you are old!" Being old is associated with physical,
social and domestic and emotional/attitudinal changes.

When a woman reaches middle-age, she slows down and her
health starts to decline. This includes a general feeling of tiredness,
pains in the legs, putting on weight, and wrinkling of the skin as
well as other health problems. The most frequently mentioned being
arthritis, heart and "sugar" (diabetes). These infirmities and diseases

prevent normal routines. Women complained that they could not perform normal tasks or participate in physical activities like dances and are restricted in going to concerts and performances. Those who must diet "miss all the good food." As respected dames in the community, they are looked up to and have important roles in giving advice to young people. The women complained that responsibilities came with age. "You are not allowed, by the rules of society, to make a mistake. Your children and society watch you," they say.

At this time there also are changes in the home. A generation gap is created when children are grown and may be working or at university. Women attributed this to the fact that children, especially daughters, now had to have a craft or career. Much more than when they were growing up, there now is an ideational and behavioral gap between parents (especially the mother who in most cases is homebound) and children. Children also get married. We should be reminded that the Indian woman, with few exceptions, is a homemaker even today. She administers domestic affairs as the ideal wife/mother is supposed to and in the nuclear family setup there is the possibility of role continuity if she is left behind when the children leave. In some cases children break with their parental homes; daughters elope or sons get involved with alcohol, slighting their kinship obligations and not caring for their parents. Older people can also be made to feel out of place. "Children married, grandchildren all over. You don't feel its your house anymore. They tell you where you may put a chair," said one. In some cases, the daughter-in-law takes over or the woman develops hobbies or interests of her own. At the time of this study, a number of women who were better educated were learning French through the Alliance Francaise. For the first time, there also were classes in aerobics. These were restricted to younger women. Indian South African women are notoriously sedentary. They move around within the confines of the home but do not exercise, walk any distances, or keep in shape physically. One of the younger women thought about changes which coincided with middle-age and stated, "Life is complete. You've had your children. Periods stop. Outlook changes. What is left is extra." This attitude was much more common among the older than the younger women. The previous quotation has an expectancy to it; an implication that the life cycle which started with birth and childhood is completed when a woman has produced and reared the next generation. "What is left is extra(!)"

Bernice Neugarten speaks of events being anticipated, being "on time" if they occur when expected. "There are two distinctions worth making: first, that it is the unanticipated life events, not the anticipated...which is likely to represent the traumatic event. Moreover, major stresses are caused by events that upset the sequence and rhythm of the life cycle...when the empty nest, grandparenthood, retirement, major illness, or widowhood occur *off time*. In this sense then, a psychology of the life cycle is not a psychology of crisis behavior so much as it is a psychology of timing" (1970:86–87). Both the timing and the events which are recognized as markers will differ from one culture to another, and also possibly from one generation to another. One major stress-producing marker is the education of the daughter — the residential change this implies, and the independence it permits. This was not the case for the older generation nor is it likely to be so for the next generation. Some women are coming to grips with it. "I feel better now, I've adjusted to the new way. We must listen to the children and vice versa," said one woman. Another put it simply, "Don't envy young people, accept it." There is also resignation. "We start out with hopes, but at old age our hopes die down." But the acceptance of menopause is generally positive. What the new generation will bring is a positive attitude about the postmenopausal years.

How do Indian South African women feel about aging? There are positive aspects. Age brings experience and understanding: it brings more leisure which allows time for religious activities. A woman has important responsibilities toward her grandchildren and in her senior status, she may proffer advice. A person who is old has lived many experiences and seen many things. She is mature and normally gets respect. Being experienced, she is more independent, may do what she chooses to do, and usually runs her own affairs to a greater extent than before. One woman smiled and said, "...and you no longer have to please the in-laws." While most of the women recognized physical changes — wrinkles and gray hair — as negative effects of aging, a few were proud of the gray, emphasizing that they didn't color it because it was becoming to a senior woman.

Aging, however, produces fears. The one most frequently expressed was that of becoming physically infirm, sick, bed-ridden, and being dependent on somebody else. This was also the reason why some women stated they did not want to become very old. Postmenopausal status removed both the desire for and obligation for sexual intercourse with the husband. Walking "with a stick" was acceptable; being able to be active around the home was desirable; being involved with the education and moral instruction of the grandchildren was essential. That is the role of a grandmother. She must maintain her stature within the family and community. This involves behavior, dress, interaction, and example. Waxing philosophical, a number of women commented on the ideal of growing old in a respected, graceful way. Though age is forced upon us, one woman hoped she "would grow old gracefully and not become orthodox (stereotyped)."

Old-age is a distinct possibility, but the infirmities which accompany it are not restricted to a particular age. Knowing about the infirmities and problems which might accompany old-age, how do Indian South African women approach this life phase?

There obviously was a certain resignation to this condition which comes to all who live long enough. Most of the women stated simply that it will come and they must accept it, but two active attitudes also emerged. First are large numbers who "pray to God to remove me before I am too old," or conversely, who pray for health and strength. One of the younger women explained, "I always tell my husband I'd like to live to fifty or fifty-five at the most, then God must take me. Too many old people are dependent on their children and they become a burden." There was a realization, born no doubt from experience, that a very old and infirm person is a burden upon a family; and for this reason, a number of women would simply prefer to die. Second, there are those who do something about aging by taking care of their health, avoiding catching cold, exercising regularly, and eating nutritious foods. One woman's regimen called for brown bread (whole wheat is even better); polished rice and potato (but not too much starch); and cutting down on oil and sugar.

In the Indian tradition, it is incumbent upon children to care for their parents. A mother would prefer to live with her son. But a son also implies a daughter-in-law. One woman who is not to be envied has five sons, and her statement that "a daughter-in-law is a hell of a thing" does not bode well for her future. Most said that they were living alone or as they could. Ideally, they would live with their husbands. This independence allowed them quiet, self-reliance, and autonomy even though the marriage relationship might be different, i.e., usually not including sexual relations. "As long as my husband doesn't mind and go looking for a younger woman, I'd like to have him along." one woman explained.

But what about alternatives? When independent living was no longer an option, old people either had to live with the children or seek some other arrangement. A number of joint-family homes have been built allowing for extended family members to live together, but many families (especially those at the lower end of the economic scale) do not have the option of co-residence. In a few cases, a small apartment or room might be added to house an aging parent. While the research was in progress, the father of one of the women died at age 105. She as the youngest surviving daughter had cared for him for many years. One alternative is for an old person to remain independent by renting part of her home to a younger person, with the understanding that assistance is part of the contract.

In Durban there is an old-age home run by the government for Indians, but it is not well operated and not very popular. In Transvaal, there simply is no home or related institution to cater to these people. What was their attitude about an old-age home? Doesn't it allow for a further break up of the extended family? One woman was quite outspoken. "My sons say they will burn it down if one is built in Laudium," she said. The reason for this strongest negative sentiment is that it becomes an excuse for children not to honor their kinship obligation. It would be easy to justify noncare for parents by pointing to the availability of an institution. This would contribute still more to the fragmentation of the kutum and the joint family and to the negative effects of social change in the Indian community. Not everybody felt that strongly about it. In general, there was a more accepting and even positive attitude about old-age homes among the younger women than among the older ones. A common sentiment was expressed in these words: "While I'll never send my mother to an old-age home, I'll go there." Another one of the younger women explained, "It is our custom to look after the aged in the home and family; but if a person can't look after herself, she must be sent to an old age home — children of today don't want old people around." Others suggested that an institution of that nature should be there only for the financially needy or the very sick. Persons who were more positive pointed out the advantages of companionship and support in a home for the aged: care for those who have no one to care for them, and friends of the same age group.

Alternatives were suggested, usually a day care center, or activity centers where old people perhaps too infirm to go visiting could be with their age mates and friends, interacting and being entertained. At night they must be cared for by their families. In the old extended family, it was explained, somebody was always home. Now it frequently happened that both parents worked and when the children were grown, there was no support for a grandparent.

As is frequently the case in societies where life expectancy is unclear and the status of women is low, these women viewed aging negatively. The major role of Indian South African women is a biological and nurturing one. They are expected to produce an heir; their greatest moment is the birth of a child; and the completion of this role occurs when they have had their last child. Menopause, which usually comes a few years later, puts a seal on their reproductive abilities. For most, especially the older and/or more traditional women, conditions are expected to deteriorate. Aging is a condition that they do not savor.

4

෫෧

Being a Woman

Introduction

Every person is socialized with certain role expectations. These are gender-based and reinforced from the earliest age by words and acts of the parental generation and by approval or disapproval of the child's behavior. In communities where gender differences are greater and where girls and boys are socialized differently, we may expect to find a greater contrast between the expected female and male roles than in present day United States society. Because the mother is the primary socializing agent, she has a better idea of gender-role expectations than would the father in the same family. Thus we can hypothesize a lag in men's conception of women's roles. This lag will be reflected in the ways men think about women's ideals and actions and in their views of themselves and their roles. In contrast, we might expect a much greater uniformity in the views of women concerning men, but particularly in their views concerning women in their own society. After all, they were the socializing agents in each case.

Nancy Chodorow (1974) has presented a very useful discussion of women's roles in which she points at the psychological boundaries between persons. In the process of identifying self, every person develops "ego boundaries, or a firm sense of self." These boundaries are quite clearly expressed vis-a-vis members of the opposite gender but not relative to a family member of the same gender. The result is that a girl grows up in a relationship where proper behavior is emulated and the boundaries between grandmother/mother/daughter are only relative ones. A woman sees herself as an extension of her mother and her daughter as an extension of herself. This, I would suggest, makes socialization easier within the same gender but also makes radical changes (e.g., secularization of women's roles) harder to accept and to integrate.

This chapter deals with the views of women regarding their roles and how they should be performed. It also discusses the image of women as contrasted with men and the way it is given expression by Indian South African women.

Role Conception and Performance

Though there is a preference for a male child, particularly if it is the firstborn, the Indian child is welcomed and loved irrespective of gender. It is a source of pride, a sign of fertility and achievement, and an investment in the future. In almost every case, the child grows up in a family context (as contrasted with single parenting) where there is a mother who loves, cares, and disciplines and a father who frequently is absent during the day — and may be apt to spoil the young child when he is at home.

The child has role models at the parental level, and if they live in the kutum or the joint family, also at the extended level of uncles and aunts and grandparents. Lynn has addressed the role modeling of parents, especially the mother (1969) and the father (1974). There is a clear distinction between the preference and adoption of sex roles, and identification with a sex role. These differences were also discussed in Brown (1958) and Lynn (1966). At the core is *sex role preference*, which pertains to the way in which the child conceives of and evaluates the role of one gender as compared to the other. Studies have dealt with this question by presenting a child with a series of pictures or objects from which an appropriate choice must be made. It is useful to keep in mind here that children are never neutral. They have been receiving stimuli since birth. "Even the fetus does not exist in a socially neutral environment. Parents have sex preferences and make gender-related attributions well before birth. There still exists in our society a clear preference for male children...it has been found that when the first child is a boy the interval before the next child is, on the average, three months longer than it is when the first child is a girl" (Unger 1979:168). Related to the sex role preference is the second criterion, *sex role adoption*. No doubt influenced by expressed preference and by socialization, a person adopts certain gender roles such as dressing, speaking, acting, or behaving in accordance with expectations for a member of that gender in that culture. Perhaps most important, influenced but not determined by the above, is *sex role identification*. This refers to internalization of the particular role and may be expressed as gender identity.

The Basis of Gender Identity

In this discussion we look at the ideal role for an Indian South African woman as seen through the responses of these women. Ideal roles involve correct and proper behavior, behavior which will be rewarded not only within the family but also in a wider context by the members of the community. Women are expected to perform as females, wives, and homemakers.

Chrysee Kline (1975:487) points out that roles must be conceptualized according to normative, behavioral, and interactional aspects. Every role must be performed in a certain way: this normative component will obviously show variation due to such factors as culture. other roles performed, context, and so forth. Roles are components of individual behavior and will be influenced by other factors in the behavioral matrix. Roles also involve at least one other person so that interaction and context may influence the expression of certain statuses. But nobody ever performs only a single role. Due to ascriptive statuses of ethnicity, gender, and age as well as achieved statuses, each role in turn influences and is influenced by others. It is useful to follow Shirley Angrist, whose study of sex roles suggests that we look at sex role constellations because a person never acts or behaves "just as a man or woman" (1972:103). It should be kept in mind, too, that roles are dynamic and change through time; or stated in a different way, the performance of a role will change as the performer ages, taking on new roles and abandoning others.

Gender differences. Indian South African women in our sample recognize the obvious differences between females and males or between girls and boys. Biological differences, however, are matched by differences in behavior and temperament which are recognized culturally.

Girls tend to be quiet, friendly, sociable, loving, and obedient. They are more homebound and in turn are protected and pampered. They tend to be more polite and want to please the mother, with the result that they are taught kitchen activities and can assist their mothers. Girls want to be attractive, which requires them to dress in bright colors, to be reserved, quiet, and submissive. "If a girl is bathed, she must be dried under her arms and in the genital area — boys get dry by themselves," said Mrs. Padayachee, a wise grandmother five times over. One of the younger women who is well educated pointed out with some resentment that Indian girls are guided as if they couldn't think for themselves. This is all part of the protection which also stipulates that a girl should not go out by herself but always be accompanied by her mother or her brother.

Boys...well that's a different story. They are noisy, naughty, rebellious, and much more active. They tend to go out more and are allowed greater freedom (there quite clearly is a relationship of permissiveness here). Boys are bossy, demanding, and dominating and "their socialization confirms this," said one of the younger women. They are assertive and mischievous and go out without any consideration for their mothers. However, at age thirteen or fourteen they change. They become introverted and quiet. They now prefer to be alone in their rooms listening to music — they become loners. Mrs. Desai had an extremely strained marriage. Her husband always sided with his mother against her, as daughter-in-law she resided in the patrilineal joint-family. She said bitterly, "Sons are mommies' babies, they listen to their mothers not their wives!"

These differences are recognized in childhood and continue into adulthood. For as girls differ from boys in behavior and treatment, so do women differ from men. This is the area where the individual, behavior, and institutions all come together.

A woman is essentially domesticated. She is involved in and enjoys household affairs and is home-loving. Women, by choice, are in the background; and this pertains especially to younger women. Even the educated younger women are subdued. In many conservative families, the women may not even serve food to men — this is done by a servant — or eat with them. Women told me that women are not allowed to sit with men at functions, e.g., a Muslim wedding. Even at home, in many cases, they would not join the company. Men frequently are served and eat before the women. Women, of course, do not go to the mosque. Their major role then is in the home. Women informants made an interesting deduction. They pointed out that *because* women are isolated and restricted and must stay home, their men tend to treat them as delicate creatures and spoil them. Another stated that women are considered sacred. Women, in the roles of wives and mothers, keep tradition alive. An oft quoted Gujerati idiom says: "Train a man and you've just trained a household, but train a woman and you've trained a nation."

On the whole, it is said a man does not encourage his wife to study or to become a professional because this would simultaneously raise her status and take her out of the home. Independence, especially in a financial sense, would change the face of Indian society. Explains one wife, "The woman is more dependent on the man than vice versa and tends to be guided, in fact, dominated, by the man. When it comes to children, the man's decisions count."

Indian men are looked up to. "The man is higher than the woman; he always deserves best," said one woman. "It is the right way," echoes another. But an older woman who has been around for a while gave a wise smile and said, "Man is the breadwinner but the woman is kept home to cook the bread."

Gender differences also imply ability. The first and most elementary difference that was recognized involved the ability to cause pregnancy and to become pregnant. "No man could have a baby" was repeatedly stated. However, as one pointed out, "they can have as many affairs as they like and never fall pregnant...if a woman tried it, she would fall pregnant the very first time."

The second area of ability which was repeatedly mentioned was in the area of homemaking. A man simply cannot run a household; he cannot cook or sew, and he certainly cannot raise the children. Guiding youngsters through childhood, especially girls, is something unique to a mother. While a father/man is necessary to lay down the law in the house and to ensure obedience, that is only the formal side; it takes a mother/woman to manage a home and to raise the children.

This suggests acceptance of the complementariness of female and male. It also suggests insistence on a higher status of and greater recognition for women.

Physiological differences. One of the most basic differences which Indian South African women recognize between women and men is the monthly change in hormonal balance and menstrual flow.

Do women, in fact, have an advantage because they menstruate, or conversely, do men have an advantage because they do not? In tallying the responses, the conclusion seemed contradictory: both women and men were said to have an advantage. When one looks at the reasoning behind the responses, the contradiction disappears.

Women have an advantage because they experience a monthly internal purification. "Old blood" is shed along with "impurities." While a woman menstruates she will hardly ever be sick. It is only when the monthly flow is interrupted that changes occur. If a woman does not menstruate, she must be pregnant. In this regard, the monthly flow not only enables women to become pregnant but becomes a useful marker of both youthfulness and pregnancy. When a woman menstruates, she "thinks she is still young," one woman stated. Women who do not menstruate and are not pregnant are prone to having problems. The "impurities" which had previously been removed by the monthly flow now "go up" causing hot flashes and also causing blood pressure to go up. Because the impurities go up, women are prone to headaches. They also get "high blood," "veins in their legs" and are prone to obesity, heart attacks, and cancer because they are no longer menstruating. Menstruating women are not allowed to engage in sexual intercourse. Muslim women are not allowed to fast or pray and must withdraw for seven days. Hindu women are not allowed to light the sacred lamp (*veleku*) in the home or go to the temple. Some women saw these restrictions as advantages, as a break in the routine.

In contrast, men do not have to go through premenstrual tension and back pain; they do not have the fear of pregnancy; they need not give birth; and they do not have to go through the "monthly bother." They are never impure and can attend the mosque, the temple, and all funerals. He can have sex at all times. However, Mrs. Abramjee stated, "My husband says shaving is men's curse — God made it that way." Most women would settle for the way God made it. They enjoy being women because of the themes and values in Indian cultural traditions with which they were raised.

Emotional and physical differences. From the discussion to this point and the numerous statements by Indian South African women, it is evident that they saw clear differences between their menfolk and themselves. These differences range from physical characteristics to emotional strength and are as much a product of nature as of nurture.

There was little disagreement regarding physical or bodily strength. Men can do the hard work around the home; they can make a living at construction, or they are seen as larger and more physical. Only two of the women in our older category, both of whom had made a living first at hawking and later as tradeswomen, felt that they could hold their own against a man. For them, muscular strength had to balance an inner strength and endurance.

In the realm of endurance, the women were sure that men were inferior (only three younger women gave the edge to the men). It was, they said, because men did not have staying power; they could not take pain or suffering and, thus, would back off or discontinue their effort. With two exceptions, all the women in this study agreed that when it came to pain and suffering, women were way ahead. The first example mentioned was that of childbirth. "Men can't bear pain — especially Indian men," said one of the older women. A younger cohort responded, "Indian men in particular are soft because their mothers spoiled them and their wives are supposed to do the same." Retorted a third, "...can you imagine a man in labor?" A man, they all agreed, wanted to be fussed over at the slightest discomfort, went to bed with a headache, disrupted the household over a runny nose, and if he had a pain behaved like a colicky baby. One of the older women who has seen fifty years of marriage and raised her family was amused at the question about who was stronger at withstanding pain. She stated, "If a woman sleeps with her husband, that's a pain; if a woman has his child, that's another pain. Hindu women are more accepting and tolerant."

In the realm of emotional strength, there was a much greater range of responses. Seventeen (58.6%) of the younger as well as eighteen (66.7%) of the older women saw men as stronger. "Men will never cry" was frequently stated, but in almost every case a clarifier was added. Among the latter were: " . . . he doesn't care if he hurts your feelings"; "because they don't care"; "because they don't have soft hearts like women." Women, on the other hand, show their emotions under stress: they confide in each other; they cry it out together. This makes it easier for women to handle grief and pain. Because they express their emotions, Hindu women are not allowed to go to a crematorium or funeral — the eldest son or closest male relative lights the fire. But being emotional makes a woman more buoyant. She can put up with a lot to maintain the respect and reputation of her home and family. In the same vein, it was suggested that "a woman can keep the home fires burning even on five cents" because she is emotionally adaptable.

Role Expectations

Domestic roles. Indian South African social and economic structure produces a community in which males are out working, leaving women alone during the day. Receptions, entertainments, and parties essentially take place on weekends because men get home late. They frequently have to drive long distances to work outside their segregated residential communities. A question arises, given both the economic circumstances and the status of males, as to whether husbands are jealous. In numerous contexts, women alluded to the fact that men might have extramarital affairs; that they frequently had girlfriends; that Muslim men could marry up to four wives; and that with the ideal of no divorce, people frequently remained married but not emotionally pair-bonded.

The majority of women in this study (twenty or 69.0% of the premenopausal and fourteen or 53.8% of the postmenopausal category) stated that their husbands were jealous. If they dressed up, even to go out with other women or with their children, some men became suspicious. If another man paid attention to a married woman or if she paid attention to another man, her husband would react. Specific examples are: "If there are men in the company and I talk to them without including him"; "If I'm friendly with male friends"; "If I dance with a stranger"; and "If I wear a see-through blouse." A young woman complained that, as a nurse, she often had to talk to or show attention to men whom they had met as a couple. Her husband got mad. Another educated woman said she could not talk on the telephone, put a cup of tea into a man's hand, see someone off at the gate; or ever go out alone except to work. Her husband "doesn't say anything, but his eyes...!"

Some men scold their wives, others insist on knowing everyone with whom they interact by phone or in person; others simply frown and look cross, or pick an argument. Those who do not get annoyed will recall past events or just become crabby and irritable if their wives have had social contact with other men.

Parenting. The question of a woman's fertility is involved in her role definition and role realization. At issue is the question whether a woman who has not had a child is really considered complete; and related to that, whether a childless marriage is lacking a necessary component.

Writing within the context of the United States and the women's movement, Rhoda Unger (1979:330) states that womenhood is not necessarily the same as motherhood. While that is true culturally and biologically, Indian South African women would disagree. For reasons of self, husband, and in-laws, an adult Indian woman must also be a mother. When asked whether a woman who has not had a child is a complete woman, nineteen (65.5%) of the premenopausal and eighteen (66.7%) of the postmenopausal women said she was not.

The reasons behind this response were psychological, emotional, and social in nature. Responses which fell into the first category suggested that a woman who has not brought a child into the world, lacks the experience or the special feeling which results in labor and birth. This bond is something a mother can only experience with her natural child, never with an adopted child. It is a complete experience. It results in that special feeling when a child calls you "Ma!" One woman suggested that to be a woman one must go through the pains of childbirth.

Others felt that there are biological and emotional components to motherhood. Without a child, there is a feeling of emptiness, as if something is missing. The experience of pregnancy tends to soften a woman, it was explained. She would have more understanding and be more patient with children.

Not having a child also involves social and religious aspects. A number of women stated that religion teaches there must be a child, and that through a child the parents love each other or come to love each other. A Tamil woman pointed out that unless a woman has had a child she cannot help with wedding rituals. There is a belief that childlessness is an affliction that can be passed on to a bride. A Hindu stated, "God created women for reproduction. It makes her complete. If a married woman dies before her husband and before she has a child, she is buried in her bridal clothes." Other women emphasized the support aspect of children. Without a child she lacks "somebody to call her own." And even more important asked one, "Who will care for you? Who will sit with you? Who will mourn for you?"

Hilda Kuper speaks to the importance of children in a woman's life but also in a marriage.

> Children are the fulfillment of marriage, and the hopes of the childless are maintained by the belief that conception is a blessing, a blessing that is demonstrated daily. The high birth rate of the Indian community is an accepted fact. Should a young wife not fall pregnant within the first year of marriage, the usual procedure is to seek a possibly purely physical defect through consultation with a doctor of medicine and also to expiate a more fundamental or spiritual misfortune. The woman is generally held responsible by the man's kin, who may in anger or disappointment insult her with her affliction which is regarded as possibly a punishment for sin in a previous life, and she, usually accompanied by one of her own kin, will try to expiate by devotions at the temple, or vows of penance to her home gods (1960:122–23).

Findings among women in our research sample overwhelmingly support this statement. In fact, twenty-seven (93.1%) of the premenopausal and twenty-five (92.6%) of the postmenopausal women confirmed that a marriage without children was not complete. One woman stated it so clearly when she said, "...because the husband *needs* a family and the wife also *likes* to have a child." The father's name is carried by the son, but even a daughter assures him status. The reason for a child in a family, though, is that it brings the young wife and husband together. It completes their union and gives them a common goal, namely, the raising and education of the child. In the process it keeps them happy and together. One of the better educated women in this study explained, "If theirs is an arranged marriage, it brings them together with a common interest; if they married for love, a child replaces their waning passion. It softens the woman and makes their relationship complete."

But a child is also important in a social sense. Husband and wife won't get bored with each other; the husband is less likely to seek extramarital affairs which could result in separation or divorce; and it will ease their old age. One woman best expressed another important consideration when she stated that marriage (without children) would not be complete. The in-laws would make her life a total disaster. "Where God meant for people to have children, couples who do not are not doing their duty. But if God doesn't want to give them children, they can't fight with God."

More immediate than supernatural sanctions or blessing are the social implication of having or not having children. What would "people" say if a woman did not have a child; or conversely, what would these same people say if she had twenty children?

The reactions of others may call for responses of a social, religious, or ritual nature. An adult married woman who does not have a child is looked down on, will feel shame, and is likely to be harassed by the in-laws. It will be suggested that the husband should marry another woman or that she might be a 'moffie' (i.e., a lesbian). The husband is never blamed other than through the suggestion that maybe he isn't home enough. In a religious context, a childless woman knows what to do but will receive advice from others concerning prayer and sacrifice. Women who have problems conceiving will go to the mosque or the temple, depending on their religious group membership. "Generally, Muslim women do not enter the mosques in South Africa for purposes of praying due to the prevailing tradition in terms of which men and women pray separately" (Meer 1969:191). Muslim women may, however, visit the back of the mosque, where they may consult with the *molana* (priest) to learn if their childlessness is Allah's will and whether anything can be done about it. The molana may sprinkle sacred water, or tie a *ta-wiz* (a piece of cloth or wool in which words from the Koran have been embroidered in black) around the loins of the woman. Hindu women may pray on their own or with a priest at the temple. Depending on the Hindu subgroup, the prayers may be addressed to any of a number of female goddesses; specifically to Kalie (the female goddess Sakti, in the form of the divine mother), Ganesha (son of

Shiva), or to Shiva himself. In addition to sacrifices or burning camphor for Shiva, a woman can make a vow. The making of vows is a distinctive religious practice for women in Hinduism. Vows entail abstention from food and ascetic rigor on certain days and on the days preceding and following them for an approved number of years. For instance, a woman might vow that if her husband or child recovers from an illness, she will not eat or will refrain from eating certain foods, on certain days for a fixed number of months or years (Bhattacharyyi 1953:202). In this case, women will vow that if they have a child, they will give the equivalent weight in gold or jewels to the poor — either personally or through the priest. Tamil believers go to the temple with an offering of fruit or coconut and present it to the priest who will pray for them. He officiates in an intercessory role and ties a yellow string around the woman's wrist. Some of this, women explained, may be blamed on a woman's previous life (Hindu believe in reincarnation) or two people getting married without the traditional blessing.

Inability to conceive may also reflect a woman's earlier lifestyle. If she remains childless, people will say that she must have lived a wild life in her early years, or she must have had an abortion before marriage. Explained one of the college lecturers in our study, "There is a lot of superstition; the in-laws especially, will say she must have been very promiscuous. That is supposed to use up the fertile eggs of a woman much as masturbation is supposed to use up good sperm in a man."

A woman who doesn't have children feels shame and is pitied, but she is also a "bad luck woman" to be avoided in certain ritual contexts. It is unlucky to see her face early in the morning; brides are not allowed to look into the face of a childless woman because they, too, may be childless; and such women can be cut out of the social life. Tamil women used herbal mixtures to counter barrenness. There are a number of leaves involved (we were unable to gather a sample of them) which are ground in their green form and made into a small ball which is swallowed. In the past, a woman might go to a temple where a priest, who goes into a trance, removes a substance from the vaginal canal that is said to be "blocking the womb." Nowadays women say they will go see a doctor. It is interesting that whereas Gujerati designates a barren woman *vanjhni* and the couple *vanjhiya*, these words are derived from the same root, but the man is not held accountable. She will be shunned by her in-laws, and despised by her husband. His family will ask him, "Are you married to a mule?"

But, says an idiom, "A house full of children is a house full of gold." So what will the public reaction be to a woman having a very large number of children? We used the number twenty thinking that this would sound preposterous, even shocking. Instead, a number of the women, especially the older ones, responded simply with, "children are luck" or "I'd like it." There were a large number of positive responses among the older as well as the younger women. Some reasons given for positive feelings were that the in-laws would be happy and that children are a gift from God. "Children are money — nobody will ask you how much money you have in the bank but how many children you have," stated a Muslim woman.

On the negative side, women said their neighbors would say they bred like goats (or dogs, or rabbits). "Maybe they're not all the children of one man...the children don't look like their daddy." It was suggested that a woman with so many children had to be a "sex maniac" or was obviously a "child-a-year woman." How such people spent their time was also questioned. "Maybe they don't have TV and have nothing better to do." someone suggested. A number of the women wondered why some type of birth control had not been used by those with very large families.

An interesting point in this context is that, once again, the husband is not blamed. He is instrumental, being used by the wife; but blame for a large family (like the blame for no children) is placed on the woman. Says Hilda Kuper:

> Children of both sexes are desired, but since sons are required to carry out funeral rites and make ancestral devotions, special rituals are sometimes performed for them. No limit is set on the size of families, but there is no injunction against family limitation as long as it does not involve acts considered morally degrading and physically harmful (1960:123).

How then did the women feel about their own families? Are they satisfied with the number of children they have, or would they have liked to have a different number of children? In the case of the postmenopausal women, the family is complete. But in the case of some of the premenopausal women, pregnancy still is a possibility; and we are dealing with the possibility of change in family size. Table 15 represents their responses to the question: On the basis of your experience, if you were a young woman starting a family would you want (none) (fewer) (same number) (more) children than you have? While the first choice among pre- and postmenopausal women is reversed, we find that respectively 69.0% and 74.0% of

TABLE 15

What Change in Number of Children
Would You Want if You Could Start Over?

	Premenopausal		Postmenopausal	
	Number	Percent	Number	Percent
None	–		–	
Fewer	6	(20.7)	12	(44.4)
Same	14	(48.3)	8	(29.6)
More	9	(31.0)	7	(25.9)

these women would prefer the same number or fewer children. The difference may be ascribed to younger women who have not completed their reproductive roles — but the difference is relatively small.

The postmenopausal women pointed out that when they were young, they didn't know about the pill, clinic, or family planning and the result was large families. Others felt that economically it was becoming too tough to have a large family if you wanted to give children an education and a good chance in life. However, those older women who desired larger families were equally convincing. "When I die my sons and daughters will sit around my coffin crying. People will say she was blessed: Look at all her children mourning for her." Another felt that "as you get older in life children are all you have. No father, no mother. If you fall they pick you up. If there are six, there are always two or three who are good."

An almost identical justification came from one of the premenopausal women: "More is better. If you have one son he can turn away. Have more and at least one will care for you." A large family fills the house with life and activity. Everyone has something to contribute. One is never lonely. Those who would prefer to have fewer children justify it on economic grounds as well. For a child to be given a chance at a good education and a quality lifestyle, parents should limit the number of children.

It is interesting that in both categories of women, those who advocated a smaller number of children gave altruistic reasons referring to the future of the child. Those who would like to have a larger number of children in almost every case did so for egotistical reasons, i.e., to support, care, or mourn for the mother. The middle-of-the-roader said it most succinctly, "...the same, emotionally I couldn't cope with more."

We now have some indication of the value of children and the considerations which enter into deciding their number. Every woman in this research responded positively to the question of whether there is value in having children. Two in the younger category, though, suggested that they might not marry again given a second chance, but they did want children because of the companionship. There are essentially three areas of response regarding the value of children. The first and overwhelming number of responses spoke of the *future value* of children as support in a parent's old age. This is, of course, a folk model which substitutes children for social security, insurance, and pensions. Women pointed out that "Girls dowries take more than they give back, but still they are there to support you in your old age." There is also a realization that conditions are changing as young people move away or do not perform their kinship obligations. A second area of response deals with the *emotional value* children have. They provide love and companionship and allow a woman to feel that she is a woman; she brought forth children; or that she could see someone she produced become an asset to the community; or that it makes a parent proud and is emotionally fulfilling. The third area of response recognizes that *the extended family is breaking down thus increasing the importance of the nuclear family.* That there had to be enough children to support each other is a response typical of the Indian community that sees support as originating essentially within the kingroup. When the kutum breaks down or the joint family disappears due to housing restrictions, there is still the business built up by a father and shared by all the sons. This is where obligation lies. Assist your brothers and sisters and expect the same support.

Image: The Modern Indian South African Woman

Everyone presents an image to others that communicates certain basic information about herself. However, there is usually a difference between what a person thinks she is projecting, i.e., her self-image, and what others actually see — her real image. The latter frequently is influenced by behavior as a woman gives expression to her conception of who she is. Speaking of womanhood among American blacks, Joyce Ladner states:

> The identity an individual assumes is crucial to an understanding of her behavior. Human behavior can best be understood

by probing into the set of individual characteristics that define her ideology, sentiments, beliefs, lifestyle and so forth. However, an individual's identity is in large part a product of her experiences in the society in which she has been socialized. The person she is, the way she comes to feel and respond to events in her environment are highly conditioned by the cultural milieu (1971:107).

But even more specific is the cultural identity which results in an expression of femininity. A number of researchers have recently dealt with this subject, e.g., Gough (1952), Lott (1981), Brownmiller (1984), and Jackson and Cash (1985). From our point of interest, the dominant finding is that the cultural component is the primary one. But cross-cultural studies of femininity are lacking, in part because being feminine is defined in very specific cultural terms which reflect roles, values, and image. Cross-cultural studies in this context give less emphasis to feminine role and image than to culture and personality studies, e.g., Mead (1935) and Kessler (1976). Because feminine roles — particularly image — are so strongly defined by cultural context, it is best to rely on the descriptions of participants in the particular culture. What makes an Indian South African woman attractive? What does she do to enhance this attractiveness?

Model

The old cliche that beauty is in the eye of the beholder is certainly true; but by asking a number of beholders, it is possible to arrive at some kind of general model of what features, characteristics, and attributes are most valued.

To arrive at this information, we asked a simple question and allowed the women to interpret it the way they wished and answer accordingly: what makes a woman attractive/beautiful? The item most frequently mentioned was dress. This meant wearing the *sari* according to religious and ethnic prescriptions, looking dignified, and matching makeup with the rest of your appearance. But external beauty was mentioned only slightly more frequent than the rest. Most of the responses are really summarized in the words of one premenopausal young woman. "To be beautiful is to be kind, good to people, and honorable. Always smile. Don't be selfish, give a helping hand to all — beauty is inside. How you think and live will show up on your face." Thus, the second most frequently mentioned item was behavior or charm, implying the general impression a woman radiates to others. This includes a friendly smile ("a sulky woman is ugly"); talking in a friendly quiet way; and gentleness. Beautiful women are also characterized by cleanliness in both their person and their attire. Only at this stage did physical attributes become important. These included, with equal frequency: way of walking, having long black hair, and having the kungum (red dot on the forehead).

Much the same picture was sketched by the postmenopausal women. The first and most frequently mentioned set of criteria were described by a Hindu. "Simplicity," she said. This involves a graceful use of clothing (once again the sari was singled out for its effect) and being soft spoken and friendly. Related to the latter is the personality and charm ("more important and lasting than looks") a woman radiates because it reflects her moral character. The third set of characteristics is more physical in nature, yet does not relate simply to external beauty. It has to do with how a woman carries herself; whether she is physically active; whether her complexion is well cared for (the use of turmeric powder — which in India is made into a yellow cream); and whether her hair is long. Attractive Indian South African women do not smoke or drink, they wear the *tali* around their necks (if they are Hindu), and they apply the kungum to the forehead. Most of these attributes describe inner qualities, and it should be remembered that "boys go out with the wildest but they settle down with the passive."

Younger women tend to dress in brighter more flashy clothing and to use more jewelry. This contributes to their attractiveness — an attraction which also seems to relate to the married men in the community. Twenty-six (89.7%) of the premenopausal and twenty-six (96.3%) of the postmenopausal women indicated that the men in their community prefer younger women. Since almost all adult males are married, this stated preference would suggest the possibility of a certain amount of extra-marital activity. According to Mrs. Chetty, "It's in a man's blood not to live with one woman." Added another: "Indians have always preferred younger women." The latter statement is true of course in that grooms normally were older and established by the time they married, frequently marrying a teenage bride. However, the context and connotation here suggests that men prefer younger women even after they are married.

One of the premenopausal women explained that in traditional village communities this created no problem. She said, "A Tamil (Hindu) married for twenty to twenty-five years then takes a second wife who is his junior by twenty years because older women lose interest in sex." This is the single most frequently mentioned reason for a man's interest in a young woman. She "makes him feel young," but he also has a manipulative power over her. The younger women in our study also placed part of the blame on the older women. "In the past," Mrs. Radia said, "older women were less critical of their figures and were less educated." Another woman said that older women let themselves go, they don't take care of themselves, and are conservative in their sex life. This may be true, but if one listens to the life histories of the older women, it is clear that they have had, in many cases, lives which were physically and emotionally draining. "Indian women age very rapidly due to the stress of the in-laws and children," explained one woman. In general, responses by the women in this category were more reflective of the husband, his aims and interests; that he had too much money; or that his needs may not have been met at home.

When we turn to the postmenopausal category, we find greater reflection on the woman. The two most frequently mentioned reasons for a man's extramarital involvement were that those younger women were prettier and had "more stamina" in their sex life. Along with physical beauty is the fact that these young women can go out to parties and dances; that they are sociable; and that men can show them off. At least in part, the fault is with the married women who may be old or sickly but frequently just look and behave that way or simply "become sluggish." But men, we were told, "go after looks not character" and many of them were thought not to be mature.

If men are attracted by physical attributes and external factors, what are they? What do women see as a perfect figure? Since there was almost no difference in the response pattern of the pre- versus the postmenopausal women, they will not be differentiated. An ideal Indian South African woman with a perfect figure is (in order of mention) tall and slim, being at least five feet six inches so that when she drapes a sari around her it will look dignified. She has: (1) long black hair, the pride of the Tamil, (2) a fair complexion or lighter skin, desirable because of South African politics, as one woman explained (du Toit 1966), (3) a "nice bust," breasts are well developed and will be shown off in a sari, (4) narrow hips, resulting in a nice waist line, (5) nice legs accentuated by high-heeled shoes, (6) a "small butt," or "bum" and yet "her backside must have shape, not [be] flat." In addition, she should walk well, have a stately carriage, have a pretty face, wear her kungum, and know what color sari suits her. In the last analysis, however, beauty is more than physical: "Some women are beautiful but when they open their mouths..."

What contributes to the attractiveness of these women? Readily mentioned is a set of undergarments which make a woman feel more womanly and feminine. However, most women in both age categories differentiated between garments worn to enhance their attractiveness in public and those worn to satisfy their husbands. Public appearance requires a padded or stiff bra that shows well if the sari is draped correctly, a long half-slip, and panties. Many women wear girdles or corsets. A woman who wears a sari will also wear a short blouse and may wear the sari above the navel and waist (as is becoming to older women) or below the waistline as a hipster. Formerly it was cooler to wear a sari while working in the fields, but now it is worn for reasons of (sexual) attractiveness. Pretty undergarments (or no undergarments) are also worn for private reasons, to satisfy husbands. These include bikini panties, see-through garments, and of course see-through pajamas, nighties, or negligees.

Every woman in the two research samples said that she wore certain kinds of clothing to make herself more attractive. "Clothing" in this context refers to the sari (for Hindu) or Punjabi dress (for Muslims). It also includes hair, makeup, and jewelry which might be applied to the forehead, ears, nose, neck, or arm, and more recently, to the ankles.

The most important item of dress, the sari, is the major garment. Hindu women always wear a sari, and most younger professional women wear saris for social or ceremonial occasions. Whether or not they are Hindu, Indian women consider the sari attractive dress for special occasions. The best saris are made of thin cashmere from Banares and may sell for anywhere from $300 to $500. French silk is also valued for formal events, but women wear cotton saris at home. The sari is draped over the right (Hindi) or the left (Tamils) shoulder, and Gujeratis give it an extra loop on one side. Pregnant women have a special drape to accentuate the body curves. Young women may go bra-less or wear a fancy open see through, or off-shoulder blouse. The hipster, which leaves the navel and waistline bare, is also more common among younger women. Blouses may have high or low necks and may have sleeves or not. For funerals women wear white cotton saris similar to those woven by Gandhi. A good cashmere sari may have gold embroidery on it and take up to six meters of material to make. To complete her outfit, a woman may wear the traditional sandals or high-heeled shoes. The secret is in selecting the right color of material to bring out a woman's beauty. No Hindu woman is completely dressed without the red kungum on her forehead; the Hindi apply the red powder to their hair. Mrs. Singh explained, "When a Hindu woman gets married, the groom sprinkles red powder, *sindhoor*, into the hair parting — halfway to the top of the head. He then places the red dot on her forehead. When a woman is widowed, the sister of the deceased husband puts the red powder back in her hair and then washes it out with plain water. From this day on she may never again put the red dot on her forehead even if she gets married again."

Muslims dress in accordance with prescriptions which have moral, social and legal dimensions. The Prophet said "...If the woman reaches the age of puberty, no part of her body should be seen but this — and he pointed to his face and hands" (Badawi nd:6). This resulted in the head cover, which is drawn over the neck leaving slits for the eyes. With few exceptions, South African Muslims are not orthodox and do not cover their faces. They do wear what has become known as the Punjabi dress. This consists of the *abha*, very narrow pants, and *ijar*, a short dress with slits on each side worn over the pants. Muslims of Indian origin wear tight pants; Muslims of Pakistani origin wear baggie ones. The slit on the side of the dress may be higher to accentuate a woman's attractiveness or lower for pregnant women. This is somewhat at odds with the prescription that "the dress must be loose enough so as not to describe the shape of a woman's body" (Badawi nd:7). One of the younger Muslim women in the study explained that she wanted a straight skirt to make her look younger. A thin woman will ask her dressmaker for a flair or something wider to "fill her up." Another woman stated that the Punjabi dress was more flattering to the figure than a sari, which might again contradict the requirement that "the dress should not be such that it attracts men's attention to the woman's beauty" (Badawi nd:8). In addition to the abha and ijar, a woman wears a scarf. This is made of about one and one-half meters of material and is wrapped around the shoulders or over the head, then around and down the neck. For older women the scarf is draped over the shoulder to cover the breasts, but younger women frequently don't wear it. The Hindi *chudidar* (broad pants) may be worn for a party. The outfit consists of a maxiskirt richly embroidered with gold and silver over which a short blouse may be worn. Often the regular Punjabi dress is also richly embroidered or decorated with sequins. Some Hindus describe it as gaudy. Such price and variety might not be in keeping with Koranic prescriptions, for the Prophet warned "whoever wears a dress of fame in this world, Allah will clothe him with a dress of humiliation in the day of resurrection, then set it afire" (Badawi nd:9).

To the disgust of may old women, young people wear ordinary dresses ("European dress looks ugly and old") or more frequently blue jeans and blouses, miniskirts, and halter tops. Needless to say, this dress is not permitted when women go to prayers.

If women should not wear such modern clothing, can they wear specific kinds of clothing to make themselves look younger? The general response was in the affirmative; all women like to look younger because that also makes them feel younger. But there were two categories of responses. First looking younger and looking modern imply European clothes like dresses, pant suits, slacks and tops, and among the youngest, miniskirts, halter tops, and similar nontraditional garb. Along with this change, young women cut and style their hair. This is acceptable to the older women because the young go out to work or go to college; but they should not sacrifice traditional dress completely and should wear it on social occasions. Second, other women would rather adapt the traditional dress, e.g., by wrapping the sari tightly to show body curves and wearing a skimpy blouse or hipster. Someone who wears the Punjabi dress can wear the pants tighter, the slits higher, and the scarf backwards over the shoulder, thus "flaunt her figure."

The image of the Indian South African women is not complete without the inevitable signs of age — gray hair and wrinkles. The former is seen as common, but something they can change; wrinkles are not. Once hair starts to turn gray, women use traditional rinses or some color dyes at a hair dresser. "It's such a shame," said one, "in women it looks old; in men it looks distinguished." Women try to prevent wrinkles with a variety of creams or moisturizers but one woman suggested that wrinkles were not a major problem among Indians who very rarely get them. This is due in part, the women explained, to "their diet with oils," "their darker skins which are thicker," the fact that they don't spend much time in the sun, and they don't put "a lot of cosmetics" on their faces.

This, then, is the cultural context within which the image of the Indian South African woman is defined. It is a context which has ethnic-linguistic, religious, and political connotations — and where male dominance influences the ways in which a woman expresses herself.

Expression

The discussion of how these women personally express the image of an aging Indian woman might well start with their acceptance of the physical signs of age.

Hair is supposed to be black and long. When grey hair starts to appear younger women might go to the salon to have it tinted or dyed black. Older women either accept the grey as a status symbol ("it doesn't bother me, I get respect and all kinds of help") or wash their hair in henna. This is a tint or dye derived from the leaves of a shrub *Lawsonia inermis* and normally is either red or brown. The red dye is called *henna* while the brown dye is called *mendhi*. Women see this not only as a traditional practice but also as nutritious for the hair. "The Muslim religion," explained one woman, "says we must accept grey hair but we younger ones dye it." Another woman with a beautiful head of grey hair said, "Whites dye it with a blue tinge; it doesn't suit our complexion." She had decided to let nature have its way.

Wrinkles are a different matter. Luckily they are less frequent in Indian women; but once they appear, there isn't much anyone can do. One woman stated, "Tamilians don't wrinkle early because we don't use cosmetics, and because of *bori*." This word is the local term for turmeric. A woman is expected to rub it on the tali once a week but also to apply it to her face for about ten minutes before her daily bath. The practice starts at her wedding. For three days before a woman gets married, eleven married women will mix turmeric (this is a ground form of the aromatic rhizome which is such an important part of curry powders) and sandalwood (the fragrant, ground-up form of the pulpwood) with rosewater to form a paste. Each of the eleven women take turns in applying the paste to the hands, face, feet, and ankles of the bride-to-be. On her wedding day, the bride is given a bath and has a beautiful glowing fresh skin. She does not need makeup. She will continue this practice to keep her skin healthy, young, and wrinkle-free.

In a number of cases women did have wrinkles and blamed it on powder (cosmetic) or that doing something about it cost too much. Asked about her reaction to wrinkles, one of the older women just smiled and said, "I've got plenty, let me know if you find anything that works."

A number of the young women pointed out that exercise would help in preventing wrinkles and aging in general. Just before this research commenced, somebody had started exercise classes at the local hotel. Women go there in the morning and have an hour of aerobics. As the practice becomes more accepted, the number of participants should increase as will the number of women who jog. There was a realization that young women had to break out of the sedentary existence which so characterizes the older women in this community.

Behavior is an area in which status differences are obvious, and clothing is also frequently a status marker. There are certain items of clothing and jewelry which women wear that are characteristic of their age and status. Certain items are simply not acceptable and indeed would be inappropriate.

What is acceptable for or expected of older Indian South African women? Clothing is generally conservative, not exposing the body or accentuating it. Colors are selected to blend with the appropriate age and complexion: thus, a sari may be peach, pink, or a similar pale or pastel color. Widows must wear white — a "saintly and pure color." The widow's sari is loosely draped over the shoulder and tucked in at the back to form a slight bulge. For Tamils, the blouse has longer sleeves and the top part is wrapped to close the neck quite snugly. A widow removes the tali from which hangs the husband's crest in gold. The tali was tied on by her husband in public on their wedding day. She may wear a gold chain instead of the yellow string but will still have a short piece of string on the bottom of the chain to hold the family tali. Different Tamil families, such as the Naidoos, Goranders, or Pillays have different shapes for their family talis. When a woman is widowed, three women take off the tali and place it in a tray of milk. At the end of one day, they will present the string and the gold tali to the widow. If she desires, she may have a ring made of it or not wear it at all. The chain, which now is simply jewelry, may be worn but it will no longer have the tali or the yellow string attached to it. The tali used to serve as wedding ring, but now they use a ring in addition. She will of course not make the red dot on her forehead.

Muslim women may also wear white, though they are more likely to use the ijar with a longer dress and a long scarf over their heads. Preferred colors are blue, gray, or black. The scarf (*burkha*) is used to cover their heads while praying.

Indian women are very fond of jewelry, especially old gold and family heirlooms. Old women should wear light gold jewelry such as a necklace and earrings or a locket. In some cases, a gold bracelet or removable nose ring will be worn. If a woman wears diamonds, pearls or rubies, they should be plain and in a simple setting.

Just as there are expected forms of dress and conduct, there also are things which an older woman should avoid, including very short or very tight dresses, pants, slacks, or jeans. She should avoid flimsy clothing, high-heeled shoes, and clothing with gold thread in the embroidery. Hindu women should not wear yellow; Gujerati (Hindu) believe black to be an ill omen and will hardly ever wear it — especially not to a wedding. Normally, old women do not wear the Punjabi dress. No older woman in this community will wear fashionable European clothing or backless dresses.

Nobody will wear imitation jewelry or colored plastic jewelry ("gaudy stuff") — if she does she's called a Christmas tree. Old women are also expected not to wear long chains or long earrings. However, "if a Muslim woman goes without bracelets, people say her husband must be deceased."

The last area in which age is quite clearly represented is that of hair style. Muslim women are not supposed to have their hair exposed; Gujerati women are supposed to plait theirs. The majority of old women comb their hair straight back against the head and tie it in a bun. An old grandmother explained that every Saturday after washing her hair she rubs it with a mixture consisting of coconut oil, rose petals, castor oil, and herbs (especially masala). This keeps the hair healthy and black. Younger women cut their hair, go for perms or other styles, all of which are frowned on by the older women. The most beautiful and correct way, it is said, is for a young girl to have straight long black hair hanging down her back.

With women spending this much time in expressing their image of the Indian woman, it is not surprising to find that most husbands are satisfied. In the younger category, there were only two women whose husbands were dissatisfied. One was told that she looked like an old woman. The only woman in the older category whose husband was dissatisfied was criticized for being overweight. Those who were satisfied either remained silent or said so by praising their wives' beauty and youthfulness or by other compliments. One husband compares his wife to her mother; another brags to his friends that his wife is ten years his junior; and a third, a Muslim, takes his wife home from a party when he find other men looking at her. His wife explains: "Muslim men are kept back and at a party they tend to look at a beautiful well dressed woman." One of the postmenopausal women, sitting comfortably in a deep chair with a cup of sweet tea on her lap, smiled at my question whether her husband was satisfied with her. "...After fifty-four years of marriage, he'd better be!" she responded.

A woman's image of herself also involves a certain degree of introspection and retrospection. In thinking about herself and her life experiences, she must remember good times in contrast to others which were not so good. At what stage does she think she was sexually most attractive, or by contrast, least attractive? In considering these conditions, our women obviously evaluated their acceptance by others as well as how they felt and the experiences they had.

The years just before and after marriage were overwhelmingly the best for both pre- and postmenopausal women; especially the year before marriage when they were admired and wanted, when proposals were being presented to their parents, and when they were in good health. For the younger category, this involves the years around ages nineteen or twenty; for the postmenopausal women it refers to ages sixteen to eighteen. The second most frequently mentioned stage comprised the reproductive years when children were small. A forty-seven-year-old woman thought about her life and said, "...When was I sexually most attractive? Now, because he has forgotten about all his girlfriends and is interested in his old wife."

In reflecting on the stage of their lives when they were sexually least attractive, there was a clear difference. A majority of the premenopausal women singled out their teenage years; looking like "Twiggy" was a common description. The second most frequent stage was during pregnancy. Of the postmenopausal women, an overwhelming majority indicated that they felt the years after menopause or the present was the stage of least attractiveness. One woman said, "Now, I've gone old."

If they could change anything about themselves, what would that be? One could expect fanciful dreams and wishes indicating dissatisfaction with their lives, their age, their condition. Instead we found acceptance and resignation. The majority of women took life as it was; two wanted to put on some weight; two wanted to lose some weight; and two wanted to become younger. Three of the postmenopausal women said that they would like to have a full head of long black hair down to their waists — one actually prayed about it. The rest agreed with Mrs. Hafeji. She is a small, overweight, sedentary woman with a smile as wide as the Ganges. Her answer was, "God made me and I'm happy."

Being a Woman

Being a woman also entails emotion and expression. It entails a feeling of achievement and fulfillment. In retrospect, a person will say that those were the good times or that was the best time of her life. It is also possible to look back at the worst time.

It has already become clear that the universe of the Indian South African woman revolves around her home, and by extension, her husband and children. It is within this setting and among these relationships that a woman enjoys her most satisfying and rewarding experiences as well as her worst. It is only natural that since marriage means financial and emotional security to women who are not educated or trained for an industrial economy, it is within marriage that they find security. The best time for both categories of women included the years just after marriage when husband and wife shared interests; when he expressed himself emotionally and sexually by being loving and caring; when they had time for each other; and when they were healthy and strong. Marriage represented a newly achieved freedom from the restrictions of the parental home where feminine activities were repressed. In many cases, marriage meant independent living so that a woman could have her own kitchen and living space. It also represented potential higher status through starting her own family; for being married was only half of her role expectation. The other half involved having babies — the stage that is the second most rewarding one for women — especially the premenopausal group who are emotionally much closer to those years. These were the years when a woman felt wanted and needed. Having her first child, particularly if it was a son, changed her status in the community. She was accepted by the in-laws, which immediately gave greater security and permanence to her marriage. Being in the childbearing stage of her life allowed for sexual interest from the husband; and a number of pregnancies, as most women have had, reaffirmed her image as woman and mother.

But if marriage and the relationships it produced represented the best years of a woman's life, then disruption in this context should produce the greatest strain and concern. It also represented the worst time. A clear majority of pre- as well as postmenopausal women stated that the times when they wished they could leave or experienced the greatest emotional stress involved their marriages, their husbands, and to a lesser extent their children. The younger women complained that husbands were unfaithful; marriages were on the rocks; there was simply no communication; husbands never apologized. Because of such conditions, one woman saw no way out. She was a nervous wreck and emotionally shattered. Second in this negative context were repeated references to problems with the in-laws including: a dominant mother-in-law; an envious sister-in-law; a brother-in-law who tried to break up the marriage. The postmenopausal women, who were much older, also positioned their worst times in the marriage context. Here, however, it involved widowhood; the death of the husband; illness of the spouse (both physical and mental, i.e., a nervous breakdown); or in two cases husbands who physically violated their wives. A number recall with resentment the early years of marriage when the in-laws dominated their lives and the husbands did not support them against unjust pressure from the husband's relatives.

The third largest number of women saw the present as their best years. For the premenopausal women the reproductive years were passed. They all stated that they did not want any more babies. Their children were in school or college, and as one woman said, she could now learn to relax. A number of women were involved in aerobics; others were taking French lessons at the French Embassy; participating in cooking or handicraft classes; and helping community welfare organizations coordinated by the Muslim or Hindu religious leaders. Many of the postmenopausal women are facing old age, widowhood, and deteriorating health. For them there is a selective remembering of childhood as their best years — years with no responsibility, no marriage, freedom to come and go, and no concern for health or immediate needs. We call it selective remembering because some women in both age groups looked back on childhood as the worst time in their lives. Many of them remember strict parents; living in poverty; the death of a parent; and being sent to relatives who did not give them love or security. One of the younger women, today educated and a qualified teacher, recalls the death of her father. She was taken out of school, and because the family lacked resources, forced into an early marriage.

The present was the only other stage singled out as good by the postmenopausal women. It involves experience, confidence, and self assuredness and represents a time when the children are on their own. Above all, it represents the time when a woman is "a granny." Being a grandmother is fulfilling. It provides someone on whom she can dote, whom she can spoil, and in whom she finds role continuity. With a live-in grandmother, parents are free to work or to be much more involved in extra-domestic activities.

The expression of her image as a woman and her role performance both coincide for Indian South Africans in the domestic setting. In relationships generated by marriage and the nuclear family, women find expression and experience their greatest pride, fulfillment, and joy, but also suffer their worst denial, resentment, and pain. In the Indian community, a woman is a wife and mother. Anything that disrupts the harmonious expression of these roles causes unhappiness and can shatter her emotional, marital, and social security.

❧

5

Lifestyles and Life Course

Introduction

There have been a number of attempts at devising or developing indices to measure the status of a particular category of the population. Some of these have had an economic focus, and others have dealt with social networking or support systems. Concepts developed by psychologists and given expression in gerontological studies have become the most sophisticated. However, due to the nature of the research subjects and the inclination of the researchers, these devices have not been tested in cross-cultural settings and for that reason frequently have little value when they are administered outside of the cultural system for which they were designed. As Gutmann remarked:

> Lacking an adequate cross-cultural theory, as well as an extensive body of cross-cultural research, we can only make educated guesses as to the relationships between social phenomena and the psychological well-being of older individuals in various societies (1980:430).

Anthropologists have been accustomed to using a life-cycle approach in their studies in part because it allows for a sequential and cyclical discussion of the potential life cycle of an individual from birth to death. Anthropologists used to view community life during an annual cycle that includes the seasons, the stages of growth and harvest, or the ritual cycle. So, too, people were viewed as occupying various stages in their expected cycle of life. These stages are ritually recognized, either by sacred or secular ritual. Almost always there was greater emphasis on or greater recognition of the potentiating stages of the life cycle than the terminating ones.

A newborn who receives a name, is nose-pierced or marked in some way as a member of the group, has potential for life. The teenager who at puberty undergoes some genital operation or is tattooed or marked has potential as wife and childbearer or as warrior and male leader. The young mother experiencing her first pregnancy has the potential of satisfying the marriage contract or producing an heir and creating a family. All of these phases are marked by ritual. The loss of these potentials, the conclusion of these phases, is not so recognized. Aging is part of the life cycle, but it represents a series of terminating stages. That death in an ancestor cult is potentiating does not have general applicability outside such socioreligious systems.

Brief mention should be made that certain East African societies, usually quoted as typical examples, are based on age grading. This means that the society is not divided vertically by kinship systems where membership in extended families, lineages, and clans gives people social status. Instead, the society is divided horizontally, by relative age, and an individual takes his social meaning from membership in an appropriate age group or from identification and residence with such a group.

Thus people's social position and status is derived from membership and association, and their roles derive from these identities. Every society in the world has some degree of age grading. Although these may not be institutionalized as they are in East Africa, a person is always older than or younger than others. To a certain degree, one graduates from one relative age grade to another — when one is recognized as "a child no more," as married, a mother, an adult, or old (see also Clausen 1972: and Riley, Johnson, and Foner 1972). Generally speaking, one gains as one matures and loses as one ages, but this is relative, and researchers frequently record an expansion of roles or an entering upon new roles as age increases.

Birren has pointed out that there is biological age in contrast to psychological age and both contrast with social age. All three are interacting. Psychological age has to do with the achievements and potentials of the individual. Social age uses the additional criterion of the extent to which the individual has acquired or performs the various social roles that his society and his immediate social group expect of a person of his age. The emphasis in psychological age is on the *capacity* to adapt, whereas in social age, the emphasis is on the *social output* or *performance* of the individual in relation to others (1960:19).

Social age in part depends on the sequencing of life events. Events which do not follow in sequence disturb the rhythm. Examples of such disturbances are pregnancy of a teenager; hysterectomy for a young woman; early widowhood; climacteric pregnancy. Status, then, is defined by the events which a person has experienced. Bernice Neugarten has commented on events occurring at the expected time — when they were anticipated — as well as the more unsettling effect of unanticipated events. She suggested that "a psychology of the life cycle is not a psychology of crisis behavior so much as it is a psychology of timing" (1970:87). But timing may be relative between different cultures and even within the same culture.

There is a need to develop cross-cultural tests so that comparative statements are possible. One attempt at devising a social events test was presented by Holmes and Rahe (1967). Their social readjustment rating scale, however, is so culturally biased that its usefulness within the United States would be questionable. It would be impossible to use it cross-culturally without major adjustments and substitution of items.

Another attempt had been developed by Neugarten, Havighurst, and Tobin (1961). They wanted to use an individual's own evaluation of his satisfaction with life. Components of a person's life which were investigated dealt with the person's enthusiasm and degree of ego-involvement in life (designated zest vs. apathy); the extent to which a person accepts personal responsibility for life or whether there is an attitude of resignation (designated resolution and fortitude); the extent to which a person had achieved life goals, or succeeded in accomplishing ideals (designated congruence between desired and achieved goals); the concept of self held by a person, including physical, psychological, and social attributes (designated self-concept); and a rating of the attitude toward life and other persons in general (designated mood tone). A person might receive a high rating on mood for being happy, optimistic, supportive, positive, or taking pleasure in life. A low rating would result from generally negative attitudes and depression. All of this resulted in a Life Satisfaction Rating Scale (LSR). A number of authors have used or adapted this scale (see discussion by Hoyt and Creech 1983), and it remains one of the standard scales because it is informant-dependent rather than heavily culturally-based. Nevertheless, it is "unwise to assume that these items measure the same thing in differing segments of the population" (Hoyt and Creech 1983:115). These differences may pertain to ethnic or other groups in the same culture (Usui et al. 1983), but they also may be influenced by the fact that events such as retirement or children leaving home are not always or uniformly experienced as stressful (Eisdorfer and Wilkie 1977).

In the discussion that follows we have included much derived from Neugarten and her associates, but the material is not presented as a rating scale or an index.

Self-Concept

Self-concept has physical as well as ideational dimensions. An individual has specific ideas about himself as a physical person in time and space as well as ideas about who he is and what his role is in the narrow or wider community. Self-concepts are arrived at both by introspection and by comparison, through which a person sees himself relative to others as taller, thinner, more active, more involved in community activities, etc. It is within this setting that a person perceives and performs a life-style and a life course. The self-concept may also influence or determine the actions which follow.

Physical

More than half, seventeen (58.6%) of the premenopausal and fourteen (51.9%) of the postmenopausal women, felt they were over-weight. The inactivity that characterizes the lives of these women and their high sugar, starch, and oil diet makes it possible for weight to become a problem. In most cases (75.9% of the pre- and 48.1% of the postmenopausal), they stated that they were lighter ten years ago. Thus, they see aging and weight increase as inevitably connected.

Indian South African women can be subdivided in terms of their activity level. Many women stated that they got plenty of exercise doing their housework and caring for the children. However, it will be recalled that most of the Indian households have servants — at least on a part-time basis. What these women were saying is that they get plenty of exercise: what actually was happening was that they were busy. One of the older women indicated that walking the length of the house was plenty of exercise for her. This may certainly be true depending on age and health; but it is also true that only two of the women in the older age category had any regimen for exercise — going for long walks. This is simultaneously cause and result of their feeling and acting old.

There is a different attitude toward age among the women in the younger category. At least half of them (and this might be representative of modern younger Indian women) either went swimming on weekday mornings when the municipal pool was reserved for them or swam in private pools, or were involved in aerobics classes or gymnastics workouts held regularly at the hotel. Others followed

TV or radio workouts with music and performed the exercises in their own homes.

Indian South African women in our study were not tall. The tallest was just over six feet in height and the shortest, four feet six inches. The average height of sixty-two inches pertains to both the younger and the older categories. In fact, the postmenopausal women as a group are slightly taller than their younger cohorts.

The number of women who smoke was higher than we had expected. Among the premenopausal group five (17.2%) smoked, and among the postmenopausal group six (22.2%) did so. They smoked an average of more than ten cigarettes a day. Only three of the older women stated that they had tried or were trying to stop smoking. There seems to be a tradition of smoking among the older women. Meer points out that two categories of women are considered exempt from the prohibition of smoking due to gender and status namely those who are educated and those who are old. "Elderly women in the more peasant and working class groups have appropriated the masculine rights to smoke and drink, and these rights are respected, as well as earned after years of service to the family" (Meer 1969:71). The women who responded positively to questions about smoking were either older women who had worked most of their lives as hawkers or saleswomen in markets and stores or the younger, more sophisticated (but not necessarily the best educated) women. It should be kept in mind that Islam prohibits these acts.

Emotional

People's self-concept is influenced by physical characteristics in comparison to those of others with whom they interact. There is also a more emotional side to this concept, influenced to a major extent by experiences and events in her life. Our attention focuses on life events in this discussion but it is necessary to recognize factors which influence the attitudes and evaluations regarding self on a day-to-day basis. The self-concept is partially a product of the cultural traditions within which people exist; thus, it is as much a product of their environment and setting as of their ideas about self.

Most of the older generation expected a woman to find fulfillment in her husband and children, and upon maturation of her children to be old and to prepare for death. This despite the fact that many had mothers and grandmothers who lived into their seventies or even eighties. Only 59% felt hopeful about the future (whereas 83% of the younger women did); 52% of the older women frequently felt lonely (only 27.5% of the younger women did); and 50% of them frequently felt depressed (only 38% of the younger women did). In total context, the postmenopausal women in this study felt more lonely, more frequently felt sad, were less optimistic about the future, found it harder to shake the blues, felt they were not as good as others, and experienced more restless sleep. These attitudes could have been generated by actual experiences or by emotional evaluations; but in part, they were almost certainly a product of women's culture in this community, a culture which contains ideational and behavioral sets regarding the status and role of women and aging. For the younger women, education has changed these ideational and behavioral expectations.

Life Events

The early research into stressors which affected most people during their lives and which were somewhat sequential was done by Holmes and Rahe (1967) in terms of readjustment. But these were events which normally took place or could be expected to take place with the passage of time and were expressed in a schedule of recent events. Not only is this list of events somewhat restricted but it also attempts an objective weighting of events rather than recognizing evaluations which are individually or subculturally variable. Needless to say, such an inventory cannot be used cross-culturally without significant adjustment.

Neugarten and Datan (1973) gave attention to life span, recognizing and differentiating between life time (expressed as chronological age), social time (used to measure passage from one age status to the next, like age-grading in stratified societies), and historical time. All three may be present and influence the life course. More recently Neugarten dealt with "life events (marriage, parenthood, climacterium, retirement, widowhood)...in terms of the accompanying changes in social roles" (1977:634). It should be remarked here that all the events, except climacterium are events which can be pinpointed by a ceremony or ritual, a birth or a death. The climacterium is a phase of transition and not an event, although the menopause (Neugarten, Kraines, and Wood 1965) itself can be discussed in this context. All of these changes should take place within an expected time frame and in an expected sequence. There is a time for marriage: but if two seventy-year-olds get married it invites comment. Parenthood should take place when the parents are young adults; retirement should take place around age 65–70; conversely, widowhood should not befall a woman in her twenties. There is an expected time pattern within each culture or at different eras within a culture.

In an important discussion, Neugarten (1970) has suggested that "it is not the occurrence of the life event itself which precipitates an adaptational crisis, for most such events are anticipated and rehearsed and the transition accomplished without shattering the sense of continuity of the life cycle. Instead, it is when such events occur 'off-time' rather than 'on-time,' for example, when grandparenthood, retirement, major illness, or widowhood occur earlier in life than expected, that crisis is experienced" (Neugarten 1977:639). We will take note of the events that Indian women themselves recognize as important and also what differences exist between the two cohort groups. We should keep in mind that an expected or culturally-valued event not occurring on time or not occurring at all may create greater stress and, thus, gain importance as a life event by its very absence. Indian women are expected to receive proposals and to be married in their early twenties. This might be considered an important life event, but its nonoccurrence is even more important. Chiriboga has expressed this eloquently: "To restrict the definition of social stress to life events is to ignore a large domain of stress experiences with potential relevance to life course investigation. Examples of such experiences include anticipations of stress, being off-time, nonevents such as not receiving an anticipated promotion or not getting married, and chronic stress conditions" (1982:600).

Experiencing menopause, as we will discuss below, is soon accepted by most women who find that they are "on-time" and age cohorts have the same experiences. Thus, menopause itself is really not a crisis and does not produce stress.

Researchers in the past frequently described psychological and psychosomatic symptoms which were supposed to be a product of the climacterium and even more specifically of the menopause. Thus Neugarten and Kraines (1965) described "menopausal symptoms" while McKinlay and Jefferys (1974) spoke of the "menopausal syndrome." That these symptoms occurred at or about the time of the menopause is not in question but causality is. More recently, researchers have emphasized that we are dealing with a coincidence of various events in the life cycle which occur about the time of the menopause. The symptoms are due to psychological stresses caused by role loss (Bart 1976; 1977) or other changes in a woman's life.

These may include children leaving home, illness or death of parents, widowhood, or similar events. Cooke and Greene, following the early work of E. S. Paykel, speak of these important life events as "exits." They explain: "These are operationally defined as any event involving the departure of others from the social field of the subject" (1981:6). Life events and accompanying stresses may be the occurrence or nonoccurrence of an event at an expected time; they may be major transitional events which are phased into the life cycle and are accompanied by status and role changes; or they may involve the exit of significant others from the individual's social field. Life events will differ in significance, in time, and in space as we move from one cultural setting to another.

As one part of this study, the participants were asked to single out the proudest moment of their lives. Table 16 presents the listing of events by the pre- and the postmenopausal women respectively. This question occurred at the end of a series of detailed questions about the best and worst things that can happen to a woman and have happened to the respondent.

Each respondent was asked to list the three proudest moments in her life. This is not quite the same as recording life events, but it identifies those events which are most highly valued within this community. Getting married is the proper thing to do and is the goal of every girl. This is reflected both in the value of a woman's own marriage and those of her children, particularly the girls. But when a child marries "within religion and caste," as one put it, it certainly is a moment of pride and gratitude. Having a child is critical particularly if it is a son (and this is reflected in the responses of the older women); it establishes a woman's status with both her husband and her in-laws. For the younger women, having a child was the single most highly valued "moment." Given the South African sociopolitical system and the status of those who are not white, the women recognized that education is the only alternative to a strong, established business venture. There were two responses which are significant, partly due to their value for this study and partly because they were given only by the younger generation. These referred to graduation and being hired for the jobs they were holding at the time of the study. Most of the older women were uneducated homemakers. Some of the younger women had degrees, were college lecturers or held good secure jobs. One woman was managing a franchise of a national financial undertaking. She was proud of the time when the director met her and praised her as "an Indian woman" achieving this rank. One woman still saved a news-

TABLE 16

The Three Proudest Moments

Event	Premenopausal	Postmenopausal
1. When I got married	15 (17.2)	13 (16.1)
2. When I had my first child	16 (18.4)	8 (9.9)
3. When I had my first son	9 (9.2)	11 (13.6)
4. When my child(ren) completed their education	9 (10.3)	11 (13.6)
5. When my child got married	2 (2.3)	9 (11.1)
6. When I graduated	11 (12.6)	–
7. When I got my current job	6 (6.9)	–
8. When my husband settled down and showed interest in me	4 (4.6)	4 (4.9)
9. When my first grandchild was born	–	8 (9.9)
10. When we got our own home	2 (2.3)	2 (2.5)
TOTAL	73	66
Since there are three responses for each, N = 3 × 29 and 3 × 27 respectively	87	81

paper cutting that reported that she made the top score of 1,000 students who took Hindi for their final year in high school. Reference to husbands was varied. In most cases the women were grateful that their husbands settled down in marriage. One older woman said he was "living with me nicely now." Husbands who had not settled down may have been philandering or waiting for their wives to produce an heir to secure the marriage. Other women were proud when people told the husbands what good wives they had — this reflected their qualities as both homemaker and wife. Being a grandmother opens a number of avenues for role continuity. Although a number of premenopausal women had grandchildren, they had enough avenues for expression and involvement, and consequently did not yet make use of the grandmother status. The last "moment" in the table refers to that two-fold achievement, a house of her own and an independent home. Housing in South Africa, especially for persons who do not belong to the privileged group, is hard to find. One woman still recalls the elation she felt when they got a brick house after living for years in a zinc cabin. An independent house allows a woman to make her own home, no longer under the eyes and authority of a mother-in-law. Said Mrs. Desai, "Getting this house was like heaven after living for twenty-seven years with my mother-in-law and surviving it."

Other proud moments, mentioned but not tabulated referred to menarche ("when I became a young girl"); religious experiences (both a hadj to Mecca and a visit with a guru in India); and family matters such as good children; having a loving family or being a good wife.

Family and Friends

The strength of tradition and the perpetuation of Indian culture is found in the vitality of the extended family. It is a reference group; a network of kin and surrogate parents; a financial support group; and a group who reinforces religious, moral, and cultural values.

Secularization of the Indian South African is directly linked to the breakdown of the extended family.

Most of the women in this study, 86.2% of the younger and 62.5% of the older, felt that the family was important. The closeness of the extended family has deteriorated, which might be cause or effect of the modern Indian father taking more interest in his nuclear family and children specifically. Residence is becoming increasingly nuclear and lifestyle more materialistic. The extended family was important in the performance of rituals and as an economic support group. Nowadays traditional rituals are decreasing and nuclear families are becoming more self-reliant. This was recognized by the women. There was general agreement that the kutum had its advantages, particularly when families were poor, coresidence was common, and the social support infrastructure absent. They point out that now the nuclear family is gaining in importance because of individual homes, involvement of the father, completeness of the parents-and-children unit, and because social, medical, and economic support systems are becoming more common.

This does not mean that women are ignoring more distant kin or paying less attention to certain members of the kutum. Many persons consider relatives among their best friends: the category "closest friend" included a kinsman for 37.9% of the pre- and 41.7% of the postmenopausal women. This may be related to the fact that members of the extended family had much contact during their formative years and in growing up together got to know each other well. The average length of the friendship with "closest friend" was 19.6 and 30.3 years respectively for pre- and postmenopausal women. The closest friend was always a woman with two exceptions in each category. Residential choices are not open to Indian South Africans and the number of urban neighborhoods available to them is limited. As expected, 65.5% of the pre- and 66.7% of the post-menopausal women had their closest friends in the same community. This tendency for networking among minority groups in South Africa confirms earlier findings relative to urban black South Africans (du Toit 1978). The implication is that a woman may visit a "closest friend" either on foot or by automobile subject to restrictions laid down by her husband. In fact 89.7% of the pre- and 79.2% of the postmenopausal women do retain and strengthen friendship ties by visiting — not a single one employs correspondence. Most homes have telephones, a handy mechanism for communication among women who are to a great extent homebound. Yet the figures for telephone conversations are well below those for personal visits.

"A friend in need is a friend indeed," states the old idiom. This is exactly what "closest friend" implies. Somebody to confide in; somebody to trust; somebody who is always available. Closest friends do things together. Two young Muslim women were studying Arabic together, two others French. A third set exercised together, and members of the same faith prayed together. Friends learn from each other and start to share life styles — like the women who were taking French cooking lessons or another who said, "I'm becoming vegetarian because of my friend." Out of such closeness, confidentiality, mutual understanding, and relaxed communication came one statement which was mentioned a number of times: "We laugh a lot when we're together." This may be the most important point for women who are so dominated and for whom communication between husband and wife is at a premium. Laughing together affords the women an opportunity to relax, to forget their daily stresses, and to unwind.

A relationship of amity can exist between relatives, friends, and neighbors or more distantly residing people, men or women, who are contacted by visit, telephone, or letter. The most likely close friend is a woman who is not a relative, lives within the city of Laudium, has been known for quite a number of years, and who will be visited in person or telephoned regularly but not corresponded with. Such friendships may, but do not necessarily, also include the husbands in visits and meal sharing.

Stressors

Life stress events will be experienced more or less severely depending on the intensity of the relationship and the emotional intimacy with the person involved. The death or departure of a distant relative may have the same effect as that of a more closely related one if the persons were emotionally and socially closely involved. Greene and Cooke (1980) suggest that women during the climacteric become vulnerable to a number of stress-producing life changes which they might have been able to handle at an earlier or later age. We should also keep in mind that during this stage of their life cycles people are more likely to experience such events as children leaving home (or even loudly proclaiming their independence), widowhood, or family breakups. The uniqueness of the South African political situation adds further stress: namely, the frequent emigration of children, siblings, or relatives who do not want to remain under apartheid.

A large number of the women in this study have experienced the permanent departure of such "significant others." They indicated what events affected their lives and what relationships were involved. Marriage, childbirth, and return of a relative were balanced with divorce, illness, retirement, departure, or death. The relatives listed in many cases extended beyond the category of immediate kin and included relatives thrice removed, e.g., Hu Si Da Da, Fa Si Do So So, Mo Br So Da and others. Although the majority of persons would be classified as immediate kin of either the wife or her husband, they also extended both patrilaterally and matrilaterally.

Social. Social stresses derive in part from familial relationships and responsibilities. Most women will designate three areas of stress: the husband, children, and (aging) parents. In many cases, the mother-in-law is singled out as a major stressor.

Among the younger women, the feeling was that marriage relations had improved. This referred to husbands who had started out with a certain degree of social clumsiness but who have been domesticated. Such awkwardness was due, in part, to an imbalance in the socialization process and in part to the dominant role of parents in the selection of a spouse. Thus, the first months of marriage frequently were bliss, but as soon as the wife was pregnant (satisfactorily performing her role) the husband frequently lost interest. Marriage then gradually improved as the husband later turned to his family, sharing their affairs and finding satisfaction in his relationship with his wife. For the older women, marriage was neither better nor worse. It was simply there...

The women were quite varied in their attitudes toward children according to different experiences. An adult son had physically attacked his widowed mother; another had qualified as a teacher and lovingly cared for his widowed mother. There were children who visited their parents daily. There were also children who had emigrated to Great Britain, Canada, or Australia without retaining contact with aging parents. Women who had children in the home complained of the breakdown in morality, the temptations of drugs, and an inability to keep the children home. These women were caught in a dilemma: they would have liked to keep their children home in an attempt to minimize exposure to a variety of temptations — especially in the area of drugs, sex, and general secularization. But they knew that in the interest of future success, the children must be involved both in education and secular behavior. Thus, 65.5% of the pre- and 57.9% of the postmenopausal women felt that their parenting role was more difficult now than it had been ten years ago. "Certainly the children are older," one woman stated, "but life is much more dangerous than it used to be."

In the realm of caring for parents, these women did not see any change. Old people were healthier now than they used to be, and medical facilities — both a hospital and a clinic — were close by in Laudium. With this in mind, most of the women did not rate parental care as a stressor. When they were asked for an overall evaluation of their conditions, only 17.2% of the pre- and 25.9% of the postmenopausal women stated that they were not too happy. Stress in some cases was personal but in most was due to strained relationships such as the divorce of a daughter, the death of a favorite grandchild, or the ill health of a husband. With few exceptions, these women had the support of their families; the younger ones living in a nuclear support group, many of the older ones being cared for by children and spoiled by grandchildren.

Other stressors were always present. These were matters of personal health or of a more distant or material kind and involved relations outside the home (with friends or neighbors), or money. Indian South Africans live very introverted lives, yet except for two or three women who had some tension with neighbors, this was not a source of stress. However, inadequate housing was considered stressful. Almost one-third of respondents in each category were dissatisfied with the apartment or house they were in and were building or applying for an improvement. Health gave some concern. Almost half of the women, slightly higher among the older respondents, stated their general health caused them concern, affected their sleep, or necessitated visiting a physician. Finances, in the form of husband's income, widow's income, or pension did cause stress to 48.2% of the pre- and 44.4% of the postmenopausal women. Widowhood created hardship for the younger women. Two women in this category lived in threadbare houses. One of them had only one son, whom she had put through college. She was looking forward to the future when he would want to support her. The other widow had three children — a teenage boy, an 18-year-old daughter who had a baby extramaritally, and a son in her early twenties, who was drunk most of the time and terrorized the family. Her future seemed dark. Among the postmenopausal women there was an interesting dichotomy. The widows were almost all living with married sons or daughters and had no immediate stress from material needs. However, a number of aged couples, especially where the husband's health was poor, were having a rough time. They had to manage on pensions or gifts from children. In two cases, they could not afford a servant and the old people were dependent on each other to run the home.

Psychological. In this context we may be dealing with genetic predispositions to stress versus reaction to stressful situations. What would be stressful to one person need not be so for a second due to personality and experimental factors. The way people react to stress will also differ.

Du Toit (1979) deals with the South African situation in terms of stress production and stress reduction. The diagram represents a cognitive model for the process of stress.

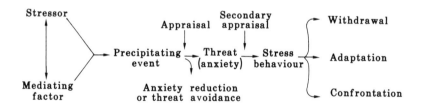

This repertoire can be designated *stress behavior* and seems to allow for at least three reactions; namely, *withdrawal* (either in neurotic avoidance of reality or suicide), *adaptation* in terms of trying to cope with new demands, or *confrontation* where the attempt is made to remold the situation to suit the individual concerned.

One thing we should keep in mind is that stress is never an 'individual affair'; it must be viewed in terms of a social context within which it occurs, which frequently precipitates it, and where solutions are often found. Stress based on social factors, such as class or caste, is frequently of a cyclical nature.

If there is a crisis which an individual, supported by his inter-action group, can cope with, then the situation returns to homeostatis. However, the threat recurs if the underlying agent of stress is still present (1979:122).

In situations of stress, whatever the cause of this stress, people attempt to cope. In certain realms, a person may be able to cope and to reduce the anxiety; in others, he may require short- or long-term assistance; in yet others he might withdraw.

According to the model developed here, most people frequently experience anxiety and are able to cope through a series of appraisals of their situation followed by appropriate action. This may involve redefining the situation as nonthreatening or responding to the threat. In both cases, anxiety reduction fol-lows. Crisis behavior must then be seen at the individual level where it operates, where it causes action, and where it reduces anxiety. But individuals do not live alone, nor are crises very often experienced alone. Crisis, then, has a very personal refer-ent, even though it always has implications on a wider inter-personal scale.

But the definition of crisis must be based on the situation and conditions of the persons or community under discussion, not in terms defined by the observer. What would be a crisis in one family, or what may result in confrontation by the mem-bers of one community, does not affect the members of another. The reason for this is that different people draw on different reservoirs for coping. The mediating factors of religious faith, fatalism, a sense of human powerlessness, and similar aspects, will have a lot of influence on what persons see as threatening or what calls for crisis action (du Toit 1979:140).

Withdrawal may be in the form of dramatically or quietly removing oneself from a stressful situation. Inability to cope may lead to suicide. In her study, *Race and Suicide in South Africa* (1976), Fatima Meer discusses in numerous case studies the stressors faced in that country and also ways out of such crises. Suicide is, of course, one quite final way of stress reduction.

Personal Satisfaction

In spite of minor stresses from a variety of sources, most women in this study were satisfied with their lives. Most of them were always ready for a joke or a laugh. The majority of them, 79.3% of the pre- and 88.5% of the postmenopausal women, thought that life had been good to them. They were satisfied with their condition despite minor problems. Those who were not blamed there dissatisfaction either on poverty or on an errant husband.

Poverty affects a relatively small percentage of Indian South Africans. Due in part to business acumen, the support of extended families and the kutum, and the role of religious aid societies (both Hindu and especially Muslim), there is relatively less poverty when Indians are compared to Coloured and black populations.

In spite of relative satisfaction with their lives ("Yes, compared to most people we have what we need!"), most of the women could think of things they would change if they could. Such responses are of course a good index of relative values but also serve as an index of conceived deprivation. Among the younger respondents, there are three repeated themes. First and most frequently mentioned was a desire for more education. "I would like to take up a career," said one. "I feel so deprived," stated another. In an earlier section, I mentioned the traditional pattern of taking girls out of school especially coeducational institutions, upon reaching menarche. Many of these girls were extremely bright and doing well in their studies. Terminating this phase of their lives and growth has resulted in permanent resentment. Some simply want more education, an increase in general knowledge. Others state clearly they would like to have a career outside the home which would get them out of the house or facilitate some local or overseas travel such as their menfolk do. Those who wish for a career mostly mention being a nurse or a teacher. Among the postmenopausal women there is a fatalistic acceptance that it is too late. Nobody in this age category mentioned a career change, though more education was valued.

The second most frequently mentioned change the women desired related to marriage. In most cases, the younger women would have preferred to marry later in life, thus allowing them some individualism and independence before being saddled with home, husband, and in-laws. For the older women, this was also the most frequently mentioned change they desired, but it was stated much more firmly. For them, not a later marriage, but no marriage. No fewer than four women stated that they would not get married if they had it to do over again. "I would never ever get married — stay single and work," said one. "I would remain single, not married," said another, "(with) no responsibilities and able to dedicate myself to my family and friends."

The third change desired was simply a little more freedom and flexibility in their daily lives. For most, this involved some travel; for others, release from the daily routine of running a home. If the husband were in business, this might mean getting involved in the business also. One evening we were invited to a delightful dinner at the home of a Muslim couple, the Abdullas. After the meal, with the aroma of spices still in the air, Shereen Abdulla raised a topic we had discussed in an earlier interview. Didn't I agree, she asked, that a woman should be allowed to work outside the home. This gave her husband the opportunity to justify the need for a woman to be in the home, to care for the family, to be there to support the children (they had only one teenage daughter) when they return from school, and to assure the comfort of the husband. Working outside the home created all kinds of opportunities for extra-marital affairs, he concluded, and he supplied enough so she need not work. At our next meeting, Shereen confirmed her great love and dedication to her husband but also allowed that on certain issues he was "as obstinate as an ox." Needless to say, she remains homebound.

Role Satisfaction

Every person, by ascription or by choice, occupies a variety of statuses. Though certain statuses are beyond the control of the person who occupies them, the role which is performed, i.e., the expression given to a particular status, can be influenced. When we look at achieved statuses and the way these are acquired, there is much greater opportunity for selection and variation on the basis of age, ethnicity, and related factors.

Chrysee Kline (1975:487) points out that roles must be conceptualized according to normative, behavioral, and interactional aspects. Every role must be performed in a certain way and the normative component will obviously show variation due to culture, other roles performed, context, and so forth. Roles are components of individual behavior and will be influenced by other factors in the behavior matrix. Roles also involve at least one other person, so interaction and context may influence the expression of certain statuses. But nobody ever performs only a single role. Due to ascriptive statuses of ethnicity, gender, and age, as well as achieved statuses, each role in turn influences and is influenced by others. It is useful to follow Shirley Angrist, whose study of sex roles suggests that we look at sex-role constellations because a person never acts or behaves "just as a man or woman" (1972:103).

Roles are dynamic and change through time; or stated in a different way, the performance of a role will change as the performer ages, taking on new roles or abandoning others. This change is due in part to different new statuses and roles (thus, realignments in the sex-role constellation), and in part to changes in aspects associated with existing roles. These aspects may relate to the norm, the behavior, or the relation of performer to others. "For the female, the various roles of worker, housewife, and mother occupy different priority positions at different points throughout the life cycle" (Kline 1975:487). Kaufert laments the paucity of cross-cultural data regarding the menopause and suggests that ethnographies may shed some light on the diversity of role changes brought about by the menopause (1982(a):183). Two recent papers dealt with such a cross-cultural review of ethnographic data (du Toit and Suggs 1983; du Toit 1986). The latter study concludes that menopause generally implies a "return to a nonreproductive state with the status and role associated with this state. Such a woman experiences an expansion of roles which is liberating" (1986:187).

During the year-long research project, four extensive interviews were conducted with each woman in the sample. These interviews were performed topically so that all the women responded to one interview schedule before we started over with the first respondent and the next interview schedule. The first interview dealt with the family history and personal background of the respondent. It discussed the family of orientation, childhood and socialization, and life experiences as an adult woman. In this way we could get a picture of family life in each community.

The second interview dealt with the subject's views about the experiences and behavior of women in her own community: prevailing attitudes regarding child-adult relationship, ideal roles for mother and grandmother; attitudes and information flow regarding menopause and related topics.

The third interview dealt with the subject's lifestyle — her physical and mental health and life course. A number of questions were of a more emotional and subjective nature regarding different feelings and relationships. It was at this stage that each woman was asked to perform a number of simple non verbal tests of a psychological nature. One of these requested the respondent to rank eight roles in the order of how important they were for her at that particular time in her life. The first or most important choice to be designated "1"; the last or lowest ranked role to be designated "8".

This particular role definition technique was developed by Pauline Bart. She applied it first to depressed middle-aged women in mental hospitals and included Jews and non-Jews and apparently black and white respondents. (These findings are discussed by Bart 1970). The eight roles, in the format and order in which they were presented to our research subjects, are presented in Table 17. To facilitate conceptualization, a set of picture cards depicting each role was prepared and women were asked to arrange the eight cards in rank order of preference/importance. The result of this part of the research was to allow for a listing of role priorities but also construction of a role constellation.

It was expected that the family and extended family would receive higher ranking; but the roles concerning parents, children, and grandparents were generally neutral in evaluation. Both categories of women refrained from assigning a high or a low rank to social-religious activities outside the home. An impressive number (increasing with the status change from pre- to postmenopausal) gave a very low rank order to working outside the home. This greater negative evaluation by the older women could be attributed to their age but also to their socialization and the times and conditions prevailing when they were young or middle-aged.

There is one other way of looking at the eight-scale ranking of roles and that is to record the statistical rank assigned each role. Table 19 presents these data.

The view presented by Table 19 confirms much of the findings derived from Table 18 but also permits the reader to see the middle-ranking categories not present in the first table.

TABLE 17

Bart's Eight Role Scale

Rank	Role
_____	Being a homemaker (A)
_____	Taking part in church, club and community activities (B)
_____	Being a companion to one's husband/partner (C)
_____	Helping parents (D)
_____	Being a sexual partner (E)
_____	Having a paying job (work outside the home) (F)
_____	Helping children (G)
_____	Being a grandparent (H)

TABLE 18

Rank Order of Roles by Indian South African Women

Role	Rank Order of Role Selection															
	1-2				3-4				5-6				7-8			
	Pre-		Post-		Pre-		Post-		Pre-		Post-		Pre-		Post-	
	#	%	#	%	#	%	#	%	#	%	#	%	#	%	#	%
C. Being a companion to one's husband/partner	22	75.9	17	62.9	4	13.8	6	22.2	2	6.9	2	7.4	1	3.4	2	7.4
A. Being a homemaker	16	55.1	15	55.5	9	31.0	3	11.1	4	13.7	9	33.3	–	–	–	–
G. Helping children	7	24.1	5	18.5	18	62.1	16	59.2	4	13.7	4	14.8	–	–	2	7.4
E. Being a sexual partner	7	24.1	1	3.7	6	20.7	5	18.5	6	20.7	12	44.4	10	34.4	9	33.3
D. Helping parents	1	3.6	5	19.2	9	32.1	6	23.1	16	57.1	8	30.7	2	7.1	7	26.9
H. Being a grandparent	1	3.4	2	7.4	3	10.3	9	33.3	4	13.8	8	29.6	21	72.4	8	29.6
B. Taking part in church, club and community activities	3	10.3	8	29.6	6	20.7	8	29.6	18	62.9	9	33.3	2	6.8	2	7.4
F. Having a paying job (work outside the home)	1	3.4	1	3.7	3	10.3	1	3.7	4	13.8	2	7.4	21	72.4	23	85.2

TABLE 19

Mean, Median and Mode of Role Ranking
by Indian South African Women

Role	Premenopausal	Postmenopausal
A. Being a homemaker		
Mean	2.6	2.9
Median	2	2
Mode	2	1
B. Taking part in church, club & community services		
Mean	4.8	4.3
Median	5	3
Mode	5–6	3
C. Being a companion to one's husband/partner		
Mean	2.0	2.7
Median	1	2
Mode	1	2
D. Helping parents		
Mean	5.0	4.7
Median	5	5
Mode	6	7
E. Being a sexual partner		
Mean	4.9	5.9
Median	5	6
Mode	7	6
F. Having a paying job (work outside the home)		
Mean	6.7	7.2
Median	7	8
Mode	8	8
G. Helping children		
Mean	3.4	3.7
Median	3	4
Mode	3	4
H. Being a grandparent		
Mean	6.6	5.0
Median	7	5
Mode	7	5–7

It is clear that role constellations can be observed. Being a homemaker and companion go hand in hand. This constellation contrasts quite clearly with other women's roles.

The Indian family is recognized for a number of characteristics, among which are the dominant role of the father; virilocal post-marital residence; homogeneity of religious and linguistic group membership; and the loving-caring service role of the wife and mother. For a wife to become a mother is of critical importance. The caring role of the mother is confirmed over and over again as the most important aspect of her being. As soon as her children start maturing, she begins to cultivate them (especially the sons) with an eye to her future status as grandmother. There is role continuity but each of these roles is unique and specific.

The question underlying this discussion is whether changes in education, health, housing, and socioeconomic conditions have also changed Indian status preferences and the roles they prefer. Are family and domestic roles still the roles of choice, or has the younger generation accepted a new orientation?

To answer this question, it is useful to look at the role selections within the context of ethnographic data. Only within the social context does a role find expression.

The Family

This refers to the first two role categories, C and A, as ranked in Table 18. Marriage, the normal and expected ritual for every Indian woman to go through, is the prerequisite for starting a family. (See discussion in Chapter III.)

Since women selected these roles quite clearly over others, it would be interesting to see how (in a different set of questions) they evaluate their marriages. The premenopausal group of respondents

TABLE 20

How Has Your Husband Treated You Over the Years?

Response	Premenopausal #	Premenopausal %	Postmenopausal #	Postmenopausal %
Very Well	7	24.1	15	55.6
Well	19	65.5	8	29.6
Not Too Well	1	3.4	1	3.7
Poorly	2	6.9	3	11.1

had a positive evaluation but not as positive as the older women. Table 20 lists these responses which cover the range of behavioral possibilities. One young woman said, "My husband treated me like a dog, he beat and kicked me and filled me with hate." An older woman explained that her husband "beat me regularly." The majority of women, however, had better marriages and were more philosophical about them. Explained one of the younger women, "Marriage in the beginning has its ups and downs — as maturity comes, so does understanding." It was in this *understanding* that most women found their companionship. Marriage, if not bliss, was certainly preferable to the alternative; and so a younger woman concluded, "We understand each other, we compromise." A number of the older women were clearer in their evaluation. Respect and fulfilling needs were frequently mentioned. Typical was old Mrs. Devchand, who in her wisdom born of Hindu philosophy remarked, "...he respected me and always supplied what I needed. That's enough." That suffices for being a companion and homemaker. Fulfillment is something that is reached in time. Good marriages are made on earth not in heaven because they require constant attention and compromise. With time, a woman finds role satisfaction in her home as her husband provides, as her family grows, and as she herself matures. Both the pre- and postmenopausal samples placed these two domestic roles at the top of their role selection. It is interesting to note that eighteen (62.1%) premenopausal women gave Role C the highest ranking, with Role A as second in preference, but the postmenopausal women reversed this rank order. Companionship and marriage are more important to the younger women; the role of homemaker is more important to the older women, all of whom were in their own homes by this stage of their lives. These two roles are the only ones in which rank order one or two was the mode.

The Mother

After the role of wife, that of mother is the most significant one for an Indian woman. Caring for the children (G) is clearly selected as the third most important role. Nobody ranked it last and a number listed it first or second.

In a related set of questions, we asked the respondents whether, in their view, a woman was a complete woman if she had not had a child, and also, whether a marriage was complete without a child. The figures in Table 21 are enlightening about the status of wife and mother.

TABLE 21

The Importance of Having a Child

| | Yes | | | | No | | | |
| | Pre- | | Post- | | Pre- | | Post- | |
	#	%	#	%	#	%	#	%
Is a woman a complete woman if she has not had a child?	10	34.5	9	33.3	19	65.5	18	66.7
Is a marriage complete if a child has not been born to it?	2	6.9	2	7.4	27	93.1	25	92.6

Given these potentially conflicting dominant roles in competition for the time, attention, and loving care of the wife/mother, how are these roles reconciled? In a different context, we asked the women whether they placed the needs of their children above their own: only two persons responded negatively. When we asked whether they would consider the needs and desires of their children above those of their husbands, fourteen (48.3%) of the premenopausal and seventeen (63.0%) of the postmenopausal women said, "yes."

As a wife and mother, the Indian woman finds complete role satisfaction. She will have gained the respect of her husband (Hiebert 1981:224), satisfied her in-laws, and laid the foundation for a full family life and a secure old age supported by her children. Although the husband prefers a son to carry on the family name, and a son may guarantee a woman a comfortable old age, it is frequently to a daughter that a woman turns, for there she is assured of empathy and support.

Bart has written quite extensively about her research on "the Jewish mother." This label implies characteristics such as family centered, doting on the children, overprotectiveness and the like. "But it is clear that you don't have to be Jewish to be a Jewish mother" (1976:79). Many Indian mothers tend to be "Jewish mothers." They tend to be overly attached to their children because their worlds focus inside the home and the family network.

The idea of a daughter's marriage is generally met with negative emotions. "I'll be sad, broken," one women said. "My right hand will be gone." Others stated the same emotion in different ways.

One common comment was that a daughter is always a daughter. A son goes out and becomes independent, but a daughter will always return for her mother to confide in. Part of the concern about a daughter's marriage stems from the likelihood that she may live with her mother-in-law and be "treated like an outsider." Mothers are also concerned about the safety and happiness of their daughters. It will be recalled that a large number of Indian marriages are either arranged by the parents or involve a proposal delivered through kinsmen to the girl's parents. The result of both possibilities is that the bride and groom do not know each other, which means a potentially bumpy start to the course of their relationship. One lady explained, "Indian marriages break up after a few weeks, not months, because Indians don't court. If they survive the first weeks and learn to understand each other and live together, then the chances of the marriage surviving is pretty good: because pregnancy used to follow quite naturally."

As to the marriage of a son, matters are quite different. It is not that there is less emotional attachment to male offspring, but daughters-in-law are possessive. There is an aphorism which expresses this: "A son is a son until he takes a wife (but a daughter is a daughter all her life)." Mothers like the extended family to continue — with the great house, the common meals, the daily gathering of members. Even where this is not possible, a mother likes a son to take one meal a day at her home or to visit her daily. If a son lives with his family, a mother gains a daughter-in-law. If he does not, his mother-in-law sees it as a gain because it frees her daughter and retains the maternal bonds. Gaining a daughter-in-law has pros and cons. One woman complained that her daughter-in-law was too modern, too critical of the old style. This caused dissension because the son frequently sided with his wife. Another told of a daughter-in-law who lived with her for fifteen years. She really felt she had gained a daughter; but when the family emigrated to England, her loss was double. In talking about the marriage of children, one frequently hears use of the term "stranger." This may be a serious matter involving violations of caste and religious or ethnic group restrictions. Or it may simply refer to the person as an outsider. Mothers are concerned that their daughters will be strangers when they leave their parental homes to marry. They are equally concerned about the kind of women their sons are going to marry — "the stranger in our midst," as one woman put it, remains a possibility. Being a "stranger" might imply differences in religion, linguistic traditions, background, and even ethnic origin.

Women are affected by the very fact of children growing up and leaving home for whatever reason. When children leave, a mother suddenly realizes that she is getting old. "I'll be lonely once they're gone. We share so much. I'll cling to one." Here is "the Jewish mother" who finds her fulfillment and happiness in the family and who feels left behind and tries to hold on to the children. "When I sit with my children I feel very happy," explained a typical family-centered woman. Women try to possess their children; they try to retain a relationship which inevitably changes as children go to school, university, work, or enter a marriage relationship. One woman expressed her emotions at the maturation of her children. "I feel sad; I feel I'm being left behind. I can't stay up with what they say and do..."

Sexuality

An interesting aspect of sexuality emerged from the analysis of our tabular data: namely, that these women separated the role of sexual partner (Role E) from that of husband's companion and other wife and homemaker roles. Neither the premenopausal women, whom one would expect to be more active sexually, nor the post-menopausal woman, many of whom have taken to sleeping alone, have given a clear rank order in their selection of this role. Although seven (24.1%) premenopausal women ranked it first or second and only one (3.7%) postmenopausal woman did, the opposite end of the scale does not confirm this preference by younger women. We find that ten (34.4%) premenopausal and nine (33.3%) postmeno-pausal women ranked the sexual partner role lowest, i.e., seventh or eighth. This is the only role in the eight-role scale that did not produce at least one dominant ranking — except for the strongly negative ranking given by the postmenopausal women. For this role, the mode was six; and twenty (74.1%) ranked the sexual partner role as sixth through eighth.

In spite of these figures, it should be noted that connubial sexuality is important to Indian women and valued by them. Rosen-thal states that "women are regarded as sensual creatures and their need for sexual satisfaction is recognized. Yet their status is unequiv-ocally subordinate to that of men" (1977:209). (See also Meer 1976:134f.)

The Extended Family

Every woman is supposed to leave her natal family and in time find fulfillment in the kutum (see discussion in Chapter III) of her husband. Serving her apprenticeship with the mother-in-law sets her on her course; having a child qualifies her; and eventually she becomes a respected member of a large extended family. As Kuper states: "Only with the passing of years and the birth and growth of her children, does the daughter-in-law become more emancipated from in-law control, and the husband-wife relationship itself branches out into many interdependent activities and joint responsibilities" (1960:133). During all these years of marriage, the woman may visit her parents — but not too often and not too long; and normally she would request permission to do so. In today's more relaxed atmosphere, rules are not so strict; but a woman does not visit around too much.

If we compare the responses for the two questions, D and H, which pertain to her own extended family, we find only two clusters of responses. Both are by premenopausal women and both are at the lower or negative end of the rating scale. In the younger category, there is no definite pattern of how they rank helping parents (Role D); but an overwhelming number, twenty-one (72.4%), rank being a grandparent (Role H) seventh or eighth. To a certain extent, as was found also among the other sample populations in this study, younger women simply do not want to think about being grandmothers because this role contains negative connotations of aging. Once a woman has grandchildren, even if she is still physically able, she would effectively have passed to the postreproductive phase of life. The postmenopausal women were equally vague in their ranking of the role of helping parents. Again this role received a negative rank but not as strongly negative as from their younger cohorts. Many of the older women actually were grandmothers so the negative connotation of aging is tempered somewhat by role performance.

What this says is that once a woman has her own family, with responsibilities and obligations toward her husband's family, that is where the priorities are; more so for the premenopausal than the postmenopausal women. The former most likely had children at home; the latter in many cases were living with a married son or daughter. Their perspective and experience may explain the difference in responses by the two categories.

Extradomestic Roles

We emphasized that the Indian woman is above all home-oriented and sedentary. Activities requiring her to leave the home,

detracting from the attention she can give her husband and children, would therefore not be popular. Something requiring her to be
away for short periods of time is preferable to spending most of the
day out of the home.

It is important to recognize that most of the men we spoke to
prefer their wives to remain at home. Ross (1971:122), speaking of
modern India, states that the major factor resulting in women entering the job market, is change in "the attitudes of fathers and husbands." It is almost as if the protection and isolation which marked
postmenarcheal schoolgirls a generation ago has been projected onto
the wife. First the father was the protector, later it was the husband.
A few of the young wives in this study sample wanted to take jobs
but their husbands refused, explaining that the household was in
greater need of their attention. This does not imply that all Indian
women stay home. Our sample included an ample representation of
nurses, college lecturers, teachers, businesswomen, etc. They are in
the minority, however, and in some cases work to assist the husband
and increase the family income.

In her thorough study of suicide in South Africa, Fatima Meer
points out that Indian women have a very hard time visualizing
themselves as anything other than wives and mothers. When they
do work outside the home, they find it difficult to integrate these
roles. Suicide frequently follows. Meer says: "This corroborates the
dim view Indian society continues to take in respect of the gainful
employment of women and accounts for their very low involvement
in gainful employment" (1976:71). Confirmatory evidence for this
statement comes from Mostert (1981:12), who states that 89.3% of
Indian women, aged twenty to fifty-nine, in the Transvaal and Natal
were not gainfully employed and were not seeking employment.
Our own findings hint at the same attitude toward employment
outside the home: 72.4% premenopausal and 85.2% postmenopausal women rated outside work (Role F) at the lowest order of
selection. "I'd rather be poor and in my own home," one woman
said, and added philosophically "...but luckily my husband's business is doing very well."

The last role to be discussed is that of taking part in church,
club, and community activities (Role B). Two matters need to be kept
in mind: formal activities (religious and social) are dominated by
males; and women experience times of ritual uncleanliness. Women
have very small roles in Islam. Among the Hindu, their activities are
concentrated in lighting the lamp and performing domestic religious
rituals. Even the washing and dressing of the deceased may only
be done by a woman who no longer menstruates. Thus, it is not

strange to find a much more positive ranking of this role among the older women. In addition, these activities all take place outside the home and would interfere with the domestic roles.

There are occasions when women involve themselves in extra-domestic activities. These are essentially cultural, welfare, and religious in nature. They tend to follow not only religious but also linguistic/ethnic lines. The Gujerati Women's Social Club, the Tamil League, or the Laudium Women's Club all have some welfare activities. The more strongly religion-based groups care for the needy, do handicrafts, or are involved in welfare (often subsidized by the government). The Laudium Women's Club gives lessons in flower arranging, sewing, knitting, and similar crafts. It also had an outreach program to organize the Training Center for the Handicapped.

But it is more specifically within religious groups that social and outreach programs are centered. The relatively few Christians operate within denominational groups (e.g., Anglican, Catholic, or Dutch Reformed Church) as welfare committees. These committees may contribute government programs which usually operate independently. The Laudium Cripple Care Association coordinates the local work of the national association, as do various child welfare organizations. Women who are in need can benefit from government pension schemes (e.g., for widows, disabled, or old age) and costs for attendance at the Laudium Clinic are cut upon presentation of a pension book. Government aid does not go far enough or reach deep enough, and that is where the Hindu and Muslim organizations take over in caring for their own.

During the early years of settlement, a great deal of secularization took place among Indian indentured laborers. They soon began to experience cultural change as customs and festivals were ignored or new religious patterns accepted. Many of these early Indians, especially those born in South Africa followed European styles of dressing, living, and talking. Their traditions had become moribund. The better educated — particularly among the passenger immigrants and visiting representatives from India — were concerned at the rapid cultural change taking place. A number of such persons tried to give meaning to the Indian culture. In 1912 a conference was held in Pietermaritzburg and focused on establishing a Hindu Maha Sabha organization to promote religious education, observe Hindu festivals, and increase women's participation in social and religious activities. This was important because it created opportunities for women who so desired to have roles outside the home. These roles could be religious or educational but always involved some aspect of welfare. Lalla explains:

Ever since its formation, the Sabha has been faced with the problem of poverty among the Hindus and the serious consequences flowing from it. It was aware that many Hindu families, unable to survive the battle for bread, had succumbed to the temptation of bartering their faith for food. Moreover, the ugly spectacle of men and women, old and young, in rags and tatters, soliciting alms in the streets, was undignifying to the Hindu community. To these derelicts of human society, Hinduism could have no meaning and to speak of charity as one of the fundamental principles of religion, smacked of hypocrisy. To combat this blot on the fair name of Hinduism, the Sabha created a charitable trust and registered it in terms of the Charitable Ordinance of the province. Funds were raised from time to time and assistance rendered. In addition bursaries were awarded to some very poor children to pursue their studies (1960:110).

The Gujerati have the *Hindu samag* that has a committee for the needy; a cultural center that receives old saris for distribution to the poor and during Diwali, provides hampers of food and clothing to the needy.

A ritual popularized by the Hindu Maha Sabha is the Deepavali (Tamil) or Diwali (Hindi). It is recognized as a public holiday in Indian schools by the Department of Education and is a time of general festivity, though expressed in different ways, among all Hindu. When explained to whites, it is likened to Christmas. That may imply a religious basis and religious rituals, but many people participate only in the secular phase of both festivities. Diwali is observed in November.

During the day, relatives and friends visit, bringing gifts (frequently in the form of sweets or other delicacies); but in the early evening, families gather in their own homes as the Hindu lamp is lit in honor of Lakshmi, the goddess of wealth. Some of the women who were members of more orthodox families lit small clay lamps which were placed in the kitchen and other parts of the home. Others lit only the main lamp. There is an atmosphere of gaiety as gifts are exchanged; and after a usually elaborate vegetarian meal, the children go out for fireworks. Diwali is, however, also a time to think of the less fortunate. Women prepare extra boxes of food for the poor to be distributed by the Central Cultural Committee. However, this kind of altruism, sharing of wealth when the goddess of prosperity is honored, does not greatly alter the condition of needy families. Women explained that they gave because of their surplus, but they knew their actions did not have any lasting effect.

Among Muslims we also find a wide range of welfare organizations, but because the faith is uniform, there is less diversity of groups involved. Women's participation, however, is restricted. They serve on madressa committees and may be involved in some of the others. The Pretoria Muslim Trust, the Muslim Youth Movement, and Mosque Committee, or the Memon Jamaat are examples of organizations involved in outreach. Within the latter organization, Baitumal is a group dealing specifically with widows and orphans. Those in need go to the wives of men who are in charge of the other committees and request assistance such as paying rent, supplying groceries, etc. Muslims have regular days of fasting, and on such occasions, charity is given to those who ask. It would seem that Muslims, with the *zakaat* system, have a better ongoing welfare program than do the Hindus. One young businessman explained that "at the end of every year (in the month of Ramadan) we must give 4.0% of all our assets (i.e., cash, clothing, jewels, etc.) to the poor. Thus, if someone has $1,000 he must give $25" (sic). Fatima Meer explains this form of taxation:

> Muhammad, alive to the fact that economic inequalities vitiated against the establishing of a true brotherhood, institutionalized a rigid system of taxation, *zakaat*, on all accumulated capital and current earnings exceeding a stipulated basic sum. There is a two and a half percent tax on all capital be it in the form of cash or kind, and a tax on current earnings, which varies from as much as one-fifth on mining enterprises, *khuns*, to one-tenth on produce, *ushr*. In the Islamic state, paid officials are responsible for collecting the tax and the central government then utilizes the money to subsidise the poor. Zakaat remains obligatory even in a non-Islamic state, and Muslims are required to elect a central committee which will be responsible for the collection and distribution of Zakaat to those in need, who may not necessarily be Muslims. In Zakaat, man has the first institutionalized concept of a welfare state, based on the principle of progressive taxation (1969:185).

Since this is religion-based taxation, the committee that administers it essentially operates out of the mosque. Women can be involved in the distribution of goods to the poor. Their primary care is for fellow believers (widows, orphans, or impoverished persons) who are in need.

The women explained another type of welfare through which money or goods are sent to the natal village in India. This is particularly true for those who were born there. In some cases, the village from which a person derives or one that was visited during a trip to India is singled out. This is particularly true among Memons.

Not only do welfare activities give women an opportunity for service and care, but they allow, or even require, that they leave the home. Extradomestic roles were not favorite roles among Indian South African women, but the postmenopausal women gave it a somewhat higher rating than their younger cohorts.

Being a Woman

Socialization provides gender identity but does not necessarily guarantee satisfaction with it. In some cases, gender conflict occurs due to hormonal imbalance at the time of early fetal diversification; in others, it may be due to childhood experiences. The women with whom we worked were all happy with their role as women, though some expressed frustration about their status vis-a-vis their husbands and males in general. In fact, it is with reference to their husbands that women found their fullest satisfaction as women and also their greatest frustration at being women.

Asked to consider at what times they most liked being women, a majority of our subjects found that satisfactory state within the marriage — specifically, in relation to their husbands. The women expressed it differently, and a larger number of premenopausal women indicated satisfaction in this context; but it always included being with the husband and children; making love; being admired or flattered; or as one woman said, "at the end of the day, everything ready, waiting for my husband to come home." There were those who simply liked the adulation they received when they were all dressed up, with their hair done and jewels in place — be this from the husband or from the opposite sex in general.

The second most frequently mentioned context within which Indian women most liked being a woman, was that of being a mother, i.e., when they were pregnant or caring for a child. It is interesting that both categories of women gave this equal weight in their selection. Two quite diverse responses rounded out these selections. An old woman stated that being a *peri pombla* (Tamil for "senior woman") gave her satisfaction because the younger ones came to her for advice. A young woman stated, "I am happiest when I can get my way around men" (e.g., in business deals). Herein is reflected the dichotomy of the two generations: the older generation

— satisfied in the home, finding fulfillment in the traditional role of "big (senior) woman" who runs her home as well as her children and daughters-in-law in contrast to the young women who are successfully competing in academics and business, previously all male realms.

What they least liked about being women also involved relationships with their husbands, the subject most often mentioned. These included husbands who abused alcohol; one who had run afoul of the law and was in jail; quite a number who caused distress for their wives by ignoring them, "trampling" on them for not being educated, and causing mental stress of a variety of kinds. Mentioned almost as frequently was menstruation. One woman complained of the pain and said that it was the worst time in her life. The women liked to be in charge of their homes and have the authority in the daily running of affairs (particularly in the big house of the extended family), but this did not include doing the chores. We have noted the presence of black servants in most homes. They relieve the women of day-to-day household responsibilities while she continues her supervisory and educational role. Almost as often as the previous issue, Indian women stated that they least liked being a woman when they were barred from things because of not being equal to men. It is also interesting that only the younger women gave this response. The same number of older women stated that they never disliked being women. Not a single one of the older women complained about not being equal to men. But not a single woman in the younger age group said she never felt frustrated because of being a woman — or at least at the way women are treated.

Because men have superior status and women are essentially homebound, one can expect that women would agree with the statement, "Life for men is more exciting and interesting than for women." This is confirmed by 76% of the pre- and 85% of the post-menopausal research samples. The reasons for this evaluation are fairly uniform: after marriage the woman is homebound, but the husband essentially uses the home as a hotel. He spends his time at work; goes on business trips, meets people, has diverse experiences, and is free to do things while a wife is "trapped." The man can have a girlfriend, has freedom in sex and can initiate an affair, which women would do at the expense of total ostracism and financial ruin. In religion, men are free to participate as they wish, but women are restricted — partly because of ritual uncleanliness. "Indian men are IT," said one. Women must get permission to do things or to go places, but men never consult their wives about their actions. What Lemu and Heeren say about Muslim women applies equally to Hindu women in this context...but not to their husbands.

> The Muslim woman's role in the home is a vitally important one to the happiness of the husband and the physical and spiritual development of their children. Her endeavor is to make her family's life sweet and joyful, and the home a place of security and peace. This and her early character-training of the children have a lasting effect on the behavior and attitudes of the next generation when they reach adolescence and adulthood (1978:19).

In many a home, wife and husband work as a team, and the woman finds recognition and status. These homes tend to be those in which women are better educated or qualified either in a profession or in business.

We have emphasized conservation and documented a stability in status and role, particularly with reference to the wife-home-maker-mother. This does not imply that there are no changes taking place. Ramasar (1966:31). speaks of "a progressive emancipation" which is taking place as education increases; family size decreases; new roles open up; and greater personal independence and social rights are allowed. She concludes:

> The modern, educated, middle class, urban wife is emerging, confronted with several difficult, mutually contradictory role situations. She too will soon be expressing dissatisfaction with her roles of housekeeper and mother since vocational opportunities and choice of roles are open to her. At the same time, if the women do not have jobs, some will seek outside interests doing voluntary work in cultural or club activities, simply because they may feel constricted by a purely domestic routine (1966:32).

Conclusion

Important attitudes emerged from the fieldwork; namely, the great value placed on marriage with its security, companionship, and relative comfort. Because younger persons are more interested in the sexual component, one would expect this companionship aspect to receive even a higher rating from them. During visits to individual homes, we were repeatedly assured — particularly by older women — that they enjoyed their life and that their universe really evolved around their homes. Only the young ones would have it any different. These are the impressions which emerged fairly early in the interviews. They were the impressions formulated by the anthropologist outsider.

The insider rating scale (even though the role categories were not devised by the respondents) confirmed that impression. There are only two rating categories where more than 60% of all respondents in a particular menopausal category agreed. The first is eighteen (62.1%) premenopausal women who gave top rating to being a companion to one's husband. The second is seventeen (62.9%) postmenopausal women who gave the lowest rating to having a paying job outside the home.

At the time of this study, despite rapid changes in education and other aspects of living, Indian South African women still give preference to traditional roles. The stability in domestic roles such as mother and its extension, grandmother, are central to their preferences. These roles are family oriented and are performed in the home.

Coping Behavior

We have looked at the mechanics of stress reduction through coping behavior. Much of stress, as the cases studied in the home and family illustrated, can be reduced by openly dealing with it. Some husbands have heard the complaints of wives who are effectively shut out of their lives once they leave the home. However, there are other areas in which stress is potential. The way people respond to real or hypothetical situations tells much about them and about the social evaluation of the context. To arrive at these evaluations, a number of hypothetical crisis situations were imagined, and the women were asked how they would cope or what their reaction would be. For many of them, there were implications of reality stemming from their own or a close relative's actual crisis experiences.

Responses are a good reflection of the social structure and the values of a community at a given time. This material represents Indian South African women, their emotions and likely actions in situations of crisis. To explore these potential crisis reactions, four hypothetical situations will be discussed:

> Suppose that as a young woman (before you had a family) you were forced by health problems to have an operation which would have prevented you from having children. How would you have reacted?

It is important in this context to remember that a woman in Indian society is really a woman only when she has a child. The wider community of friends and neighbors also comments about a childless woman and rejoices at the birth of an infant. Inability to have a child would, thus, create emotional stress, disappointment, and a feeling of emptiness.

It is not strange that some women indicated that they would keep quiet about it. One explained, "It's a terrible thing, particularly in this community. He may look for another wife." This action is open to Muslims and was mentioned by three women. A number of women said that in such a crisis they would just keep quiet and hope for the best or not mention it to a fiance. "My family too will remain quiet, otherwise nobody will marry me." The great majority however, would discuss it with the husband, who could decide whether the marriage should continue or whether there was to be a second wife to bear children. Another response, found predominantly among younger women, was that they would not marry, or if married, would attempt to dissolve it (...the Indian community says, "No children, no marriage"). Those who said they would not marry would go into social or hospital work.

There does not seem to be any opposition to adoption; fully two-thirds of the women in each category mentioned it as a likely action. Some women, however, qualified this by indicating that they would rear a child of a family member.

> Suppose that as a newly married woman, your husband has an accident that leaves him sterile. What would your reaction be?

In this question the situation is reversed, and the decision lies with the woman. However, only two of the older and one of the younger women said they would divorce the husband. The premenopausal woman explained, "If he was half a man I don't think I'd remain married to him." A larger number of women mused that if they were not yet married, they certainly would not marry a man with this condition. "During the first two years it would not make a difference, but as the years went by it would become an issue. Every woman wants a child." Once two people were married they would accept it and work it out. One explained, "We don't just divorce";

and a second stated, "Hindu marriage is a commitment for life irrespective of children."

There is a certain degree of fatalism or divine providence in other responses. With a shrug of her shoulder, one woman suggested that it was in the hands of Allah; and from another came the thought, "God did it; we cannot fight with God."

Once again, adoption was seen as a possible action, the decision being the husband's. But the emphasis was placed on the relationship which existed. That was most important.

> Suppose that as a forty-three-year-old woman you discover that you are pregnant. To whom would you talk or turn for advice and support?

One of the first women at whom this question was directed gave a self-conscious little laugh and said, "I'm forty-three years old and I am pregnant!" The majority of women, however, by this age have long completed the reproductive phase of their lives and many are grandmothers. It is in being pregnant at the same time your own daughter is pregnant (or already a mother) that women see the dilemma. Their first, nearly universal reaction was one of discomfort. The words used to express this were embarrassed, shocked, upset, ashamed, disgraced, or shy. One young woman blurted out, "I'll commit suicide...." Two of the older women said, "I'll die." One explained, "I did once miss my period and almost worried myself to death."

Women explained that they wouldn't be able to live with having grown children or worried about abnormality of the child. "I'll get mad at him (my husband) and go ahead and have the child." The woman who said this was a Muslim and claimed that Muslims are not permitted abortion. But to a certain stage of this development, abortion is permitted. According to the Koran the fetal development is a slow process:

12. Man We did create
    From a quintessence (of clay);
13. Then We placed him
    As (a drop of) sperm
    In a place of rest,
    Firmly fixed;
14. Then We made the sperm
    Into a clot of congealed blood;
    Then of that clot We made

A (foetus) lump; then We
Made out of that lump
Bones and clothed the bones
With flesh; then We developed
Out of it another creature.
So blessed be God,
The Best to create! (SURA XIII:12,13,14)

The first binding verdict on abortion was given by Hazrat Ali Talib, the son-in-law of the Prophet, when he declared that the embryo could not be regarded as a living child until the beginning of the seventh stage which, according to Jurists, has been set as the middle of the fifth month from the day of conception. Thus, termination of pregnancy before this period cannot be considered to be infanticide. According to the Hanafi Law, pregnancy can be terminated within 120 days (Brijbhushan 1980:80–81).

Feelings about abortion are not structured by religious group membership. Of the younger women, 40.0% said they would not have an abortion; but in the older category, only 29.6% are definite in this regard. An older woman justified not having an abortion "because it spoils your health." Another said she would feel embarrassed and ashamed and hide her pregnancy under her sari; a third said that she'd feel very shy and disgraced but have the baby, using the Afrikaans idiom, a *laat lammetjie* (literally, a late lamb). One of the younger women suggested having the baby "as a bonus for my old age." A second indicated that she would most likely have an abortion to avoid the embarrassment.

The women in both age categories stated that they would discuss their predicament with their gynecologist, relatives, or friends. Those consulting the physician would do so to confirm pregnancy and to assure that they would expect it to be a safe one. However, if the gynecologist recommended an abortion, most said they would terminate the pregnancy. In order of frequency, the next person to be consulted is the husband. In most cases, the women were sure that the husband would be delighted since men like large families. A smaller number would discuss their condition with a daughter or the other children and this was a way of overcoming their feeling of embarrassment. One woman said she would talk to her daughter and ask her to help seek an abortion. A few of the women indicated that they would turn to their best friends for advice and support.

Two of the younger and three of the older women thought that it would be exciting or that they would be very happy experiencing another pregnancy at that age. Speaking of Muslim women in the Middle East, where husbands put the same emphasis on family, Minai points out: "Most have defined themselves solely as wives and mothers, and see their entire purpose in life coming to a close. Out of panic, they sometimes try to have just one more child, who will rejuvenate them in their husbands' eyes more effectively than a face life" (1981:194).

Suppose you were a thirty-eight-year-old woman, the mother of two children, both of whom had been killed in an automobile accident. How would you react to this?

The universal reaction would, of course, be one of shock, devastation, and depression leading gradually to an evaluation of the situation. There was some expression of fatalism in accepting what God puts out for you, or accepting it as part of your *karma* (life course).

Would these women, given the age at which this hypothetical disaster was to occur, think of starting another family? No fewer than 69.0% of the premenopausal and 66.6% of the postmenopausal category indicated that they would have another child or children. One stated, "It would leave a great gap in my life — after quite a while I will try again..." Most of those who said they would have another pregnancy made it clear that it would not be a replacement pregnancy because each child was special and unique. Only four women indicated that they would consult a gynecologist before having another child, and most were sure that their husbands would want another. One woman who was experiencing bouts of severe depression during this time explained that her (favorite) son had, in fact, been killed in an automobile accident a year before.

One other woman said, "I would be heartbroken. I would not have another child at that age or after that shock. A woman will be emotionally scarred and think back: why didn't we have more children?" Those who would not have another child of their own (and some of those who would consider another pregnancy) indicated that they certainly would consider adoption. Of the younger women, 20.7%, and of the older, 11.1% saw adoption as a way of having a family without risking a pregnancy at that age.

We find in these coping strategies a restatement of the weight placed on the nuclear family. Children are at the center of a woman's life, and they are the cement that binds a man and a woman into a family. In spite of numerous statements which are critical of Indian men and their own husbands in many cases, women do place a premium on the marriage relationship and on the bonds of communication and support. Other members of the nuclear family, especially a daughter, are closer to an adult woman than are her friends. Blood is thicker than water, and keeping those relationships healthy is greatly valued. Yet, when it comes to the question of potential threats to health, the medical specialist is recognized, consulted, and listened to.

Life Cycle Perceptions

Introduction

Every person has some perception of various stages in the lives of those around him and of his own stage vis-a-vis those of others. Thus, a person recognizes others as being young, middle-aged, or old and himself as older than some but younger than others. Such life cycle perceptions generate not only cognitive behavioral patterns which are gender linked, but also ideals of interactional relationships.

The life cycle, if one thinks about it, is actually a fairly straight line (much like the dotted line used by psychologists to ascertain past-present-future orientation of test subjects). It starts at birth, or before, and runs for various lengths depending on the individual until death, or after. If there is belief in an after life, especially among people who practice an ancestor cult, there may be continued interaction beyond the last breath. But essentially it is the period when people are living and interacting that is of critical importance. Ask someone what life-span stages he recognizes and you will have an indication of the stages or events that were important in his life or are considered important to members of that particular community. Such stages are frequently marked by some ritual or ceremony, or they may simply be seen as important for men or women, separately.

When the Indian South African women were asked about stages for women and stages for men, some interesting differences emerged. Stages punctuate the life course because other people recognize them as important; but in retrospect, looking at his own life course a person tends to become subjective and to integrate personal events and experiences. Stages may also be described by the emotional rather than structural features which characterize them.

For women the following composite was presented:

a. Infancy
b. Childhood
c. Teenage: This stage was variously described as consisting of puberty or falling in love.
d. Married: Characteristic or coterminous are moving out of the family home and "trouble with in-laws."
e. Childbirth: Here women mentioned childbirth or birth of first child. Substages which were mentioned are achieving a goal and subsequent children.
f. Childrearing.
g. Children marry: This naturally leads into the important stage of having grandchildren. A number of women referred to this stage as "respectability."
h. Change of life.
i. Old age: coterminous with this stage is widowhood and being very lonely.
j. Death.

Incorporated in these stages and markers are all the important social events and conditions which count for Indian women. In the context of male activities, life stages as seen by the women are quite different:

a. Infant.
b. Childhood.
c. Puberty: voice breaks.
d. Premarital control.
e. Marriage: characteristics mentioned by a number of women were: learn to be dependable; responsible for household; and become provider. It is interesting that this maturity is reached *after* marriage. Said one woman, "Indian men mature very late in life." Added another, "Men mature later, about thirty."
f. Parent.
g. Old age: Informants said that this is when the working years are over. Others explained that it is very difficult for men to accept.

A third group felt that grandchildren were not critical to men. Once again we are dealing with role continuity for women, whereas men retire from their accustomed roles.

Conceptual

Rather than deal with the details of stages recognized by informants and enumerated above, this discussion will look at a more general breakdown of childhood years, middle years, and late years or old age. These categories are relative, and some of the women, despite their years, defy classification. In general there is a fairly clearcut division.

The early years. The critical question here is what distinguishes a child from a woman?

Indian women were quite clear about the characteristics of girls. They are immature, like to play, are self-centered and childish. They have no worries and don't know right from wrong, essentially because they have "small bodies and small brains, and must be taught everything." They must learn to help in the kitchen, assume responsibility, and bathe themselves. They must have an escort as they mature and want to go out.

The girl becomes a woman: 76% of the younger and 71% of the older women in the study linked this specifically with first menstruation. Matters change now that she is "a young girl," she has "come to her age" and can get married. She now is taboo in the kitchen for five days every month. She becomes moody and starts to be attractive. She notices boys and becomes secretive.

The trend toward later marriage is noteworthy, because in earlier times marriage frequently followed menarche. A number of the younger women pointed out that maturity came only at about age seventeen as girls are educated and become part of the adult world. However, one grandmother explained, "Indian girls mature earlier mentally and physically as compared to whites. The mother role begins early." Another of the older women suggested, "A child's blood has a lot of heat — it cools down as she matures and starts thinking on her own."

When asked about the best time in a woman's life, a significant number (37.9% of the pre- and 33.3% of the postmenopausal women) indicated the teenage years just before marriage. It is interesting that this life stage is variously defined by the two relative age categories. The older women spoke about a girl's teen years from about fourteen to nineteen as a time when "spring has bloomed up" in her life;

when she is important, popular, free, "without responsibilities...
(but) then come the in-laws." These girls are young and beautiful
and are to be courted or proposed to. Younger women in the research
sample defined this premarital stage as teenage or up to the middle
twenties. Young Indian women today do not see marriage as the first
priority. Most want some tertiary education or want to work and
gain some experience rather than just to go from one kitchen to
another. One of these younger women, a Hindu, stated that the
courtship period was the best time in a woman's life. It is a time
which "promises to bring the moon." Hindus, she reminded us, are
more liberal and once engaged may go out freely — unlike Muslims.

Menarche and its cultural significance in this community will
be discussed contextually in the next chapter. Suffice to mention
here that it does not have the same importance for the present generation as it had for their mothers and grandmothers.

The middle years. Marriage is supposed to bring maturity as a
woman assumes responsibility in a kitchen, looks after herself
(instead of being told), is free to choose and act, and is more aware
of herself as she matures physically. It has been said that she has
lost her virginity, one can see it in her face and in her behavior. Her
posture changes — she becomes more lady-like and conscious of
herself. At this time, too, authority over her changes from the father
to the husband. The girl wants to be an adult, but the adult is conscious that old age is approaching. For this reason one woman saw
the difference between a girl and a woman essentially as one of
orientation: "A child wants to be big; a woman wants to be young
again."

About the same number of pre- and postmenopausal women
preferred the time which immediately followed marriage before the
birth of the first child..."before problems start." During this time,
there might be a honeymoon, especially valued if it was not an
arranged marriage. The bride could expect full attention from the
groom and they have time for each other. However, nature and societal expectations dictate that pregnancy soon follow. The same
number who preferred the postmarital phase also preferred the
years between twenty and thirty when there are small children and
the wife is accepted by the in-laws. During those years they felt
healthy and strong enough to do everything. The next phase indicated was from thirty to forty-five years old. A larger number of pre-
than postmenopausal women preferred this stage. As one expressed
it, "You've found your niche. You're married and have ironed out the

problems. The children are independent." This is an age when women are involved in extradomestic activities or when they have time for self-enrichment activities.

A larger number of postmenopausal women found it attractive when all the children were married and they could settle down. They were contented and happy and most likely would have some grandchildren so they could "sit back and enjoy life."

The middle years represent the prime of a woman's life, but they are variously defined and valued for a variety of reasons. It is interesting that these years have different meanings for the two age categories and that there is a preference for different stages of this middle-age period. The younger women emphasize the earlier of these years and the freedom they have to spend time on themselves and their experience and qualifications. The older women see the postmenopausal stage of life as one during which they can sit back. Their role as mother has been completed, they have served their need to provide a family. Accepted by husbands, in-laws, and children, they relax. Needless to say, each of the two categories of women view their lives and those of others in terms of their own socialization and experience. They represent two chronological phases in the culture of Indian South African women.

The late years. For many women in our research sample, the transition from the middle to the late years is signified by the cessation of menstruation — the end of the reproductive years. After this they don't get the monthly sickness, their minds are at ease, and they lose interest in sexual intercourse. After the change of life they also tend to become moody, sickly, tensed up and more reserved.

At this stage in their lives a number of major changes occur: they gradually withdraw from housework and start to spend more time on religion and their grandchildren. It is said that an old woman cannot do housework other than cooking, and in the latter she is unsurpassed. She can peel vegetables, clean rice or prepare *dhal*. She can peel garlic, slice ginger, mix spices, and prepare the best *masala*. These are all sedentary activities. For this reason, too, older women can sit on the floor and sew *godras* (patchwork quilts). They make *atjar* (pickle), which would spoil if a younger woman making it were to experience menstruation.

Women in this life phase also turn more to religion. They pray more both at home and in the Hindu temple; Muslim women do five prayers a day and read the Koran (while menstruating they were prevented from doing this for ten days every month); and Tamil women pray morning and evening.

Older women are looked to for advice and guidance; they never give the wrong advice. That advice, derived from experience as well as insight and understanding, is accepted even by men. Their wisdom pertains to: moral life, particularly in guiding grand-children; family affairs, in which they act to keep family bonds strong; and rituals. The latter include attending funerals — they may bathe and dress a corpse in preparation for burial or cremation — ; going to weddings; engaging in the Hindu's month of fasting before the *Diwali*; lighting the lamp; and giving the ritual bath. They know how to bathe a sick baby and rub in a home remedy. Some see this as superstitious, but the older women know a lot about herbal medi-cines and their healing qualities. They are also involved in cleaning the temple. Older women are thought of as quite manly, i.e., domi-neering. In the family context, they have time for their grand-children and show great patience with them. Said one young woman, "[grandmothers] are warm, loving, comforting; every child has a birthright to have a *dosima*. Her house is headquarters the kids say!"

As the late years progress, an old woman has less to do and may be handicapped by physical or emotional deficiencies. Some can't accept changes, e.g., in ways of raising children, and want to treat their daughters-in-law as they were treated. They are critical and envious of the younger generation. Some start to nag, com-plain, mind other people's business, be tired, critical, or garrulous. Some old ladies become very neat — perfectionists — and are critical of everybody else. Others do not care for themselves and become slovenly in person and dress. A Tamil child who sits hunched forward, dresses shabbily, or is catty toward others will be reprimanded for acting like a *pati* (old woman). Old women dwell on the past, the good old days, and in time may experience memory loss or repeat things over and over. "Old Indian women normally do not work, they sit in a corner and fade away...."

Experiential

The previous description dealt with ways in which women conceive of the three major phases in the life cycle. How did the women in our study experience them? Rather than look at these phases in a lengthy descriptive account, our approach was to highlight them in terms of good and bad experiences. These included the kinds of experiences to which Indian South African women might be exposed or the actual events that they experienced.

The early years. What is the worst thing that can happen to an Indian girl before marriage? The majority of the women, 63% of the pre- and 69% of the postmenopausal women indicated that a girl who got pregnant (lost or spoiled her good name) would be branded for life. She might be thrown out by her family and would not be able to get married. One old woman stated, "In the old days, for a girl to grow up and get old without a proposal of marriage was the worst thing that could happen to her. Today, it is getting into trouble — getting pregnant." It should be kept in mind that after the wedding night, the husband may decide that his wife was not a virgin and "had been with another man." This, too, is grounds for separation. But an interesting variation emerged; 22.2% of the younger women stated that the worst thing that could happen to a woman was being raped. Not a single woman in the older age category mentioned rape, which suggests that times are changing and that rape has become a more common occurrence. One of the young respondents explained, "She'll be afraid of men even in marriage. Everyone would look at her in disgust. She'd be marked in society — a social stigma — and if married, her husband could divorce her. This is why most rape cases are not "reported." A third experience, though mentioned by only a few women, was being jilted by a boyfriend or fiance. This also left a stigma which people remembered. Here the women emphasized that interethnic and interreligious unions were bad because breakup was likely. Two women also considered illness which might result in sterility..."if sterile, no child...if no child, no marriage."

Fully 80% of the total sample thought that the worst thing that could happen to a young woman was anything that might affect her chances to appear clean and unsoiled — that might hamper her chances of making a good match in marriage.

When we asked the women about their own experiences and the events which they remembered with negative emotions, nothing as dramatic emerged. Nevertheless, a major theme of resentment emerges. Among the younger women, 41%, and among the older generation, 37% resented having been forced to leave school or not even being able to go to school in the first place. The reasons for this are diverse but include being the only daughter and needed about the house; the death of a mother, with the same result; reaching menarche (a large number left school at age twelve); or having to get married. One young woman explained that she refused to stay home. "I wanted to go to school and ran out into the street. But my mother came after me and dragged me back into the house and beat me." Another relates that her parents forced her to go to a girls' school after age twelve in spite of the fact that the school did not teach mathematics and science as did the coeducational school down the street. She said, "The result was that I did not qualify to go to university. After matric I wasted four years at home being obedient to my parents. Then at age twenty-one I defied my parents and went for nurses training." The second most frequently mentioned reason for morose recollections of childhood concern conflicts between the girls' choices of boyfriends and strict parents or arranged engagements. The reasons are diverse: one or the other belonging to the same linguistic group but a lower caste; being matched by parents with somebody much older; a boyfriend leaving her for "greener pastures," i.e., another girl or a future somewhere else; or nonacceptance by the boy's family. A third and unexpectedly large number, of women recalled the death of a mother (or father or sibling) as dramatically changing their lives. In some cases, the child was shunted from one relative to another or lived with an older sibling or step mother. One young woman gave poignant expression to this loss. "My mother died when I was a little over a year old. I never knew her and was cared for by my older sister. I missed never having been cuddled. I had two nephews who were always being picked up and I was left out!" In the same vein, three women expressed the shock of insecurity when they learned that their fathers, all Muslims, were taking second wives. In one case, there was a big happy family — father, mother, and seven sisters — but not a son for the father; so under Islamic law, he took a second wife.

But what about the happy side of life? What is the best thing that can happen to a young girl? There is no doubt about the ideal situation; parents permit and support the young girl's education. No fewer than thirteen (45%) of the younger and ten (37%) of the older women stated that education gives a woman more independence, permits her to have her own career. She could be a professional, expand her horizons or go overseas, and have support in case of widowhood. She could also remain single, not needing a husband for financial security. In addition, a number of women felt that just having the opportunity to travel abroad, to enjoy life before settling down in marriage, was an ideal.

The second major area in which good things can occur is in the love relationship. Here, ten (34.5%) of the younger and eight (30.0%) of the older women said it was best for a woman if she met the right man ("right" was variously clarified as meaning "rich" or "good"). But having somebody who cares about her has another connotation: "She finds out that she is good enough to be proposed to," and this raises her sense of self-worth. Having a boyfriend, meeting the right boy, and learning about life are all secondary to the critical familial context. So the very best thing for a girl is "to truly fall in love with the right person and have no parent problems."

These are, of course, ideals — education, experiences, and, finally, the right fellow who comes courting. How do the experiences of Indian women match these ideals? What do they in fact remember about their youth? We have already seen that the education ideal was rudely frustrated in many cases, especially among the older generation. Only one of the older women said that the best thing that happened to her was passing her nursing exam. Of the younger women, however, nine (31.0%) recalled schooling: qualifying for a nursing diploma; learning Gujerati or Hindi (examination papers were sent from and graded in India); going to college in Bombay; going to university or graduating from a teacher's training college. Three women also recalled the thrill of landing a good job or earning their first paycheck.

The thing that many (eleven persons, 40.7%) of the older women and about one-third (nine persons, 30.0%) of the younger women see as the best thing that happened to them as young women was meeting and being proposed to by the right guy, their future husbands. It gave them pride, assured them that somebody really cared, and introduced them to their major role as wives (and mothers).

A large number of women remembered being loved and cared for or even spoiled by their parents, but especially the father. The fact that they were girls, either the eldest or the youngest or simply vulnerable, seems to have contributed. They still remember fondly how father complimented one on her cooking; gave special attention to another; or gave lots of practical education about the modern world to a third. Older women remember such things as a gift of jewelry or being asked to help father in the store. One young woman recounted; "On my ninth birthday, my father held out a hand full of coins and allowed me to pick money and buy my own present...he died the next year." The most memorable childhood event of one of the older ladies occurred when she was eleven years old: "We went to play on the mine dumps near our home in Kimberley, and I picked up three small marbles (*blink klippertjies*, she added in Afrikaans). Dad took them and said he would buy something. They were diamonds and he bought three shops."

Childhood experiences and memories include both the bad and the good. People remember those things which make an impact at the time, depending on their state of mind. But childhood, especially with marriage at a young age and arranged unions, flows into adulthood as the girl becomes a wife and enters a new set of relationships. She has left her parental home and cannot return.

The middle years. The middle years are years of maturation, of bonding and fruition. What then do Indian South African women see as the worst and the best that can happen during this stage of life?

Negative experiences almost all involve husbands and marriages. The worst thing that can happen to a woman during these years is the loss of her husband, either through death (31.0% of the younger and 22.2% of the older women); divorce (17.2% of the younger and 11.1% of the older); or an affair (17.2% of the younger and 7.4% of the older). The women included the latter because when that happened, they lost confidence in themselves. They could not divorce, either because Hindus don't divorce or they could not initiate such action. We should recall that an Indian woman is totally dependent on her husband. When she is widowed she loses "her guide, her support, and the father of her children." She cannot fend for herself because, in most cases, she is uneducated and lacks a profession. Widows are cut off from social and ritual functions. They may not marry again, and other women always think widows or divorcees are out to get their husbands. A Tamil woman said that not being allowed to marry again means "you have no companion, no shoulder to cry on." Almost as upsetting for Muslim women was the traumatic prospect of the husband taking a second wife. A woman "cannot share her man." The shoe being on the other foot is equally disturbing, i.e., for the woman to have an affair. Having an affair or becoming a rape victim will result in her husband leaving her, social ostracism, and isolation because she cannot return to her parental home.

Luckily, relatively few women have actually had to face what they consider the worst thing that could happen to them. One husband deserted his wife with a six week old baby; another tossed a mug of boiling water down the front of his wife's body; and a number have been beaten by their husbands. In other cases, the husband abused alcohol or sometimes went out with girlfriends. Twelve of the postmenopausal women were widowed; the husband of a young teacher was gravely ill while this study was carried out. We visited him on two occasions, and shortly before the end of the project he died.

The second major strain which the women had to contend with was in-laws. Either the mother-in-law ill-treated (both physically and mentally) the young woman or jealousy on the part of the husband's other relatives caused strain. There is always the possibility that the modern girls will cause stress by taking the sons away to other houses or other towns.

A number of specific stresses should be mentioned. One of the older women told of the comfort and social harmony they had known while living at the old Asiatic Bazaar. When the Group Areas Act was passed, they and other Indians had to move to Laudium, with its impersonal newness. Another woman told of her son's birth by Caesarian — he remained in the hospital for two months; a third explained the worry associated with the biopsy of lumps in her breast, which luckily turned out to be benign.

What is the best thing that can happen to an adult woman? It goes almost without saying that if the worst things involve the marital state, the best things would be seen in the same context. In fact, ten (34.5%) of the pre- and seventeen (63.0%) of the postmenopausal women said that the best thing that could happen to them as adult women would be to get a good husband, have a loving husband and children, or have a happy family. This again confirms the domestic family-centered universe of Indian women. A further eight (27.6%) of the pre- and two (7.4%) of the postmenopausal women stated that if a woman became pregnant and satisfied the in-laws, that would be the best thing that could happen to her. However, among the younger women there were other values. Three of them felt that the best things to experience would be freedom and a career; three others valued overseas travel, finding fulfillment in taking French, art, cooking, etc., or simply the freedom to pursue whatever she wished, provided it didn't interfere with her homemaker role.

How do the actual experiences of women in the Indian community compare with their future? In reality, the emphasis is not on the husband (mentioned by only two of the younger and three of the older women) but on children. A total of sixteen (55.2%) of the pre- and fourteen (51.8%) of the postmenopausal women stated that having the first baby was a high point for them. Within these totals, six of the younger and three of the older women specifically mentioned a son. Six of the older and only one of the younger mentioned a daughter, the rest simply indicating "my first baby." It is significant that the older women for whom there very often is an emotional supporting bond between mother and daughter, indicate the feminine gender of the first child. The younger women were still close to the in-law pressure to produce a son, so emphasized the birth of a son. Mrs. Alli had three daughters and then had a tubal ligation because her medical history suggested she should not have any more children. Because of pressure from the in-laws, she had corrective surgery: a successful pregnancy resulted in a son being born. Another pregnancy, "one last shot at age thirty-seven" also produced a son for another woman; and a third had her first child after four and one-half years of marriage. As individuals with separate lives, experiences, and backgrounds, these Indian women recognized a variety of events as being memorable — or even the best thing that happened to them. These range from leaving a mother-in-law's home, to acquiring separate housing, being an only child, having a son, graduating from college. Valued events differ as widely as experiences. The older the women become, the more diverse and rich these experiences.

The late years. Even younger, better educated, and career-oriented women, still want the security of children and home. What then is the worst thing that can happen to an old woman?

A majority of the Indian South African women (fourteen (51.8%) of the pre- and seventeen (58.6%) of the postmenopausal) stated that being shunned by her children, assaulted by a child, or abandoned by the children would be the worst experience. If a woman is destitute and not cared for, if she has no recourse, if she is placed in an old age home, it would be tragic and unacceptable. In spite of the rich descriptions and prototypes of the mother-in-law role, the shoe is now on the other foot. Three women indicated that things would be bad if a woman did not have a good daughter-in-law. Another major area which could spell disaster for a woman in her late years has to do with the general subject of health. Ten (37.0%) of the older and eight (27.6%) of the younger women thought that to be bedridden, paralyzed, blind, infirm, or in some other way both useless and dependent on others was the worst thing that she could experience. Being a widow created loneliness; being old meant that she would have no social life; being destitute meant that she would require welfare; but in all these cases she would be able to function and help herself. She would retain a certain independence and pride. But when she became totally dependent, that would be the end.

None of the women in this study were bedridden; a number of the oldest women were very proud of their mobility. Health, then, was not the major concern. There were women experiencing illness (diabetes and high blood pressure were common) or simply finding it impossible to do what they were used to doing. However, the major problems of these women were worry and concern about interpersonal relations and the actions of their relatives. In a number of cases, the husband was ill or was drinking too much. One woman worried that her two sons drank too much and fought with their wives. A mother was worried about her children; another's son was getting a divorce; and a third sighed that she thought her worries were over when she saw her last child married. It was a common complaint of the old people that life was moving by them, and the children and grandchildren were too busy. "Loneliness," said one, "is a disease of its own."

But the coin has two sides. What is the best experience for an Indian woman in her late years? One old woman who worked from age seventeen until the time of this study, when she was sixty-nine, was quite blunt, "There is nothing good; old age is old age." Another woman, a grandmother living with her son and his family, thought the best thing was for an old woman "just to sit — everything is put in her hands by children and grandchildren." The greater majority felt that the best thing for an old woman is to be cared for by her children. No fewer than twenty (70.0%) and nineteen (70.1%) of the pre- and postmenopausal women respectively saw this as the ideal. For a woman to be able to perform her role as grandmother; to remain in one place rather than move from home to home; to have someone to love and care for her (in four cases the daughter-in-law was specifically mentioned), and for somebody to bury her when she's dead. Not to have to worry about material things would certainly help, but some of the younger women thought that winning a jackpot and being able to visit Mecca or India would be wonderful. There was a core of homemakers who saw perfect old age as being treated as a full person, not an appendage; having work or an occupation, or to be considered useful around the house; having a baby; and dying peacefully. Added one of the younger women, "And dying before my husband dies."

Conclusion

With discussion of the life style and life course also arises the question of how times are changing. Every woman, in part through the accounts of family members and friends, had a means of comparison with living conditions in the past. There was a tendency to glorify the past, to remember selectively, or to find fault with the present. Were those really the good old days? To get some perspective on this question, we asked the women whether they would have preferred to grow up fifty years ago or today — and be reminded that a number of the older women did in fact reach puberty and their teens around 1935, i.e., fifty years before they were confronted with this question.

A number of women simply exclaimed that they could not compare; it was inconceivable to some of the less educated that there might be a (hypothetical) choice: and others just did not respond — fewer of the older women than the younger. Among those who did reply, twenty-three (95.8%) of the younger and fourteen (77.7%) of the older women, respectively, selected the present. The reasons for the variations of choice are due in part to experience. In the younger category, only one woman said that she would pick fifty years ago because costs were lower and "the world was not as fast and rushed." All the others thought that their ancestors had too hard a time. Life was primitive, people were narrow-minded, and there were no cars or houses for Indians in those days. They felt that today many options are open to old ladies. Middle-aged people can travel and read. Women now have better career opportunities, including being self-employed, though stress is higher. On a more practical note, the women reminded us that "mothers-in-law don't torture daughters-in-law nowadays;" women today have better relationships with their husbands; and whereas fifty years ago, "people just let themselves go and at age thirty-five they felt and behaved like a grandmother," the women of today can age more gracefully.

Four postmenopausal women thought that they would have preferred to grow old fifty years ago. They argued that violence and crime were not as bad as today; things were cheaper; food was plentiful; and the cost of living was lower, which certainly made it easier to raise children. Others who had come through the same postdepression years and raised children during rationing in World War II pointed out that Indians were too poor in those days; things were too unsettled, there was a lack of comfort. Today, women are freer; they are more advanced and can go out to work, or get a better education and enjoy an all around higher status.

The overall vote was that the present certainly offered more to the Indian South African woman. She would not change places with her mother or aunt.

6

ಜ಼

Perspectives on Health

Introduction

In the absence of medical records, statements about health assume the character of ethnographic data; and self-reporting of such data is clouded by subjectivity. But there can be two perspectives on health. The first pertains to documentation of illness episodes, healer-patient interaction, patient role; diagnosis; prescription and medication. Healing may also pertain to a folk model or derive from cosmopolitan systems. There is, however, another perspective on health that derives from personal experiences or episodes, perspectives on such experiences by others, and attitudes and conclusions about these.

Addressing the attitudes about health and sickness in South Africa, Kuper has contrasted the three major ethnic-cultural traditions:

> In South African White society the emphasis is on the application of scientific knowledge — i.e., knowledge based on controlled experimentation; among the Africans, serious illness is most frequently attributed to an external personal agent (an evil-doer) exercising powers beyond empirical verification; and among the South African Hindu the main responsibility is placed on the moral and religious behavior of the individual and the reaction of the Divine, through its many manifestations which by their very nature are above or beyond human scrutiny. The Western microscope and laboratory; the African divining bones and secret medicines; the Hindu Temple and sacred mantras; these are broadly symbolic of three distinctive cultural approaches to disease in South Africa (1960:260).

We note repeatedly the role of the molana or the priest — particularly in the area of reproductive health — and of sacrifices or of promises of these.

This discussion will deal with the experiences and perspectives of Indian South African women and with their views about health. It will also discuss reproductive health and sexuality. Since we are dealing with two sets of age cohorts, pre- and postmenopausal, respectively, it is possible to contrast maturational, reproductive, and health experiences for these two groups.

Profile of Health

Physical

Most people who are ill or who suffer a lack of health are conscious of it. Sometimes people think there is something wrong and psychosomatic ailments result. It can be expected that people who have a great deal of free time or time to contemplate their condition would also be more subjective about it. A minority of the Indian women in the study consider themselves to be in good health. Most (sixteen or 55.2% of the pre- and thirteen or 48.1% of the post-menopausal women) see themselves as "fairly" healthy, while four (14.8%) of the older age category consider themselves in poor health. This self-evaluation is obviously a product of subjectivity (some self-pity) but also results from a lifetime at least partly spent in slum shacks without the amenities of modern urban civilization. Malnutrition, unhygienic conditions, and in many cases a lifetime of physical labor did leave their marks. Mrs. Moodley was a woman in her early sixties who as a girl of ten started to assist her mother as a hawker. All her life she has spent her days carrying the wide, flat hawkers basket on her left arm, dispensing purchases from the right. The result is massive deformation of the left forearm. This was also present to some extent in the right forearm onto which she periodically switched her load. Other women complained of foot, leg, or lower back problems from being on their feet all day. It should be added that due to cooking methods, high sugar consumption and a general lack of activity, Indian women tend to be overweight which places greater stress on the feet and legs. Indian women also have had most of the common childhood diseases (see Table 22) while growing up; measles being the most common.

The availability of a clinic, a hospital, and private practitioners in the community allowed ready access to medical consultation, all used quite frequently. As can be expected, however, there was a degree of self-diagnosis and self-treatment with over-the-counter drugs, medication prescribed for a friend or relative, or home remedies.

TABLE 22

Childhood Diseases Suffered by Indian South African Women

	Premenopausal		Postmenopausal	
	Number	Percent	Number	Percent
Mumps	18	(62.1)	12	(46.2)
Measles	25	(86.2)	21	(80.8)
Chickenpox	15	(51.7)	6	(23.1)
Whooping Cough	4	(13.8)	5	(19.2)
Scarlet Fever	2	(6.9)	–	
Diphtheria	2	(6.9)	–	

There is usually a distinction between perceived behavior and real actions. We wanted adult and older women to give us their impression of who visits a doctor more often: young, middle-aged, or old women. Of the middle-aged women, thirteen (44.8%) thought that their age cohorts were the most frequent visitors to doctors' offices; of the older age group, fourteen (51.9%) thought that their age cohorts saw the doctor more. The middle-aged thought the young, and the old thought the middle-aged would be the least likely to visit doctors.

There were a variety of ailments and complaints. The most common problems according to the premenopausal category of respondents are gynecological problems, high blood pressure, and arthritis, followed by "sugar" (diabetes). Among the postmenopausal women, the complaints involve high blood pressure, arthritis, and "sugar," followed by gynecological problems. The older women tended to be more stoic about discomforts, and one of them proffered the view that "young women now-a-days can't stand pain like we did; they take tablets for everything." In the area of "high blood," as it is called, women pointed out that real or expected, friends diagnose friends and share medicine. This is, of course, a common trait in folk medicine — a half-empty bottle may remain in the kitchen or bathroom cabinet indefinitely and be used for similar symptoms among relatives or friends.

Much the same impression about males visiting a doctor was held by these women. Very few boys were thought ever to visit a doctor. Of the premenopausal women, fourteen (48.3%) thought middle-aged men, and thirteen (44.8%) thought old men visit the doctor most frequently. Among the postmenopausal women, nine (33.3%) thought middle-aged men and sixteen (59.3%) thought old men were the most likely to visit a doctor. One of the women, however, pointed out that old men don't like to see doctors very much; they only go when their wives take them. The most common complaints and problems which take men to a physician are related to the heart (angina and other cardiac pains or pressure) and diabetes. Of much lower frequency is arthritis and high blood pressure.

To arrive at a profile of physical discomforts and complaints and contrast the two relative age categories, the women were presented with a list of discomforts frequently associated with the climacterium. To arrive at such a profile, Greene and Cooke have suggested:

> There are really [therefore] two hypotheses relating to severity and incidence of symptoms at this time of life. One relates to the increase in symptoms during the climacterium, the other is what particular association if any, this increase may have with the menopause. A survey of symptoms in the general population should therefore include a group of younger women regarded as preclimacteric and a group of older women regarded as postclimacteric. Similarly there are two corresponding hypotheses regarding the aetiology of symptoms at the climacterium and menopause (1980:487).

The list of symptoms included irritability, feeling blue or distressed, backache, cold sweat, hot flushes or flashes, trouble sleeping, forgetfulness, nervous tension, and others, a total of twenty-four items. The women were asked to indicate whether they had experienced these during the past month.

There were only two items in which the two categories of women contrasted clearly: dizzy spells and experiencing pins and needles in hands and feet. In both cases the premenopausal women answered positively (62.0% for each of the questions). Most of the postmenopausal women indicated that they did not experience these symptoms (only 37.0% and 33.3% respectively).

The only three items which both categories did experience were forgetfulness, irritability, and lack of energy. By contrast, there were a number of symptoms for which we expected to find a differentiation but did not. The confirmation-denial ratio between pre- and postmenopausal women was almost identical when asked about cold sweat, hot flushes or flashes, bladder infection, and fluid retention.

We would expect a clear contrast between pre- and postmenopausal women who represent two different stages in the climacterium, but this did not occur. Though we expected the older category to suffer physical symptoms, results were either inconclusive or reversed — with the younger category indicating that they did experience the symptoms although the older category did not.

In spite of the fact that many of these women grew up in conditions of poverty, poor hygiene, or ghetto life, they were relatively free of childhood diseases. This might be partly because girls were so housebound and protected. The only childhood disease which appears with great frequency among both categories of women is measles. Of the premenopausal category, twenty-five (86.2%) had suffered measles while twenty-one (80.8%) of the postmenopausal women had. The greater protection and the lower frequency of social contact, e.g., not going to school at all or being withdrawn upon reaching menarche, does seem to have an influence on the incidence of diseases. It will be recalled that protection and isolation of young girls was much more pronounced during the childhood years of the older women than those of the younger ones. Table 22 shows that except for whooping cough, the younger women suffered more frequently from each of the childhood diseases than did their older cohorts. Measles was the most commonly experienced disease.

At the time of this study, about half the women in each category were taking medication prescribed by a physician. This ranged from treatment for heart and diabetes to blood pressure and various aches. There were also quite a number who used over the counter drugs such as dispirin (aspirin), Panado (Tylenol), and migril (migraine pills) as well as medication for menstrual pains and headaches. A number of women used home remedies. Some of these derived from India and were brought over by immigrants or more recently imported (e.g., a digestion herb that calms the stomach). Most of the home remedies employ what are locally called "Dutch remedies." (See Appendix.) These are various extracts in concentrated form that are sold in an assortment of small bottles. A number of the older women used *Witdulsies* for heart palpitations; *Haarlemensis* oil for gall stones; *Versterkdruppels* for appetite and palpitations; peppermint drops for indigestion, and *Harmansdrup* as a general tonic. The women said, however, that such tonics are better if they mix their own and add the desired components. One of these contains condensed milk, honey, water, and "Turlington borsdruppels." Another, which must be prepared fresh every day, contains the yellow of one egg, honey, raw linseed oil, Lennon's cough medicine, and "Turlington borsdruppels." Nothing sold in a pharmacy is said to touch its effectiveness in stopping a cough or loosening the hold of a stubborn winter chest cold.

Psychological/Emotional

Most people face a certain degree of emotional stress, either continuous or recurrent, and cope quite effectively. Others suffer bouts of depression or headaches during which medication is required, and over the counter painkillers are usually sufficient. Fewer still require a physician's care or institutionalization. In our sample, six (20.7%) of the pre- and three (11.1%) of the postmenopausal women had experienced serious emotional or psychological problems and had sought professional help. This usually was at Weskoppies Psychiatric Unit. This hospital was established in 1891 as the *Krankzinnigengesticht* (literally "lunatic asylum"), but care for mentally disturbed persons in South Africa was never seriously considered.

In 1966, when the prime minister of the day, Dr. H. F. Verwoerd, was assassinated by a knife-wielding mentally ill person, concern was given structure. A committee was appointed to look into and to revise the Mental Disorders Act (Act No. 38 of 1916). Under the guidelines promulgated in a new Mental Health Act (Act No. 18 of 1973), treatment and care aimed toward prevention and promoting mental health rather than coping with disease. This positive development culminated four years later in the Health Act (Act No. 63 of 1977) under which all mental health services were integrated into a comprehensive health service. One of its positive results was a network of community based services for treatment and aftercare which links up with psychiatric hospitals — in this area, with Weskoppies (for general background see Le Roux 1971 and Meyer 1979).

For the younger women in this study, two cases involved prolonged intensive pressure from the mother-in-law (in one case as a result of the woman's childlessness, which ultimately proved to be caused by the husband's sterility); two cases involved severe depression, one caused by an alcoholic husband and another attributed to a womanizing husband; one woman had a nervous breakdown when her son was killed in an automobile accident; and a last case was "nerves."

With the postmenopausal women, all three cases involved depression related to their children: the son who physically attacked his mother; a son who divorced after prolonged bitter fighting with his wife; and a daughter whose husband left her (never to return) on her wedding night.

In a number of cases, relatives had been treated for serious emotional or psychological problems. These were slightly more frequent: 34.5% of the pre- and 18.5% of the postmenopausal women had relatives who were treated or who were mentally defective. There were a mother's brother or a daughter's daughter who were retarded, but one woman had two retarded children by a first husband (she had two normal children by a second husband).

Family History

That certain complaints and diseases run in families was evident; women in this study indicated health problems they shared with relatives. Most of these are, in fact, the same conditions which emerged in earlier questioning.

The most common problems which women shared with their mothers were high blood pressure (hypertension) and diabetes. The first of these has become a problem to the older women, especially. In a number of cases, it was also found in a woman, her sisters, and their mother. Several women reported that their mothers had "sugar" (diabetes) that resulted in leg amputation, gangrene in both legs, blindness (due to diabetes), or other complications.

A number of women indicated that they knew what osteoporosis was and volunteered information about relatives. Questions about dowagers hump, a break of the hip, and similar inquiries as well as observation of the women, themselves, established the likelihood of osteoporosis. Our concern about the prevalence of osteoporosis derives from its likely presence among postmenopausal women and the coincidence among Indian South African women of a lack of exercise and a lack of exposure to the sun (suggesting a deficiency in Vitamin D). In their medical history, women reported the frequent occurrence of diabetes, high blood pressure, and arthritis. These seem to be associated not only with family histories but also with osteoporosis. In the case of high blood pressure, diuretics which are prescribed to control the condition may have a detrimental effect on calcium balance and thus on bone mass. Research also suggests an association between low levels of dietary calcium and low levels of blood calcium ionized for bone formation (McCarron 1982; McCarron et al. 1981). Bone loss is also associated with rheumatoid arthritis. A common complaint among Indian women includes both rheumatoid and osteoarthritis, which is more clearly associated with degeneration due to age. Arthritis and osteoporosis are commonly associated, but it is not clear why. When painful arthritis affects the joints, it further limits the activity level of these women. Some medications, prescribed to ameliorate the condition e.g., cortisone, may contribute to even further bone loss.

Dowager's hump, symptomatic of fractured or collapsed vertebrae, was evident in only three of the older women but reported for mothers, elder sisters, mother's mothers, father's mothers in order of frequency. The reason for fewer mentions of the latter two relatives is that these people were not known to them or that they were in India. Hip fracture, i.e., the loss of cortical bone and ultimate breaking of the upper part of the femur, is reported as common. Two women reported fracturing their hips: this had also happened to mothers, a mother's mother, a mother's sister, and an elder sister. One woman explained that her mother died from complications after fracturing her hip. Complicated conditions resulting from confinement, especially of sedentary women, constitute a major health threat — including thrombosis or fat embolism, and even more likely, pneumonia.

Other conditions associated with families were overactive thyroid, kidney complications, asthma, and cancer. One case, certainly not present in the daughter, was cancer of the tongue reported for an old woman from India who chewed betel nut daily. This could have been coincidence because this connection has not been reported before.

Reproductive Health

Reproductive health involves management and care. Within this general area we would include hygiene, prevention of exposure to deleterious contacts, actions which prevent potentially harmful conditions; and a positive regimen of actions and health services.

Not all peoples have access to such knowledge or such services, and not all within a population use such knowledge and services to the full. One would expect that the young would be better informed than the old; that those who were better educated would have greater knowledge in this area of living; that urbanites would have better access to clinical services than those living in rural areas; and that those with greater material wealth would be able to afford services and medications when necessary. Lastly, should complications develop, one would expect fewer reproductive problems among the younger, better educated, urban women who are less likely to be impecunious or impoverished.

The women in this study are clearly differentiated by relative age, though all are urban residents. Relative education coincides with relative age as all the younger women have had some education, and most have had more than the minimum four years.

Preventive

Regular visits to a physician or clinic and regular self-examination is recommended in any preventive health program. For women this would include breast examination, inspection of the vulva for obvious irregularities which could reflect infections, irritations, or hormone changes, and a pap smear.

During the twelve months preceding our study, fifteen (51.7%) of the pre- and eleven (40.7%) of the postmenopausal women had visited a doctor or a nurse for a breast examination. When asked whether they examined their own breasts for possible cysts or tumors, seventeen (58.6%) of the pre- and thirteen (48.1%) of the postmenopausal women stated that they had done so at various intervals in the past. Only twelve (41.4%) of the pre- and ten (37.0%) of the postmenopausal women indicated that they regularly examined their own breasts on a monthly basis. This seems to be an area where a community health program can be very effective (see Table 23). Of particular concern would be those who know how but do not perform self-examination as well as the 25% of all women who claim not to know how to do this.

TABLE 23

Frequency of Breast Self-examination by Indian South African Women

Frequency	Premenopausal		Postmenopausal	
	Number	Percent	Number	Percent
At least once a month	12	41.4	10	37.0
Once every two to three months	3	10.3	2	7.4
Less often	2	6.9	1	3.7
Never	5	17.2	7	25.9
Don't know how to do so	7	24.1	7	25.9

Pap smears are recommended annually. A clinic with a division concentrating on reproductive health and a hospital are present in the small community of Laudium, yet few women have this diagnostic test done regularly. Only fifteen (51.7%) of the pre- and five (18.5%) of the postmenopausal women indicated that they had had a pap smear during the twelve months preceding our study.

Corrective

By the appellation "corrective" I mean those cases in which something has been done, either in healing or curing, or having surgery. The treatment in almost all cases was aimed at correcting something which bothered the women and was decided upon by the physician.

In-between bleeding was a problem for seven (24.1%) of the pre- and only two (7.4%) of the postmenopausal women. It is entirely possible that those who have not menstruated for a decade or two do not recall such irregularities. Most of those who did experience it consulted a physician, and one consulted a homeopath. For infections, the numbers increase, as seventeen (58.6%) of the pre- and six (22.2%) of the postmenopausal women had suffered from them. A number of women simply designated "yeast infection," although others specified trichomoniasis and moniliasis. The latter is very common in women who are diabetic (or pregnant). Another complained of "infection of the tubes;" two of the older women said they each had an "inflamed uterus." One woman had various problems for which she visited the hospital's out-patient section and received medication. She was not told what she had. One of the older women explained that she used to suffer from "a cold in the bladder." The remedy she used was an old one from India. "You mix some bluing (indigo) in hot water and pour it into a pee pot. Then sit on it for a while. Repeat this three times with hot water and the bladder problem will be gone."

Advances in medicine and the availability of services are reflected in the actions of these two categories of women. Only two of the older women had tubal ligations, but twelve (41.4%) of the younger women have had this procedure performed. It represents, simultaneously, familiarity with modern medical techniques and the decision to drastically enforce birth control. This is, of course, not final. One young woman had a tubal ligation after the birth of her third child — all girls. Some time later she consulted an astrologer who stated that he "saw" a son in the family. A reverse operation was performed and her next pregnancy produced a son.

As in the previous discussion, a much larger percentage of the younger women have had a D & C. Dilation and curettage (performed for a variety of reasons from cleansing before gynecological surgery to abortion) seems to have been performed on these women for two primary reasons: following a miscarriage (thus related to fertility) and diagnosing abnormal bleeding and blood clotting. Twenty (69.0%) of the premenopausal women had experienced a D & C (one had had four), in almost every case following a miscarriage; one for the removal of a small tumor. Of the older women, six (22.2%) had had this treatment, mostly for miscarriages; one following a stillbirth; one for heavy bleeding; and one for clotting and abdominal pain.

It will be recalled that one criterion for selection of this research sample was that those in the younger category should still be menstruating; those who were postmenopausal should have reached that stage from natural aging rather than surgery. While all the women had their uteri, we did not find anyone from whom only one ovary had been removed.

There was a simple lack of knowledge about breast self-examination. There were four (13.8%) of the pre- and three (11.1%) of the postmenopausal women who have had breast surgery. In almost every case it was to remove a "milk gland" or a "milk lump" (also called fibroadenoma) or a benign cyst. Only one young woman, following a mammogram, was under observation because of a lump in the high risk tissue of her breast. There have been no cases of either radiation treatment or chemotherapy.

Sexually Transmitted Disease

Only one woman responded positively to a question about having had or having been exposed to venereal disease, which she got from her husband.

Post Reproductive Health

At this point we need to discuss attitudes and beliefs about the health of postmenopausal women. Are there certain forms of discomfort or diseases to which they are more susceptible? Are there illnesses that only postmenopausal women get?

About half the number of women in each of the categories (55.2% of the pre- and 48.1% of the postmenopausal) thought that women who had experienced menopause were more susceptible to certain illnesses. These included, in order of their mention: diabetes, arthritis, hypertension, heart and weight problems. The reasons for these are seen as diseases that have been dormant, the physical body deteriorating, the woman being less active, and simple old age. The single problem mentioned more than any other concerned the cessation of menstruation. Women were very clear on the relationship, as they saw it, between flow and health. "The blood doesn't change," said one of the younger women, "and so the body is not cleaned out and the woman gets high blood." Another young woman explained, "If you don't lose it, naturally it goes to your head." Some of the older women had similar beliefs. Women who had no more flow lacked resistance. The old blood caused pressure and headaches, due to impurities. "The blood doesn't run, dirty blood is slow," one explained. "If given a blood test it is very thick and dark." More psychological in nature is the explanation for migraines. "Migraine is a psychological substitute for no more periods," a young woman explained.

Among the older and perhaps more traditional, there also is a very strong feeling about removal of body organs. The Memon maintain that "the womb is the pillar of the body." By removing it, the body will suffer much as a building does if the center pillar is removed.

Are there specific diseases linked to age, diseases that only post-menopausal women get? Once again, more of the younger women thought so, but the majority (69.0% of the pre- and 88.9% of the postmenopausal) disagreed. They also mentioned "sugar" and called "high blood" the single most important example (due to "excess of blood in the body") of age-related illness. Heart attack was no threat while a woman still menstruated. For those who had to stand a lot, there was the danger of "verical veins" (vericose veins).

Sexuality

One aspect which all people share is an idea of attraction and attractiveness. This is translated into cultural patterns of dress, decoration, and behavior. It finds expression in sexuality and patterns of reproduction.

Looking back over the years, we all can select a certain stage or period of years when we were most attractive in a physical sense; most satisfied in a physical sense; most satisfied in a relationship; or most appreciated. In retrospect, there are specific changes that certainly would have improved matters, or so we think.

In this section we will discuss attraction and satisfaction in a subjective sense. We will also deal with reproduction and with sexual expression. In each case, the younger, better educated, more active pre-menopausal Indian South African women will be contrasted with their elder, less educated, more sedentary cohorts.

General

Personal. At what stage, or age, of your life were you sexually most satisfied? This question will provoke a range of responses in any audience, responses based on subjective experience and interactional contexts. For Indian women, sexuality was always with the family context, i.e., postmarital, but the answers are based on the experiences each woman had. Although four of the women in the younger category had always been happy and felt sexually satisfied, one postmenopausal woman said, "Never. He used to come to me once or twice a month. He slept with the child." Another said, without elaborating, "After the change of life." In most cases, change of life also implied change of sleeping arrangements as sexuality decreased. The largest single answer among the younger women was "Now!" implying the late thirties and forties, with reproductive years behind them and children growing up. One woman stated explicitly, "...after my tubal ligation." The older women selected equally the years before children were born and the years when there were small children in the home. This was a bit of nostalgia, thinking back on the old days when the husband showed interest and expressed it in a physical way. Only one woman in this group preferred it when the children were grown "and my husband and I could appreciate each other."

In many cases the attention of the husband had been redirected, e.g., to his business or to another person. In other cases increasing age had affected the health or activity of the husband, and two of the women were widowed. But if they could venture a wish, what change would they like to see in their husbands?

The predominant reply (especially among the younger women) to this inquiry, which sounded almost like a rehearsed response, was one which described a more considerate, communicative companion. In various ways, using a variety of descriptions, these Indian women yearned for a husband who was more tolerant and understanding, who communicated instead of hiding behind a newspaper; who was more "domesticated" or "homely," who was more loving and caring. They would like their husbands to be less moody and argumentative, not scream and shout or get irritated so easily (this would also influence the way a husband spoke to his wife), to practice self control, and to be less private and withdrawn. Others would see the husband "not be such a spoiled brat that I must do everything for him — pick up, clean, do gardening, cook, raise the kids — while he plays snooker and cards." In many cases the husband was described as domineering, stubborn, autocratic — a typical male — and the wife suggested that she certainly would like to change that.

A number of women would like to see the physical side of companionship improve. One would have the husband "more romantic," another would want to "recreate our love life," and yet another, "just go out more."

From the older women, one dominant theme emerged: a clear majority would like to see the husband's health improved or restored. Two would have him sexually more active. In fact, one wished her husband was "stronger — also sexually — the longer he takes to reach orgasm the tireder he makes me." A second major theme from the widows is the simple wish "just to have him here," or "to have him back, even if he's old, just to be together..."

And what about themselves, what changes would they like to see? The younger women produced two major response patterns, one dealing with personal and behavioral themes, the other clearly physical. Some of the women would be more tolerant, less impatient, more considerate and understanding, less temperamental, control their tempers, be more unselfish, less stubborn, and talk less. Others would want to be shorter, taller, slimmer, or young again. This last response, combined with "healthy" was the dominant ideal of the older women. Some individuals would go back and study, be single again and leave the country, never marry, and in the case of a Hindu widow, marry again. A number would like to have been sexually happier or more responsive. However, a number of women said they would not change anything, in the words of one, "I'm O.K. the way God left me!"

A dominant theme in the study of Indian South African women is schooling or education. Women bemoan the fact that they were forced to leave school, usually at menarche, that they could not study because boys were given preference. To return to studies or have another opportunity was the dream of many women with whom we talked. But what do they think is the general male response to women's education? Do men prefer the less educated, domestic woman or the better educated one who can participate in his world and offer him challenges? It certainly would have been interesting to pose this question to a sample of male respondents, but since that was not possible, we have only the women's view. The response pattern of the two relative age categories is quite similar. Among the

premenopausal women, nine (31.0%) said the men appreciated
uneducated women more and seventeen (58.6%) said they appreciated them less. Among the postmenopausal women, nine (33.3%)
said men appreciated uneducated women more and sixteen (59.3%)
said they appreciated them less. The rest see no difference. The
reasons for these responses are of course quite varied, but a
common theme emerges: educated or uneducated, the wife's
primary role is in front of the stove. Whether she works of not,
when the husband sits down he expects a well prepared plate of
food.

Uneducated women were preferred because they offered no
competition to the man's dominant status. This means that the man
could control them and "keep them in their place." This place, of
course, was the kitchen. Educated women must go out, spend some
time outside the home and become independent; but most Indian
men "would not want the woman to be 'dom' (an Afrikaans word
meaning mindless or dull) so they can take advantage of her." Indian
men "like their wives to be submissive. They can boss them because
women were stupid and obeyed them." An educated wife is seen as
a competitor, "It gives them a complex." But one of the older women
pointed out that at least there were fewer divorces because women
were in their place in the kitchen.

In many cases, it was felt, men prefer educated women provided they are still submissive. One woman clearly expressed this
generational conflict. "When his parents come to visit, I may not sit
down and remain in the company. I must serve them and be at a
distance. When his friends come, I may sit down with them and
discuss." It is clear that this represents a new generation, that an
educated man appreciates an educated woman, and that a wife who
can help with the income is valued. Educated women are better
company. The wife must be a little bit clever, but not too clever, and
must not compete with or threaten her husband. What emerges is a
delicate partnership, a balancing of "equals" where the husband can
show off his educated wife, but — and this is critical — she is still a
wife. A number of both younger and older women's responses
agreed with Mrs. Pillay's, "Men nowadays like better educated
women but keep them in the kitchen. You can be sick or dying but
must still do what they want...."

Normal. When we discuss normal sexuality among Indian
South African women, we are dealing with heterosexual behavior.
This can be limited even further to intimate relations between
married partners. A certain amount of variation of sexual expression

does occur, and extramarital relations are becoming more common; but the most frequent and certainly the acceptable expression of sexual relationships occurs within marriage. Normal sexuality involves a degree of noncoital or precoital activities, in the form of foreplay, and such activities in the marital relationship are sanctioned as acceptable behavior because they are aimed at satisfying the husband. This general area of sexuality, attitudes about it, socialization, and performance are intertwined with beliefs which are religious, moral, medical, and legal. All these aspects find expression in the intimate relations between a woman and a man.

Given male dominance in Indian society and the man's role in interpersonal relations (within and outside of marriage), we can also expect this dominance to carry over into the normative in sexuality. Males are in control of sexual expression. They have a demand-right on sexual intercourse, the freedom (though not the sanction) to express it extramaritally, the physical and economic power to force it on their wives, and the anatomical makeup to experience satisfaction (often at the expense of the woman). Men have been brought up this way, and women have been socialized to accept their husbands and to submit to their wants. To a major extent, this is a product of a socioeconomic system where the man represented economic security and the woman represented provision for all his wants and unquestioning submissiveness. As women become better educated and enter the professions, these old values are being questioned. This will affect the status of the male in Indian society and the basic structure of the family.

Most of the women in this study sample stated that it was not acceptable or proper to have sexual intercourse with a person to whom one is not married. Only one (3.4%) of the pre- and two (7.4%) of the post-menopausal women found conditions which might justify it. Such an excuse is that "some people's marriages are not working and extramarital relations help it along." By far the greater majority found it to be "a crime and a disgrace," something that can create trouble for the injured spouse or lead to divorce in which children lose a father or mother. It "could lead to suicide or murder." If people have such leanings, they should not get married because "marriage is a certificate to sex, a moral guide to social behavior; adultery has severe religious and social implications."

The majority of women blamed such activities on men, even suggesting that it is in their nature or that it is more acceptable for men. "If a woman has an affair, she is condemned — a man might be forgiven. Men do it more often, they are always exempted." A woman who engages in an extramarital affair "loses her self-respect, and think of the implications if she falls pregnant!" The husband would be fully justified in divorcing a wife who has such an affair; but if the husband is involved, his wife will have (only) "ill-feelings." Women cannot divorce. But a growing number of women are getting involved in extra-marital relations. "In Laudium it is occurring more among women. The Indian Welfare Society is concerned. It is because women are alone at home all day. There are even cases where schoolboys are involved," one young woman explained. States an old woman, "It used to be men, now women are also naughty."

The strongest condemnation comes from Muslims. "It is the worst sin in the Muslim marriage vow," states a believer. "Islam enjoins marriage. It forbids all forms of sexual relationships outside marriage (i.e., pre- or extramatrimonial relations)." (Ahmad 1974:16). It is *haraam* (not permissible in a sacred sense) to go near a woman if the man is not married to her, and a child born out of wedlock would be called a haraam child. Haraam should be contrasted with *halal* (permissible) as is the slaughter of sacrificial meat. One Muslim woman suggested that Muslims do not engage in such activities, but Hindu are more likely to do these things. Another stated that Hindu and Tamil are more likely. Tamil point out that "Tamil marriages are sacred," and Hindu women say, "Hindu are staunch, they will be last in line" for such things. The most likely culprits are Christians and Muslims. "Extramarital relation is morally wrong because it hurts somebody else. It is more acceptable for Muslims — their wives tolerate it. They have a legal wife and a common law wife — up to four." Another volunteered that because Muslims have four wives "they are said to be very hot-natured." Added another, "The Muslims are the hot-blooded ones — anything in a skirt will do. They have no respect for non-Muslim women." And still another suggested that "It is common among Muslims. For them sex is nothing, its like eating bread and butter." Luckily morality or the lack thereof is not decided by popular vote, but two categories come out of this discussion under heavy suspicion: the man and Muslims.

It needs to be emphasized that socialization creates behavioral images and prepares a person for roles played in later life. This is also why socialization, derived as it is from the past and existing behavioral patterns does not prepare people for changing conditions. What little sex education and role socialization there is in Indian families are based on the values and experiences of an older female generation. Hilda Kuper points out: "South African Hindus continue a cultural tradition in which sex is elaborated in religion and literature, the act of sex is not regarded as a direct release of physical desire but as a religious consummation only to be indulged in after marriage and primarily for the purpose of reproduction. While coitus is recognized as essential for conception among mortal men, creativity rests ultimately with the Divinity" (1960:122). Children are raised in an atmosphere in which sexual expression is avoided before marriage and is even after marriage surrounded by a series of taboos. These pertain to place, manner of expression, and state of ritual cleanliness.

In many cases girls, upon reaching menarche, were withdrawn from school rather than being sent to a coeducational institution. Girls were not expected to meet boys, and for many, there was limited contact until the parents arranged a marriage. Such strict rules, derived from Indian culture and found among Hindu, is just as strongly expressed among Muslims. These rules are derived from the Koran. Lemu and Heeren explain that:

The Muslim way of life excludes the boyfriend/girlfriend system, mixed parties, dancing between men and women, taking alcohol or drugs, and other facets of the Western way of life which are well known to provide the situation from which premarital and extra-marital sexual relations develop. Social entertainments in Islam are generally either within the family and close friends of the family, or among men and women in separate groups. Sex outside marriage is considered in Islamic law not only as a sin but as a crime which is punished under the law in the same way as theft or murder. The punishment for it applies equally to the man and woman and is severe and deterrent in its effect (1978:25).

Sexual expression among Indian South Africans, both Hindu and Muslims, should ideally be limited to married persons. Even within marriage it should follow proper avenues for expression as the wife plays her role and the husband his. It is the husband who initiates sexual activity. Of the younger women, twenty-six (87.7%) stated that the husband initiates sexual involvement and three (10.3%) said that both could start it. Of the older category of women, twenty-five (92.6%) stated that it was proper for the man to express or to demonstrate an interest, although one each thought that the woman could take the initiative or that it could be a mutual interest of husband and wife. Women can stimulate their libido, an older woman suggested, by eating a red chalk which they purchase in Indian shops. This is sure to stimulate them sexually. Another older woman saw a potential problem if a wife has "feeling" but the husband has slept with another woman and doesn't have "feeling."

Because of increasing openness and education, young women today are better off than their mothers, whose socialization taught them that the man was dominant and they should be submissive. There was little preparation for the wedding night and no warning of how to cope with intimacy. Rosenthal conducted an interesting study on female sexuality among Gujerati speakers in Johannesburg not far from the community under discussion here. She states:

> There are, however, factors that may possibly inhibit female sexual expression. Many young female informants claimed that the poor sex education which the Indian girl receives in her parents' home does not prepare her psychologically for a successful sexual union with her husband. A twenty-year-old unmarried girl told me: 'Our mothers do not teach us about sex. When a girl starts to menstruate at the age of about twelve, her mother tells her to stop talking to boys and not to go near men. The girl does not know what will happen to her if she goes near a man. She thinks that something terrible will happen to her. She grows up to think of sex as something disgusting'....Older women, on the other hand, did not think that it was necessary for girls to learn about sex from their mothers, and maintained that it was the husband's duty to teach a young bride. In arranged marriage the man is a relative stranger. The wedding night is traumatic because the girl is pounced upon by a strange man. Men do not try to be gentle on their wedding nights. They practically rape their wives. This leaves a scar, and after that the girl feels that sex is repulsive. She can't give herself to her husband, and there is no close relationship between husband and wife. In a love match, on the other hand, you know your guy inside out, and you are not scared to sleep with him (1977:208–09).

Coming out of a first sexual experience of this nature frequently resulted in sexual maladjustment, feelings of uncertainty, guilt, and fear. The bride, often no more than a girl, must adjust to a strange home, a new family of in-laws, and unsympathetic mother-in-law, an insecure husband who knows little, and doesn't support her emotionally. And on top of all of this, sexual intimacy with a relative stranger.

If she does not succeed in rising to all these conflicts, she is flung into a state of extreme anomie. Though inter-sexual mingling has relaxed the young girl's sexual education, the family's fears about sexual breaches have not changed. The transition from childhood to womanhood continues to be fraught with conflict, and these conflicts account for the high suicide rate of young Indian girls both married and never-married (Meer 1976:136).

Those who survive and adjust to the new relationship arrive, in time, at a modus vivendi or even, in many cases, at an amicable relationship. Sexual expression takes on a pattern where there is at least predictability and certainly, in many cases, enjoyment. A number of the women explained that their moments of greatest pleasure involved being in bed with their husbands. As familiarity increased and understanding grew, so would expectations be met and relaxation be achieved in events surrounding the sexual act.

The expression of sexuality involves atmosphere, words, and touch. Together these create an ambience which is both relaxing and stimulating. Some of the younger Indian women explained that sexual foreplay and stimulation were usually restricted to late at night before bedtime or early morning before rising. Part of this was due to having children or other relatives in the home, and in many cases because the new couple resided in the Big House with the extended family of the husband. Mrs. Abdulla explained how this setting, plus the requirement of a ritual bath after sexual intercourse, influenced the life of a newly-married Muslim woman. "Earlier all had to bathe and wash their hair on Friday. So, Thursday night was generally the time for sex so that others (parents, brothers, and sisters) would not know about sex having taken place. If you and the husband had sex on other nights, you would have to bathe before breakfast and appear with wet hair. I used to get up at 4 a.m. to wash my hair so as not to get to breakfast table with wet hair on other days."

Foreplay involved kissing and touching. It involved "saying nice things" or "saying gentle words." As time wore on they might "smooch a little." The husband would fondle the wife's breasts and body. But such foreplay, said an older woman, is for young couples — "sex is for childbearing," not relaxation. Responded a younger woman, "Well, you couldn't just act, you must be aroused." Another older woman, when asked about foreplay replied, "I wouldn't say there was much — just sex and get it over with. Young people who watch videos and T.V. have experimental sexual play."

Experimental sexual play and using different positions in sexual intercourse are acceptable "if both parties are willing," according to one of the younger women. An older cohort saw it differently. "It depends on what the husband tells you to do. In the Indian community you listen to your husband." A Tamil-speaking Hindu woman explained, "We have been taught at home that the husband can go out to other women as he pleases, as long as he returns home. And he must be served (sexually) by his wife, who must be grateful because she has a roof over her head. Now professional women won't accept it." But the majority are still products of childhood and teenage socialization.

> In spite of considerable westernization, then, the orthodox Gujerati Indian feminine ideal remains that of a pure virgin who becomes a chaste, loyal wife. The woman's body, and particularly her genital tract, are regarded by both men and women as the property of the man who married her. Indeed the very social environment of an Indian woman is designed to preserve her premarital and postmarital chastity for the man who owns her. Even young westernized women regard their bodies as the property of their future husbands...it is chiefly the feminine ideal which demeans women, in that it defines them as the sexual property of men. The fact that sexual feelings in women are recognized, simply leads to their being kept under stricter supervision in order to prevent them straying, and to preserve their sexual purity for their husbands. (Rosenthal 1977:207–09)

Nonetheless whether the husband decrees or the couple jointly decides, experiments or change in position is said to "break the monotony." Almost all the women in our study said they usually employ the face to face or "natural" position (also referred to in the literature as the "missionary position"). The exceptions were one older woman who indicated the side to side position, facing each other. When asked about other positions, there was a range of responses. Since these positions were explained in some detail, one might expect that they were also used. The greatest range, as might be expected, was explained by the younger women. When asked to list "positions for sexual intercourse" the majority of women mentioned the man on top, face-to-face position. Others that were mentioned or explained (in order of frequency) included: side-by-side, face-to-face; standing, face-to-face; sitting, face-to-face ("use a chair, this is a good position to become pregnant"); woman on top, face-to-face; woman kneeling, man supine; "back position". This latter was explained as: "enter from the rear — not anally." Another woman called it "dog style" but explained "it is not good because it makes your backside very big." It was also pointed out that anal and group sex is forbidden by Islam. One person mentioned "in a car." We did not discuss the make or size of car nor the position this might require. Older women were much more restricted in the range of positions mentioned and thought that the "young liberated ones" were less inhibited. One of the latter suggested that "satisfaction varies; a woman may not reach climax without using different positions."

When asked whether women discuss these things, one of the younger, more liberal Hindu women explained, "Yes, we women talk about it. My sister gave me a copy of the book *Karma Sutra* which tells us how to keep the husbands happy — it gives all the positions. Before marriage at a bridal shower, girls sit around and tease the bride about what will happen." This might take place among peer-group members, but very little is discussed between members of different generations. There is one more superstition which might mitigate against sexual experimentation in well lit or mirrored bedrooms, and that is the old belief that a woman is not allowed to see herself in the act. This suggests a traditional, patterned sexual behavior among the older women with the emphasis on reproduction and the belief that such activities should cease after experiencing menopause. When we asked whether old people have sexual relations, the responses of the older women covered quite a range. One woman in her early fifties, with a naughty twinkle in her eyes, said, "Almost every night — some of my friends must take a bath almost every morning." Another stated, "The feelings are the same, only the strength is less." However, the majority agreed with statement that "you've got feelings but you do not show it." This results in women having separate beds, or separate rooms if they live in a large house. In part this is done to avoid a show of love in the presence of adult children. It will be recalled that a late pregnancy is embarrassing because of having grown children. Here, too, old people are expected to act old and to play the role. One of the older women in the study, who speaks English haltingly (having come from India) explained, "Our Indians have too much nonsense way. Me and the husband not sit together or sleep together because of adult children." While the younger generation may behave differently by the time they are old, they currently endorse the view of how the old people are expected to behave. When asked whether old people have sexual relations, the common response was that women stop at about fifty or sixty years of age, or when the children are grown. At this age they "start indulging more on the spiritual plain, more ascetic." Another mused " . . . probably less, more companionship and real love, not just sex." Others felt that there would be no foreplay and less of the rest because they have less vitality and energy. Five of the younger women thought that old people's sexual expression would be about "same as us," or would involve sexual intercourse weekly, biweekly, or monthly.

In part due to expectations of the children and in part because of their own prototypes, postmenopausal Indian women either cease or severely curtail expression of their sexuality. One younger woman had the example of her mother-in-law, who at age forty-eight had a separate bed. Older people reinforce this by not expressing or acting out their feelings toward each other. They are, in fact, both product and cause of their asexual condition. In contrast, their younger cohorts can be expected to be more open about sex, to demand a share of it, and to see sex as recreational as well as for reproduction. One can also expect to find their expression of sexuality, both in coitus and in love play, to continue into the later years.

If age, for many, becomes a barrier to heterosexual expression, there were always periods when sexuality and especially coitus was taboo. As far as Muslim men are concerned, the holy month of Ramadan was a time when "they try to abstain during the night, but must abstain during the day." If coitus does occur during the night, the man must bathe before sunrise. For Hindu men, there is the month of *Purtasi* when they are expected to fast and also abstain. One woman stated that she and her husband always have separate beds when fasting. When asked whether there were times when men should not engage in sexual intercourse, one young woman said, "I wish there was, but unfortunately not." Another did not concern herself with abstention but stated, "If he wants it, you simply have to give it to him or else you drive your husband away. In Laudium many women drive their husbands away because they say this is aching or this is painful." Most of the women would welcome regular times when men should abstain from heterosexual coitus. At least while they are still menstruating, they have such a time of reprieve on a regular basis.

Most of the women stated that a woman should not engage in coitus while she is experiencing flow. Some explained that "it's not dangerous, just messy," while Muslims said "it is not hygienic, it is wrong." There are two distinct times of ritual abstention: these are *al-haiz* (menstrual flow) and *an-nifas* (postnatal bleeding). Palanpuri (1980:20–21) points out that the woman is allowed:

> To sleep with, fondle, love, caress the husband but she must keep her body covered from her navel to her knee provided there is no possibility of sexual intercourse which is haraam (forbidden) during haiz and is considered a major (*kabira*) sin....If haiz stops after ten days are complete, then it is permissible to have sexual intercourse before she has taken a bath, though it is better after the bath. If bleeding stops before ten days, then sexual intercourse is not allowed before she has taken a bath (1980:2021).

After childbirth, a woman must abstain for forty days. She is not permitted to touch the Koran for religious purposes during these times of impurity, but she may touch the Koran if it is for the "purpose of learning or teaching it to others" (Badawi 1979:26).

The Muslim women in this research sample recognize the forty-day postpartum taboo. "She's raw inside," one of the older Muslim women stated. Another added that Allah will punish the couple with venereal disease. This excuse was quite common among Muslim and non-Muslim alike when discussing abstention during menstrual flow. In most cases, it is believed that the husband will get venereal disease because she is unclean. One suggested the "man can catch a germ," and two used the Afrikaans word *vuilsiekte* (literally dirty or unhygienic disease, a common appellation for venereal disease). A third warned that the man can get "a swelling of the penis."

There also was a fear of "falling pregnant." Another older woman warned, "If a woman falls pregnant during that time, it will be a very naughty, fidgety child." Other reasons for avoiding coitus during flow are that the"mouth of the womb is open and infection can take place" or that "she is losing blood and intercourse can irritate her." One woman stated that to avoid infection a woman should abstain from coitus after the seventh month of pregnancy; another expressed a folk belief that a woman must not engage in sex if her children have measles as this will endanger their health even further.

Pregnancy

Most of the women included in this study had at least a super-
ficial idea of when conception was most likely to take place and
what the causative role of coitus was in this process.

Decorous. There is, however, a common understanding about
what actions lead to having children and in which context having a
child is acceptable. Most of the women, twenty-four (82.8%) in the
pre- and twenty-four (88.9%) in the postmenopausal category, stated
that an unmarried woman should at all costs not have a child. This
included avoiding compromising situations which might lead to
pregnancy, becoming pregnant, or carrying the child with the possibility of abortion mentioned. However, another woman said, "It
is wrong to sleep with a man if you're not married. But it is less
wrong than having an abortion. If you didn't fear God, why fear the
people. Have the child and give it up for adoption."

"Fearing the people" of which this woman spoke pertains to
the very negative reaction against premarital pregnancy. The term
'social ostracism' used by one young woman, might summarize it.
The woman's name and her family status will be ruined. Her parents may deny her, or her mother may commit suicide in shame.
The Muslims, a young woman explained, fault the girl if she has
sexual intercourse before marriage. Even if she gets married while
pregnant, the child will not be recognized and will always be a bas-
tard. The child is a haraam child But one of the older women stated,
"Yes, she shouldn't become pregnant, but if she does she can't
throw the baby away. She must have the child; it is innocent." In
fact, all the women, five (17.2%) pre- and three (11.1%) postmenopausal, who stated that a woman could have a child if she was not
married agreed with this statement. Nobody, save one, sanctioned
premarital sexuality or pregnancies (many decried the frequency
with which it was now occurring). As one woman explained, "If
you're a mother of girls, you know of the possibility." There was
only one young woman who found grounds for a premarital
pregnancy. She said, "Sometimes a girl may be lonely. She may not
want to get married but want someone to care for. One cannot adopt
a child if she is not married."

Many women recognize that premarital sexuality is increasing.
They recognize that while the parents are out, children may visit
back and forth. High school and college kids have increased freedom and are not always chaperoned as young persons were a generation ago. Secular stimuli are all over — on television, in cinemas,

and especially on video. While this research was being conducted, there was a major scandal concerning videos being loaned to school children and shown at the home of a young fellow whose parents were absent during the day. There were threats of closing down the video store, by force if needs be. Finally the children were reprimanded and life returned to normal. A nurse who worked in the public clinic stated that during the few years she had worked there the number of premarital pregnancies had increased tremendously. "It is becoming more acceptable among the girls. At first they would be afraid. Now, when they miss a period they come. Earlier, girls would come late in their pregnancy. Now we see at least two a week at the antenatal clinic. They give open information, even the name of the boy. Mostly these are lower and middle socioeconomic groups. The wealthy ones are most likely taken elsewhere. Half of them get married before the end of the pregnancy."

One of the concerns expressed is what happens to a woman who is not married? If her parents do not take her in, who will care for her? It is essential that a child have a family unit for security and upbringing. So who decides when and whether or not to have a child? Is it the man's (husband's) decision, the woman's (wife's), or both? "Both," say the majority, seventeen (58.6%) of the pre- and fifteen (55.5%) of the postmenopausal women. "It is only fair," said a young woman. "After all, she must bear and care for it, give love and attention; and he must be able to support it." One of the older women said, "Yes, parents should discuss and plan it, and nowadays this does occur. In my day, as it comes they said 'God gave'!" Parentage is a joint venture, security and affection must both be guaranteed before there is a decision to have another child. But, as the figures show, these lofty ideals are arrived at jointly by only slightly over half of the women. Eleven (37.9%) of the pre- and ten (37.0%) of the post-menopausal women said that it is in fact the man who decides about having children. This male decision is said to be Tamil custom. One woman thought that in their case it was really his parents who decided. Indian men do "like many children," or Indian men "don't care about the number of children" are phrases heard frequently. A small minority, one (3.5%) of the pre- and two (7.4%) of the postmenopausal women said that the woman should decide. "After all, she's the one who carried the child" and she can in fact decide if she simply "stops sleeping with her husband." That was, for many of the older women, the sole method of birth control. As one said, "We never discussed it — we didn't know we could have prevented it." We will return to the question of prevention and birth control but first must deal with beliefs concerning fertility and sexual intercourse.

Developmental. There is a great deal of uncertainty and confusion concerning the reproductive life and fertility of women. This pertains as much to its onset as to its termination. Some of this same confusion pervades beliefs about pregnancy and fetal development.

Minimum age for pregnancy to occur ranges from seven to seventeen, though the majority of both categories of women in this study clustered their responses around ages twelve to fourteen, where twenty-three (79.3%) of the pre- and eighteen (69.2%) of the postmenopausal women clustered. A majority of women also linked this reproductive capacity to menstruation or puberty. However, a number of women offered a qualifier. One suggested, "...if her glands are strong;" another, that it really depends on the male since the "man determines pregnancy." The critical fact, however, was menstruation. In the old Hindu tradition, a girl could be married at any age but could not sleep with the husband before age fifteen. Women also suggested that the old Islamic law was that when a girl began to menstruate she *must* marry, but no confirmation could be found for such a law or even a suggested line of action. Nor, for that matter, could we find confirmation that "when a girl has her first period she *can* marry and become pregnant."

If there is a biological marker which determines when girls reach fertility, what is the case with boys? Suggestions for the onset of fertility (the age when "he can cause a girl to become pregnant") ranged from eight to twenty. At the lower end of this age range, one woman said, "Even at eight a boy has his feelings." Mrs. Maharaj using the Gujerati term stated, "As soon as he has *veeria*" (sexual fluid — can be male and female). A third saw the practical side of the matter. "At fifteen," she said, "when he has a girl friend." The clustering of responses was around fifteen: the answers of twenty (68.9%) of the pre- and seventeen (62.9%) of the postmenopausal women fell into the age range fourteen to sixteen years of age. A number of the younger women indicated "puberty" but except for one who spoke of "voice change," this stage was not clarified.

Much the same age range pertained to the stage of life when a woman was too old to become pregnant. Nearly all the women recognized that there was an age when reproductive capacity decreased or ceased, but this age which referred to potential was much later than the accepted age when she should stop her reproductive life.

Both age categories of women in the study sample presented a reproductive age which ceased anywhere from age thirty-seven to ninety. There is a majority of responses which fall into the age range forty-five to fifty-five, though it is not a clear clustering. Twenty (68.9%) of the premenopausal women and twenty-one (60.7%) of the postmenopausal women said that reproductive capacity ceased during these years. A majority linked it specifically to menopause or change of life. One woman suggested that most women don't "fall pregnant after thirty-seven." It would seem she was merging ideal and potential behavior. Others saw the biological connection. "When menstruation ends," there is "no more blood to form a baby." A Gujerati-speaking woman explained, "When the veeria becomes dry, a woman cannot become pregnant. It comes at different ages. It results in the loss of interest in sex and the avoidance of sex." A Muslim woman however, pointed out that a woman can still fall pregnant at seventy. "Our prophet, Jusuf prayed to Allah for a child; and though he was 120 and his wife Miryam was eighty-two they had a son" she stated. It would seem that this woman was confused between Jusuf and Miryam (Josef and Mary, the mother of Jesus) and Zakariya, for in the Koran, sura XIX (also called the sura of Miryam) starts out with Zakariya bemoaning the fact that his "wife is barren" and he has "grown quite decrepit from old age." They then had a son whom they named Yahya — or Truth. The parallel Biblical account appears in Luke 1. where Zacharias and his wife Elizabeth "well stricken in years" had a son, John (the Baptist).

If Zakariya's wife set the limits for women, does he set the range for men? Can a man be too old to cause a pregnancy? "No," say the majority: but seven (24.1%) of the pre- and five (18.5%) of the postmenopausal women say that he can be too old. When we asked at what age a man was too old to cause a pregnancy, responses ranged from fifty to ninety; and now only six (24.0%) and thirteen (54.2%), respectively, stated he was never too old. It would seem that some responses are influenced by actual cases, perhaps even a spouse, who became infertile or impotent. The majority quoted cases of old men, even octogenarians, who married teenage brides and had children. "A man's veeria never dries," said one Hindu woman. Another had good grounds for her statement: "Men just get old, they don't have a change of life."

Knowing (or not knowing) what the age limits are for reproductive potential, how much do these women know about the physiology of reproduction and what causes pregnancy?

Physiological. Almost universally the women said pregnancy was caused by sexual intercourse or variations such as sex, mating with a partner, or sleeping with a man. From what we already know about the likelihood of separate beds after the reproductive phase has been completed, it was interesting that one of the older women explained that pregnancy follows "when the man comes to sleep with you." There is a certain inevitability here. Another said, "If you sleep with your husband, after a month you become pregnant. Why I do not know."

This lack of knowledge about how or why was particularly a characteristic of the older age category. A number of them admitted to not knowing why or not being clear on what occurred. "You just discover that you're expecting," explained one of the older women. Others were equally uninformed. The Hindu woman, Mrs. Maharaj, explained, "The man leaves something (veeria). This is made up of blood. The woman also has veeria. The two combine and make a baby." Slightly better informed are the older women who used some of the terms: "The man squirts (this is the woman who interjects Afrikaans terms; she used *in skiet*, literally to "shoot in") liquid into the womb. Then the womb closes and a baby grows." Another one explained, "The male egg and the female egg meet in the womb and combine;" or "The sperm goes into the uterus and forms into eggs that grow" or "If the womb opens up, his nature comes into you." Three responses call for special mention. One suggested coitus interruptus because "If he leaves it in, the water goes in, then you don't see your periods." A second anticipates the aging ovary associated with the climacteric years, for "At pregnancy the egg goes into the ovary to grow. If the ovary is weak the egg will come out." And finally, in various contexts these women have remarked on the relationship between blood and aging, health and conception. It is only logical that if menstruation stops, temporarily at pregnancy or permanently at menopause, the absence of bleeding has to be explained. So sexual intercourse causes a "union of the man's blood (white like starch) and the woman's blood (real red) in the womb and a child grows"; or "The male sperm starts growing as it combines with the blood of the woman" (six women gave this response); and finally, following intercourse "semen coagulates and blood circulates with it and a baby forms."

The younger women are better educated and experienced their reproductive years when hospital, clinics, family planning units, and public openness were all available and more advanced than for the previous generation. More than half of these women explained, some with a great deal of elaboration, that "the male sperm fertilizes the egg and enters the womb where the baby grows." Less precise but echoing back to the blood metaphor were two replies: "Sperm and periods (blood) form into a child" and "The man's sperm goes in and forms into a baby as it mixes with her blood." The vagueness increases as women explain how "the male sperm combines with the female sperm," "the man's nature mixes with the woman's nature;" "male and female parts combine." Using some more impressive terms, two of the young women explained that "male sperm and women's hormones combine to form a baby" and that "the male serum going down the tubes through the ovaries of the woman, fertilizes the female cells."

It is clear that most women recognize the need for a man and a woman, for a union of the sexes, and for the intromission of the male element or sperm. However, twenty-seven (93.1%) of the younger and only twenty-one (77.8%) of the older women recognized that only one sexual union could be sufficient for conception to result. One of the younger women qualified her response with "it depends on the sperm reaching its destination." Older women stated: "it depends on your luck," or "at least four or five times with the same man," and finally Mrs. Maharaj insisted again that it depends on how strong the man is, i.e., his "feelings" and his veeria because the woman doesn't have control.

A question which naturally arises is since a woman doesn't have much control, what would happen if more than one man had sexual intercourse with her? Would it affect the pregnancy? Would it affect the fetus if the woman is already pregnant? The most common response to the first question was that the woman would not know who was the father of her child, and one woman added, "That is why Islam forbids two husbands." The next most common answers were that it could produce emotional problems or health dangers because "another blood would enter the womb." There is also the danger of a miscarriage because "the two men's bloods" might not be compatible, or because "two male fluids destroy each other. That is why street women don't become pregnant." However, one young woman saw no potential danger because the "womb closes up completely and serum will not enter…the womb is closed for nine months."

But does sexual intercourse always cause pregnancy? The implication being that the monthly cycle produces days of relative safety from conception and others when ovulation occurs. If pregnancy does not result from coitus, what causes pregnancy in one case and not in another? The majority of women in both categories thought that pregnancy does not inevitably follow coitus. However, four women in each group, 13.8% and 14.8%, respectively, said that intercourse always resulted in pregnancy. Among those who argued that it did not always follow, one of the older women was quite clear in her explanation of why this was so. She said, "Sometimes the husband is an infertile man or the wife is an 'unbearable' woman." Others explained that conception could result only if the woman's womb opens: "She presses it during intercourse and it opens." Or "There must be a certain germ in it that goes in only at certain times — at other times it slips away." And finally, a psychological explanation: "If the woman is very nervous this causes the ovaries to close before time."

Quite a number of women in both age categories shrugged their shoulders and said that nobody knows why. "It must be in God's hands," or "Well, it's Allah's will." There were those who did not venture an explanation stating that "We Indians don't discuss these things."

But a number of the younger women knew that the rhythm method had something to do with peak periods of fertility and relatively safe periods if the aim is to avoid pregnancy. One explained that "eight days before and eight days after a woman's period are good times to get pregnant, in between is safe." Another suggested "the first two weeks after period ends is most fertile;" and a third explained that the most fertile period was "up to ten days after the period ends because the womb is still open." (See discussion below.)

Knowing that the womb is open at certain times would then be important information if somebody wanted to insure that conception will take place. A number of possibilities were considered in this context: the use of foods or medicines to assist in conception taking place; certain coital positions to assist in bringing about pregnancy; and the aid of the supernatural to achieve the desired end.

A number of the younger women stated that a healthy diet, with plenty of protein and calcium was important, or that a woman should be relaxed because tension or stress might hinder conception. There were the inevitable spokeswomen for the old Dutch remedies, especially *versterkdruppels*, (see Addendum A) and of course they knew about fertility drugs which a woman could use if all else fails — but they also saw a danger of multiple births. The best way, some felt, was to consult with the gynecologist.

In discussing the most common response to the question of conception, it is necessary to tarry briefly in anthropological theory.

In his classic study of magic and religion, Frazer discussed sympathetic magic. By this he understood the belief held by many peoples that things act on each other at a distance through a secret sympathy. Thus, things which are separated in space can affect each other as if they were in contact. This overall belief and the wide range of practices which give expression to it are actually constituted of two principles based on the law of similarity and the law of contact. The former gave rise to homeopathic magic also called imitative magic. The latter gave rise to contagious magic. Frazer summarizes these two forms: "First, that like produces like, or that an effect resembles its cause; and second, that things which have once been in contact with each other continue to act on each other at a distance after the physical contact has been severed." (1954:11)

Of interest for our present discussion is the way in which the *sympathy* is reached through a historical tradition which accepted the law of *similarity*. Homeopathic magic finds expression in two beliefs among Indian South African women. In the first, expressed by women in both the younger and older age categories, women are told to find "a coconut and inside when the milk dries, there will be a *small baby coconut* — do not cut it, give it to the woman whole to swallow." Others used the word "seed" which should be swallowed and would produce a child.

Even more common was the prescription of a folk medicine preparation in which the contents varied; glue was the one element present in all recipes. Glue from the eucalyptus tree (known locally as the blue gum tree) should be mixed with sugar. A more elaborate preparation calls for a mixture of *suwa* (fennel), *ajma* (a whole small seed, perhaps mustard; it must not be crushed), *gund* (glue), and *ghoor* (brown lumpy sugar). It is possible that we have both the glue and the little seed serving as homeopathic elements. Variations include: mix almond, gund, and milk; or boil a tea of ground almond and gund and drink a teaspoon full daily for three days.

Another example, this time from a Muslim woman, is to take an apple to the molana. He will write a special prayer on it; and the woman must eat the apple, thereby internalizing and activating the prayer.

Somewhat more pedestrian and possibly more medical is the prescription to boil a tea of fennel and drink it. It is said to "clear up inflammation in the uterus and will also help menstrual cramps and getting pregnant." Somebody else suggested that living on rice for a while did wonders for her.

When the discussion turned to the physical aspect of coital position, responses were fewer. We wanted to know whether certain positions were more helpful in achieving conception. Most women simply stated that they had no problems. A number of women in both age categories suggested ways of assuring that the male fluid did not leak out. This aim could be achieved by placing bricks under the bed to tilt the lower (foot) end up. This causes the semen to stay in. She could also "use a pillow under her backside to lift her up and prevent the serum from leaking out." Or, in the absence of these material aids, she should remain on the bed following intercourse and not get up immediately.

Even with all the medical and physical support some women are still not able to achieve or hold a pregnancy. For them the only avenue left is the help of God/Allah. In fact twenty-six (89.7%) of the pre- and twenty-three (85.2%) of the postmenopausal women thought that God/Allah could help. The range is quite diverse and includes the Hindu recognition of Shiva and others, the Muslim recognition of Allah, and the Christian recognition of God.

Fatima Meer discusses and analyzes in some detail the Hindu temples which over more than a century have been built in South Africa.

> The temple manifests faith in life and after life and in the whole ordered system of the cosmos. When there is illness or trouble in the house or at work, it is to the temple and its icons that Hindus turn. South African *vihanas* or temples vary from the humble, to the elaborate, where sculptured domes like great white iced cakes, pinnacled with golden urns, give the all-powerful formless God, a myriad form (1969:159).

These temples have sculptures, icons, and other artistic expressions of Shiva, Vishnu, and Sakti (or Marieaman), the three major dieties — as well as others. Vows are frequently made in situations of need or crisis on a kind of conditional basis: If my request is granted, then I will perform certain actions or make certain gifts. One young woman took longer to get pregnant than her mother had hoped. "My mother took a vow for me. If I had a child, she would place the child in the arms of Marieamam — the temple at Isipingo is dedicated to Marieaman." When she had her baby, her mother took the grandchild to the Natal south coast and placed it in the arms of the statue. Mrs. Gani says that when she reached menarche, her mother took her to a Tamil lady who read her signs and said that the whole family, but especially the daughter, should fast on Mondays. This will assure happiness, fertility, and a good life. (Mrs. Gani, it will be recalled had three daughters, and after a reverse of a tubal ligation, a son). Another Hindu woman explained that "one who wants a baby may *kavady*, e.g., carry a plank or frame of wood on her shoulders for miles and usually go into a trance. She prepares for this by fasting for ten days; and on the day of the sacrifice, she may not even have milk. During the trance some stick needles in their tongues."

Meer discusses kavady, its expression and its meaning for Indian South Africans. It includes carrying a burden, self-flagellation by having a needle pierce the tongue or hooks inserted in the flesh, and fire walking. For Hindus these rituals "constitute a salvation technique or mode of devotion which, according to Hindu rationalization appeals to a temperament, usually associated with the working class. It is essentially salvation through action, karma, which in this case is ritual, and Bhakti. Daily ritual requires time, and all are not able to afford such time..." (1969:155). Many, like the woman we have discussed, assume the burden and perform it on special ritual days between January and May, the Hindu months of Thai and Chitray. Hilda Kuper (1960:218-9) also gives information about kavady and, in fact, discusses a case similar to the one we refer to: namely, a woman who took a vow to do kavady if she became pregnant.

Less dramatic vows can also be taken such as giving up rice for ten days or until the baby is born; buying brass cymbals for the temple, or making a promissory gift of money or food to the hospital or to the poor. In the same religious context, one woman explained that she went to the temple where some old ladies tied a yellow string (*murd'pe*, colored by the yellow turmeric powder) on her wrist. That evening she was supposed to tie it to the bed, window, or door and leave it there until she was pregnant. After the baby was born, she had to go back to the temple to pray again. The vow, in one way or another, is very widespread. One woman recounted that her husband vowed that if she conceived, he would slaughter a goat every year for three years, giving the meat to the poor. At home she lit the lamp and prepared a sacrifice of camphor, fruit, milk, and coconut for Shiva. A small amount was put in the fire while the family ate the rest.

An interesting case involved an educated young woman who had spoken previously of hormonal imbalance, blocked fallopian tubes, and a woman who was not ovulating — i.e., a relatively well-informed person. But, she explained if a woman experiences problems becoming pregnant, her mother must make *roti* (flat bread) and divide it into twenty-one sections to be eaten separately for twenty-one days. The mother prays over everything and gives it to the daughter. It helped her and it helped a lot of people.

The Ayurvedic system classifies foods into those that have cooling or heating qualities. This is carried over into the theory of humors which are influenced by relative heat (for more detail see Leslie 1969). Although there are regional variations in which foods are seen as "cold" or "hot" (Taylor 1976), the system is extremely widespread. One of the Gujerati women in our study sample, in her late thirties, suggested that if a woman cannot get pregnant, there is too much heat in the body and she must eat "cold" foods. Among these she listed *gundar* (an herb) which will be mixed into a fudge. Also fennel seed which is boiled to make a tea, or a "very cold" drink like *thoot maria* (whole mustard seeds) in milk. As in previous cases, the woman had used this treatment and it resulted in conception.

Among Muslims there is a greater uniformity. The role of the molana is quite central in this regard as is the fact that the believers must learn Arabic to read the Koran. In spite of this, there are some variations. One of the younger women stated that she went to the molana, who ascertained through the book of divination if someone was jealous of her. He then prayed over her and gave her some sacred water to drink. Another fasted for seven days, praying every morning and evening while reading a paragraph from the Koran. She was also instructed to go to a saint's tomb in Durban or India or preferably to the *kabaa* in Mecca. If she went to India, she would also get herbal treatment of roots and leaves. So here the Indian cultural tradition is blended with Islam. But, and this is the last word, there is almost a certain predestination, because God's will is final. "It's up to us to ask; it's up to God to grant," she concluded. Along the same lines, another woman explained, "Pray; it won't make any difference because it is pre-ordained, but you profit from praying in your next life. Some people go to the molana, but I believe only in praying."

Those who go to the molana frequently receive a *ta'wee*, or string which a woman ties around her waist. It is a blessed tie and often is combined with sacred water or a prayer. One woman gave quite a lengthy description of "a prayer in the Koran to Jusuf and his wife where you ask for a son. I did this. Then I recited the ninety-nine most beautiful names of Allah — one is specifically for a son. I also followed a number of dietary restrictions and the times when sexual intercourse could take place to assure a son. I did all of these things and had a beautiful little girl."

And so, in spite of sacrifice and rituals and prayers and kavady and molana and personal regimen, some women still don't conceive. One of the older women, weather-beaten, wise and philosophical mused, "...I guess she just doesn't have the egg in her womb."

Birth Control

Birth control is nothing new in human history, but in most cases it involved the gradual withdrawal from sexual activity by women as they aged. For the Indian South Africans whom we are discussing, pregnancies after age thirty-five to forty were quite exceptional. However, if a woman started her reproductive life in her late teens when most marriages among the older generation took place, she could have been pregnant or lactating most of those fifteen to twenty years. It was not uncommon to find old women who told of their own histories or those of their mothers, for whom fifteen pregnancies were quite common.

In the 1930s South Africa established its first Family Planning Association, which provided information on birth control and maternal care. This was done initially through social workers and nurses. In time, a number of clinics were established in larger urban centers. "The clinics that were run by the Family Planning Association, with the exception of the present clinic in Johannesburg, were handed over to the State in about 1974 for financial reasons..." (Jardine 1984:7). Perhaps more important than financial reasons was the fact that a national program of family planning was initiated that year.

As a direct outflow of statements by the state president during the opening of the 1974 Parliament, South Africa developed a national family planning program. This consisted of first doing a number of surveys among the different population groups, covering such aspects as fecundity, fertility, family size, marriage, economic and education status, and a variety of other topics. *The National Family Planning Programme* states as aims:

a. to publicize, within the next five years, the idea of family planning among all adults and to endeavour to involve in family planning service 50% of all women who are exposed to the risk of conception;
b. to establish effective family planning services in all health organizations so that the service will be within easy reach of all persons (Department of Health 1974).

In the educational program, person-to-person guidance is of primary importance to ensure personal conviction, decision-making and the practice of family planning. This was to be achieved through the mass media and on an individual basis at clinics and by advisors. Family planning information was available to all family members — especially adolescents — in terms of decision-making about birth control. Thirty-seven percent of the Indian segment of South Africa's population is under the age of fifteen years old. Town clinics were located close to shopping areas and bus terminals where women could avail themselves of services and be assured of privacy and speed (Report 1984:45).

At the beginning of 1978, the Department of Health, Welfare and Pensions, whose task involves implementing the National Family Planning Programme, requested the Human Sciences Research Council to conduct extensive research in this field (Erasmus 1981). The result is a large number of systematic surveys which give good baseline data for empirical studies and also for studies of changing attitudes and practices.

Our own research, while essentially aimed at understanding the climacteric, dealt with family planning both as philosophical issue and as practical behavior. Most women thought that family planning was good; that a woman could have a satisfactory number or too many children; and that it was only fair to children and parents alike if a couple set some practical limit on the number of children they have. This is particularly true given the current economic situation.

Information. While natural means of birth control and an informal agreement about family planning may have been present among Indian women and men, the use of contraceptives is something that was accepted only recently. Many of the older women stated that such knowledge and devices were unavailable to them. Almost every woman in our sample agreed that it was good, at some stage, to avoid pregnancy. The sole exceptions were a premenopausal woman who said, "Fate will prescribe the number of children," and two postmenopausal women who felt that it was nice to have a lot of children.

The reasons for which women were positive about birth control were varied. The most common expression involved the time a mother would have to give support, emotional attention, love, and security to the children. When they are further apart, the elder ones can help with the younger. It is also important for the mother's health "to give your body a rest." It gives "a woman more strength."

One woman told of her mother who was always tired and run down. She had had a baby every eleven months — a total of twelve. The third popular reason for endorsing birth control was an economic one. Given the current cost of living, it is simply impossible to give children what they need, and this includes a good education, if the number is not limited. But the old people frequently used a qualifier: "Yes, it is good because things are too expensive, but it is not healthy to avoid pregnancy."

Suggesting an Indian cultural value, most of the women — Hindu and Muslim alike — indicated that the husbands were the hardest to convince about birth control. Speaking of Indian women in general, Brijbhushan states:

> Whatever the men may say, though, the women are overwhelmingly in favor of birth control. 'What do the men care about how many children they have?' said one, 'They have only to feed and clothe them if they can and ignore them if they can't. It is the woman who has to bear the brunt. She carries the child within herself for 9 months, then she has to feed and look after it. I really wish someone would find some way where we can have children when we want them and stop when we don't want them.' 'We are not cows and buffaloes that we should go on breeding every year,' said a mother of six. 'It is not that I would wish ill to any of my children. God forbid. But if they had not been born I certainly would not have missed having them.' 'Please tell me some way in which I can stop having children,' pleaded a young woman. Married five years she was already pregnant for the third time. 'Husbands,' she blushed, 'are not careful about; such things. It is only we poor women who have to suffer' (1980:81).

The area where the major difference emerged between the two research samples was that of having been instructed by somebody in the use of contraceptives. This normally would involve a gynecologist, other physician, or a nurse at the clinic. Of the premenopausal women, twenty-three (79.3%) stated that they had been so instructed; only four (14.8%) of the postmenopausal women had been instructed in the use of birth control devices.

Practice. How do the various methods and devices compare both in familiarity and in acceptance? This question can best be answered by briefly discussing the most commonly used methods of birth control.

'The pill,' referring to any of a number of oral contraceptives, is a relatively recent development becoming available during the 1960s. In South Africa "hormonal contraceptives are listed under Schedule 4 of the Medicines and Related Substances Control Act (Act 101 of 1965) and therefore may be prescribed or sold only by a medical doctor, dentist or veterinary surgeon or sold by a pharmacist or his assistant on the prescription of a doctor, dentist or veterinary surgeon. If such a prescription takes the form of an oral instruction to the pharmacist a written prescription should be given to the pharmacist within seven days by way of confirmation of the original prescription (Theron 1987:22).

Most of the women in this study had heard about the pill (one pre- and seven (25.9%) postmenopausal women said they had not heard about it), and most of them thought it was effective. Although twenty-two (75.9%) of the younger women were using or had used this device, only two (7.4%) of the older women indicated they had used it. One of the latter warned that the pill caused "heart trouble;" another said, "It makes you fat and gives you headaches." But the majority gave it the best overall rating for effectiveness.

One woman told of going on the pill after the birth of her second son (he was too close to the first). She used it for three years and found that she was losing skin pigmentation. When her physician took away the prescription her skin improved; and at the time of the study, only slight traces of blotchiness were present. In terms of effectiveness, every woman has her own experience as the only empirical evidence. One told of using the pill for two or three years and still getting pregnant twice. Another has been on the pill for twenty-four years, having a total of five children at planned intervals when she discontinued the pill for that purpose. All of these women were of course in the younger category. Repeatedly, the older women would say, "We didn't know anything; there were no clinics then."

The IUD, intrauterine contraceptive device, can be either medicated (bioactive) or nonmedicated (passive). Of the latter, the Lippes Loop is best known and locally quite widely referred to by the African term *shogololo* (centipede) because of its coils. Twenty-seven (93.1%) of the younger and thirteen (48.1%) of the older women had heard of the IUD method; most did not really know about its effectiveness; and only eleven (37.9%) in the younger and nobody in the older category had ever been fitted with such a birth control device. One woman was quite outspoken about her view of its effectiveness.

She explained, "The gynecologist fitted me with a loop but I still fell pregnant; when the baby was born the loop came out with the baby. Nurse told me the baby was born clutching this thing in her hand." One of the older women lamented, "When we were having babies, they only had the diaphragm — we've learned about these other things from our daughters."

The diaphragm/cervical cap was known to thirteen (44.8%) of the pre- and nine (33.3%) of the postmenopausal women. Very few vouched for its safety but the majority claim not to have enough knowledge about it. There were only two women, both premenopausal, who said they had used this device. One of them explained that she was fitted for it and instructed by a physician but was not told to use a spermicidal gel with the device.

Sterilization, though reversible in some cases, would be the choice of women or couples who had completed the reproductive phase of their lives. All the younger and two-thirds of the older women know about this, but only eleven (37.9%) of the younger and two (7.4%) of the older women had drastically terminated their reproductive lives in this manner. The reason for using the term "drastic" is that her reproductive capacity is an Indian woman's passport to marriage and security. One of the younger women explained, " . . . It's final, if our husband dies you can't have children for a new husband." Unless, of course, it wasn't done correctly. At least three women indicated that they had wanted a tubal ligation but that their husbands had refused.

A number in the older category were quite loquacious about their lack of knowledge while they were sexually active. "We were stupid; we didn't know anything . . . babies came quickly at first. People said drink Epsom salts. I tried anything," recounted one. Another explained, "At that time we didn't know about birth control but had babies when we slept together." The logical result was that birth control meant that they avoided sexual intercourse for fear of pregnancy. Some employed withdrawal or the rhythm method, which one explains is "the natural female cycle." Others told of a capsule (suppository?) which they bought at the chemist. It was called 'the wife's friend.' "You inserted it. We were stupid, we just pushed it up and never thought where it went." Two other older women explained that this "wife's friend" was inserted into the womb and would prevent conception from occurring.

The injection of contraceptive progestogen (Depo Provera and Nur-Isterate) first came on the market in 1959 and was not used much until a decade later. It is approved for contraceptive use in many countries, but the FDA has not approved it for use in the United States partly because it has a negative effect on the subsequent fertility of women — due perhaps, to severe suppression of the hypothalamus and pituitary. Theron, writing about South Africa states:

— DMPA does not cause endometrial cancer in humans.
— No evidence of any increased risk of cervical malignancy has been found.
— The finding of breast tumors in beagle dogs cannot be transposed to humans. Studies on humans have shown no increased incidence of breast tumors or malignancy.
— Despite intensive investigation the only clinical metabolic effect attributed to Depo Provera is weight gain.
— Heavy vaginal bleeding requiring therapeutic intervention is rare.
— Fertility is not impaired permanently (1987:88).

"The injection" has become a very common and popular form of birth control with all groups in South Africa. "The advantage," said one of the younger women, "is that you go once every three months to get the injection."

The condom, or "French leather," as some of the older women referred to it, places responsibility on the male and for that reason was not popular. In fact, the husbands of only seven (24.1%) of the younger and three (11.1%) of the older women had used it, though a larger number indicated that they had heard about it. A survey of attitudes towards fertility and family planning, carried out a decade before our study among Indian South Africans in Transvaal concluded: "Family planning is apparently accepted in principle by most Indian men. The acceptors are heavily concentrated in the younger age group, higher educational level categories, higher income groups, urban areas and particularly among the adherents of the Hindu religion" (du Plessis 1974:17). The French leather (a corruption of the British slang term "French letter"), or condom, was one of the only devices readily available before the middle or late sixties. One of the older women explained, "I never used anything; I made my husband use a condom; he was different, not like Indian men." The implication being that he readily consented to using it. Consent is only half the answer, however, as explained by another of her age cohorts. "I told my husband to buy condoms. He did but they didn't work because he forgot to use them — that was before family planning. We have eight children."

Male authority has been discussed in various contexts of this study. One of the older women said that after her last unwanted pregnancy the physician gave her birth control pills. "I did not use them; I wanted sterilization. My husband wouldn't give permission." Whether sterilization legally falls within the realm of contraceptives is one of those gray areas. Theron (1987:21), discussing the legal position, states: "A married person may not prohibit a supplier from providing contraceptives to his/her spouse." Nevertheless, most people would consult about their use. Sterilization, as one woman said, is so final; and this may be the grounds for the husband's refusal.

Since abortion is not legal in South Africa, there is greater emphasis on the use of contraceptive devices. Those who use them have simply discovered their use belatedly. One of the older age group recognized that contraception must work "because we had fifteen children, and many of the young women today have two or three...." Another suggested that women didn't get pregnant as frequently as when she was young, and there must then be a reason. But one of her age cohorts shook her head (indicating disgust) saying. "They're not dependable but also unhealthy and unnatural." Echoed another, "If God said you're going to have twelve children, you'll have twelve in spite of using these devices." And of course, abstention is the last possibility which was in fact employed by some of the older women when they progressed beyond reproductive age. One of them said that she had been a good wife, but regarding sex, when she had had her children "...then I was finished with my old man."

Abortion

Abortion here refers to causing miscarriage of a fetus, either killing it in the process or intending to do so if it is living at removal. Such acts are governed by the Abortion and Sterilization Act (Act 2 of 1975) and restrict such acts to a state controlled institution where the operation must be performed by a physician.

The circumstances under which a legal abortion may be performed are set out in the Act:

1. Where a woman's life is in danger or her health is seriously threatened;
2. Where there is a serious threat to the woman's mental health:

3. Where there are physical or mental defects to the unborn child;
4. Where pregnancy is due to alleged rape or incest;
5. Where pregnancy is due to unlawful intercourse with a female idiot or imbecile.

Sentiments. A very simple question we asked the women in our study was whether a woman who becomes pregnant must give birth. Twenty-six (89.7%) of the pre- and twenty-six (96.3%) of the postmenopausal women answered in the affirmative. What alternative is there to God's will? Muslims believe if a woman is pregnant, she must have the baby; any action would be going counter to what God has willed. Abortion is a sin. These were common responses. But what if there are unwanted pregnancies?

One disturbing fact found among a number of the Indian women was that they explained with clarity that they avoided sexual intercourse for a week after menstruation ended and again for a week before menstruation started because these were the most dangerous times for conception. This misinformation is confirmed in a study by Lotter and van Tonder.

The Chatsworth investigation reveals a considerable degree of ignorance with regard to the "safe" period. Only 25 percent of the women intimated that they knew that conception can only occur at certain times during the woman's cycle. Of this subgroup, a mere 34 per cent indicated that conception is most probable roughly in the middle of the menstruation cycle. Only 9 percent of the women were consequently able to supply the correct answer to the question concerned.

It is possible that many of the women answered the above-mentioned questions evasively since they considered them too personal or delicate and that a larger percentage of the women possessed knowledge of the fact that conception *can* normally occur at a specific time only.

If this was in fact the case, it is probable that a larger percentage of Indian women possess *incorrect* (as against *no*) information than the above-mentioned data suggest since, as opposed to 34 per cent of those persons who ventured a response and supplied the correct answer, 59 per cent stated that conception is most probable *just after menstruation*. It is consequently probable that Indian couples who wish to avoid conception without using other appliances and methods will tend, after a period of abstinence in what they regard as the "dangerous period," to have sexual intercourse or resume it at precisely that time in the woman's cycle when conception will most probably ensue from sexual intercourse (1975:30).

Such misinformation may have its origin in India. It will be recalled that cultural ties to India are maintained by visitations and the immigration of brides. Mandelbaum, dealing with the subject of fertility in India states: "It is popularly believed that a woman's most fertile period comes in the days immediately following the cessation of menstruation and that the rest of the menstrual cycle is 'safer'" (1974:64).

It being admitted that there may have been pregnancies unwanted because of timing, age, or some other reason, we followed up. Was there ever justification for an abortion? Again the generational difference was clear, as thirteen (44.8%) of the pre-, but only six (22.2%) of the postmenopausal women agreed that there were. Reasons which were acceptable would fall within the law: a defective or deformed fetus; danger to the mother's life; rape, danger to the physical or emotional state of the mother. In all other cases, to use the words of old Mrs. Kassim, "Have the child and give it up for adoption." However, their innocent reaction to this moral question belies the information they have and practices many have attempted to achieve abortion. Illegality of a practice generates a diversity and richness of ways to circumvent it. In the same light, many of the beliefs and practices have deep roots in Indian culture.

Methods. The first method of achieving an abortion not within the parameters of the law is to use a physician who is a family friend. "The doctor will syringe the woman in her private parts and two days later everything comes out of the womb." A case was mentioned in which a local physician performed an abortion for a family with whom he was close friends. An alternative was to go overseas and while visiting a relative also have an abortion.

Much more common is what is called "back door nurses" or "back street abortions." This involves a person with some knowledge going to private homes when so requested, and entering surreptitiously through the back door. One nurse/midwife at the local hospital is said to be available for such service and to be quite good. The problem is that when things go wrong, the "expert" frequently disappears. One of the older women explained, "Back door nurses do it at home, then they just leave the girl who had complications and she must be taken to the hospital."

Having heard about or perhaps experienced an abortion, others think of self-administration. Two of the older age group were well informed in this regard. Said one, "You buy a syringe and then force soap water and glycerine into your womb. "Added the other, "You use an object like a wire to scrape the uterus and cause bleeding." Is the mere fact of bleeding another example of imitative magic and the desire for a more normal bleeding to return? This woman did not suggest dislodging the blastocyst from the uterine wall.

On the other hand, most things, at least in the intestines can be moved by a strong bowel movement. It is not strange that some women suggested that an unwanted pregnancy could be terminated by using a very strong laxative; an overdose of Epsom salts or castor oil; or by eating plenty of dates.

It was, however, in the area of folk preparations where the greatest diversity appeared. Folk preparations use herbs, kitchen products, and old remedies. Some rely on heat as the critical element. Heat, when applied to ingestion, included "hot" food such as *goram*, thus foods in Ayurvedic classification of hot/cold, as well as drinking hot gin and other preparations (to be discussed) which must have a high temperature. Heat can also apply to water and women are advised to take a hot shower, or a hot bath. One suggestion was to give a woman liquor and let her sit in a hot bath. A woman who was six to eight weeks pregnant took six aspirins and two packets of Epsom salts and sat in a very hot bath. She aborted. Another element in folk preparations is the degree of bitterness (causing personal discomfort). Women must ingest quinine, very bitter herbs, tamarind juice (which is acid rather than bitter) or drink two or three cups of very strong black coffee in the morning (this instruction to a tea-drinking people!) All of these, it seems, are actions which will result in discomfort for the woman. In the same vein, one woman advocated the wearing of a very stiff corset or a prophylactic. Dutch medicine, especially *Jamaika gemmer* (see Appendix A), can also be boiled and mixed with gin and cloves. One woman stated that this preparation worked twice for her. "It is very painful like childbirth, but it is effective."

Only one woman in each age category admitted to having induced an abortion. (These are not openly admitted to and not listed in the fertility figures discussed above.) One other woman in the younger age category still had a very small baby when she "fell pregnant for the fourth time; and for health and emotional reasons, I got an abortion. I had a signed permission from my husband."

Three elements appear with frequency: heat (as in hot baths), hot drinks, and gin and cloves. Together or in combination with other products these are the most common.

Variations

This discussion will turn to variations of sexual expression though they may at some point relate to heterosexual expression and to coitus.

Experimentation. Exploration and experimentation characterize children. This is one way for them to learn. Parents realize this with a shock because they, themselves, grew up in such a protected domestic environment. Girls were restricted to the home after menarche, chaperoned, and finally proposed to by a relative of the future husband. Today parents look on in disbelief at the speed of moral changes and complain about "these fast times." Orthodox families attempt to retain many of the traditional values with which they grew up. They attempt to imprint religious and familial pre-scriptions of conduct and are open with children about the dangers of immorality. Some women explained that they discussed matters with their daughters that they were never told about because they didn't need to know such things until they got married. In most cases today, preteens are better informed than these women were at the time of marriage.

Very young children start their sex education in the company of siblings, cousins, and friends. The primary reason is curiosity. By exploring their own bodies, questions are raised about anatomical makeup and possibly about pleasurable stimuli. They become inquisitive and seek opportunities to confirm the presence of these in others. Women tell of the games that young children play. These all have the same theme. The games are "doctor-doctor," "doctor-nurse," "house-house," "father-mother" and similar games which create opportunities for closeness and touch. The doctor and nurse have to prod and feel and explore. The mommy and daddy, with the youngest ones being their children, sleep together and pat each other. One younger woman in the study sample told of a little girl sitting on her six-year-old son "saying they're making babies." Another little girl of six is "having a drink" and "sleeps with an eleven-year-old boy as they play house-house. Another told of a four-year-old son of a neighbor who came over to play and told her daughter to take off her underwear so they could feel each other.

Women recognize that some of this is innocent childhood play, some of it pure curiosity; but in preteens it causes concern. A teacher told of a standard three (fifth grade) boy pushing a mirror under the desk to see whether the girl in front of him wore underwear. Unfortunately, the adults grew up at a time when they had little information; but they were also protected. Not all of them recognize that because children spend time outside the home and in coeducational schools, that protection is no longer there. They, as parents, must be more open and supply information. One woman told us that her ten-year-old son watched a lot of television. She was shocked when he asked her what "sexual" means; she just ignored him. This response was more typical of the older women, only seven (28.0%) of whom found the cross-gender child-play acceptable in contrast to twelve (44.4%) in the younger category.

At what age does innocent curiosity and anatomical exploration take on sexual connotations? We know that the endocrine system is activated in the prepubertal years as the hypothalamus and pituitary secrete hormone releasing factors and gonadotropins, but does interest in and activity of a sexual nature coincide with these hormonal changes? Asked how old Indian children were when they first learned about sex, women responded with ages ranging from five or six all the way to sixteen years old. Most suggested, for both boys and girls, an inquisitiveness starting around eight or nine, stimulated in part by coeducational schools. Much of what mothers complain about or see as precocious to us would seem normal growth and education. For instance, a mother said her nine-year-old knew "all about where babies come from," and her seven-year-old daughter "knows why her uncle's wife is fat." Another said her eight-year-old daughter told her that a neighbor was expecting a baby. One of the progressive young women, a physician's wife, wanted to tell her daughters (ten and eleven years old respectively) prior to menstruation, but "they knew everything...even the youngest, age seven."

One of the older women summarized it well. "Today's children are so old fashioned [this is an idiomatic expression indicating 'smart'], they know what we learned at marriage. Much of it they learn at school. You know, we didn't even know what mother and father were doing in bed." Knowledge is definitely fueled by television and videos. Girls are said to learn earlier because mothers do confide in them and discuss changes, such as menarche which will occur. If there is a grandmother in the home, a special camaraderie develops between her and the granddaughter. Boys are not talked to in this respect because the "Indian community keeps a boy in a glass case." Boys are said to be "either more clever or more inquisi-tive" and coeducational schools are fertile ground for information. This is where a nine-year-old boy and girl were found in the school toilet taking off their clothes. This is where young children "do mis-chief" to use the euphemism of one of the older women. Another emphatically stated that separate school for boys and girls are better, and a third complained, "You just don't know nowadays with children away at school and college." At least one young girl, who had been sent to a Catholic girls' school, recognized its advantages. She was overheard 'arguing with an age mate and said: "You'll real-ize how good my school is when you get pregnant!"

Serious consciousness of and interest in the opposite sex comes with the teenage years. There is some sex education in stan-dard six (eighth grade) in Indian schools, but at this age "it's in their bodies, you can't stop it." One of the younger women, no doubt the mother of a teenage son, said that serious interest in girls appears "when he starts loafing."

Dating and courtship start with finding excuses to be together; meeting at or after school; writing notes to each other; going to places of entertainment; and walking home together. Physical con-tact, shy at first, starts with holding hands, placing an arm around the partner, and "hanging on each other." Embracing and cuddling leads to kissing, and later to necking and petting and exploring. For teenagers to be thus involved is acceptable. Parents recognize that this is a new age and new ways are the norm. One young woman just shook her head in disbelief when she told that "a carload of girls arrived, grabbed my seventeen-year-old son, threw him in the car and roared off." "Indian girls sure are changing," said another. But when private relationships become more serious, when it turns to heavy petting, when they "act mad-like," parents are concerned. "A boy can take off his pants here and tomorrow he'll still be a man; a girl loses her name."

In the traditional Indian family, daughters were protected, were taken out of school, and parents hoped to get them married off before they "lost their name." Ideally first sexual intercourse was within marriage, with the groom. Most of the women in this study see that as the ideal and certainly try to protect their children from premarital sexual experimentation, but they also state that many a teenager "is spoiled." In fact, when asked at what age first sexual intercourse occurred, responses ranged from nine to twenty, both extremes mentioned by women in the older category; guesses among the younger women ranged from thirteen to nineteen. Mean and median being fifteen and sixteen, respectively. One Muslim woman said that it did not occur among Muslim because it was not allowed; another confirmed this, suggesting that such actions were typical of Hindu and Tamil. Another stated that even though not allowed, there were a number of cases where people had to marry. Yet another reported a "shocking number of premarital pregnancies among the Muslims."

Two women recounted actual cases of teenage pregnancies. One young girl was beaten so badly by her family that she died. Another case, recounted by a lecturer at the local college, involved one of a number of pregnancies at the college. A seventeen-year-old became pregnant. Her parents forced her to marry the boy who was a drop out and a drug addict. She had twins but could not cope with personal problems and her studies as well.

In spite of the fact that women see the Indian community as conservative, religious, and guided by family values and morality, "boys and girls transgress" and not only the "naughty" ones, as one older woman suggested. Indian children in the 1980s grow up with new freedoms in homes where there nearly always is a TV and a video player. These show secular programs and frequently quite explicit actions. While we were in the field, parents were preparing a case against a local video store owner for renting videos to a twelve-year-old who showed them at his home while the parents were out. The claim of community members was that the store owner did not practice constraint in what he rented to kids. A further note of concern involves general publications. South Africa has a very strict pornography law, and many a visitor or returning traveler has had *Playboy* and similar publications confiscated. Yet equally explicit photographs and descriptions appear weekly in the *Sunday Times* or romantic women's magazines.

Masturbation. It is generally agreed that masturbation occurs more frequently among adolescent males than females (Masters, Johnson and Kolodny 1988:240–41). Indian South African women hold the same view. However, only 65.5% of the younger and 33.3% of the older women thought that it was even present among the youngsters. The women once again believed it to result from exploration of the body, "experiencing that sensation," and sometimes from accompanying dreams and visions. One woman explained, "I do know boys get acne on their faces which is related to it."

Children who explore their bodies, expose themselves, or give expression to sexual urges were frowned upon in traditional Indian society and may have elicited punishment. Speaking of Indian South Africans a generation ago, Hilda Kuper emphasizes the conservative and proper behavior she encountered.

> Sex is stressed, but its natural expression is surrounded by a series of prohibitions. Adults impress on the children that it is "wrong." "bad" and "dirty" to expose themselves or handle themselves publicly. Even in babies, nakedness is considered an embarrassment and there is constant emphasis on modesty. One of the few sentences I learnt through hearing it constantly repeated was "Nanga rahana bura hey" (to be naked is bad). Behind this early inhibition appears to be the religious attitude to chastity, and the belief that immodesty will "spoil" the individual for marriage, and make him, or her, unable to produce the ideal child. A Hindu child is trained to anticipate retribution both for unknown sins committed in a former existence and for those committed in this life which will affect its rebirth.
> From the time a child can understand, he is conditioned to responsible social participation limited by the mental and physical capacity of his age. The tasks that he is given are essentially useful, and his efforts are critically appraised. For the average South African Indian child there is no period of irresponsible play, no world of toys, no fairy make believe. Little girls in particular are little ladies whose feminine charms are encouraged and developed. They usually have their ears pierced at 5–7 years for earrings and the presents they receive from kin are jewelry and clothing. They are trained to speak quietly, and to walk lightly (1960:155–156).

Thus, children might discover themselves in private and they may express themselves in private; but it is not acceptable behavior. Parents scold or punish children who masturbate or take the child to a psychologist. The reason for this concern is that it is seen as unnatural and unhealthy. "People feel that a girl is losing her egg cells when she masturbates — boys lose sperm and won't be able to father children." It is also believed to "go to their head" and interfere with a child's normal development and marriage. However, others argued that it "gives them relaxation if they're very hot natured," and "boys will go off their heads if they don't do it."

If it is seen as immature exploration among adolescents, this same explanation cannot be given for adults who masturbate. In our total sample, twenty-two (75.9%) of the pre- and ten (37.0%) of the postmenopausal women who responded said that adults did masturbate. A minority of them (41.4% and 18.5%, respectively) found it acceptable behavior. Most of the discussion occurred with the younger women — the postmenopausal women stated that it was unhealthy and that women never masturbated, one claimed that women can't masturbate. Those younger ones who did respond thought that it occurred among men who were virile and whose wives were pregnant, under the postparturition taboo, menstruating, or away. Not wishing to be unfaithful to their wives, these men would masturbate. It is also possible that bachelors or persons in an arranged marriage (who do not get along) might perform this act. While it is mostly men who masturbate, a woman explained, "A wife might do it if she is depressed or blue — not wanting to wake her husband." Another expected that it followed "wet dreams or absence of the marriage partner. Mostly men do it but it is quite general for a woman to have an orgasm while sleeping or while awake — if she's desperate."

Those who found justification for this practice thought that men could rid themselves of urges and tensions, prevent themselves from "going off their heads," and it certainly was preferable to extramarital affairs. One woman suggested, "If a man can't stand being without sex, he must take it that way." One woman explained, "A woman friend told me when her husband is away, she just uses a candle to help herself out." In the majority, however, were the voices of those who saw this act as not normal — "you've got your partner." A common sentiment was expressed by the young woman who said, "My mind puts sex in the marriage context only."

It would seem that in children masturbation is viewed in a neutral, even sympathetic way. There it is seen as innocent, exploratory, and a part of discovery and growth. In adults, the act would be justified only for men who are subject to a temporary sexual taboo.

Homosexuality. Normally, in this condition, gender identity and gender role do not coincide; and there is sexual activity between members of the same sex. This may apply to both females and males. The term *lesbian* is used for females, and *homosexual* for males, but a large number of Indian women used the Afrikaans term *moffie* for both.

In the study sample, thirteen (44.8%) pre- and eight (29.6%) postmenopausal women thought that there were Indian children who practiced homosexual acts. It is blamed on "this fast world," seen as a result of curiosity, and strongly discouraged. Explained one woman, "My grandson went to a party dressed like Boy George. We told him we didn't want a moffie in our family."

Among adults it is a different matter. These persons would normally not be a part of a family. Twenty-one (72.4%) pre- and eleven (40.7%) in postmenopausal women stated that there were adult homosexuals in the Indian community. Among the opposite responses, it was said that the Indian community was too conservative. On the whole, it was thought that it was more typical of males: not one person thought that it was preponderantly a female phenomenon. Twenty-one (72.4%) younger and ten (41.7%) older women thought that homosexuality was concentrated among men — the rest saw it as equally distributed. It was not acceptable behavior, and only two of these heterosexual women stated that it was acceptable.

It was believed to be a characteristic of male hairdressers. One man who "interferes with young boys" was mentioned. He had dragged a young boy into a vacant lot. Others thought that men were just more noticeable and open. There was one case of two women living together, and someone suggested that theirs was a lesbian relationship.

One woman thought that homosexuality was common among the Tamil; another that a lot of young Muslims were homosexuals; a third countered that it was not permitted in Islam. Ideally, a Muslim should not even undress or bathe in the presence of others except a spouse. The Prophet is reported to have said: "Let no man look at the private parts of another man. And let no woman look at the parts of another woman" (Badawi 1979:30).

The popular reaction to homosexuality is negative. It ranges from sympathy ("something must have gone wrong in their lives"); to concern ("it's abnormal behavior;" "they have psychological problems and should go to a counselor"); and disgust ("I hate it;" "It's unnatural"). Some saw it as opposed to the divine plan ("Man and woman belong together the way God made them to compliment each other;" "God has created partners and so, to have it with your own sex will be unnatural"), others as dangerous ("it gives you AIDS"); and still others viewed it as silly or funny. There was only one conciliatory voice who said, "If God made it, we must accept it."

Experience

Heterosexual relationships are seen as normal, and therefore, as the ideal. While not all relationships were harmonious — some

TABLE 24

Frequency of Sexual Intercourse by Indian South African Women

Frequency	Premenopausal		Postmenopausal	
	Number	Percent	Number	Percent
Daily	2	7.4	–	–
Two/Three times per week	17	63.0	8	66.6
Weekly	8	29.6	1	8.3
Monthly	–	–	3	25.0
N/A	2	–	15	–

due to an arranged marriages or unsympathetic or selfish husbands — sexual relationships were always defined as involving woman and man, ideally wife and husband. Heterosexual coitus is both ideal and norm. From an institutional and a religious point of view, this intercourse should occur within marriage.

Sexual intercourse serves as an expression of love but also as a way either to satisfy the husband or calm him down. In other words, the wife does not necessarily receive direct sexual satisfaction in this service act. Nevertheless twenty-seven (93.1%) of the pre- and twelve (46.2%) of the postmenopausal women say they have regular sexual intercourse. Table 24 presents the range of "regular" as indicated by these women.

Those women who have severely curtailed the frequency of sexual intercourse state that they did so due to a lack of "feeling." One older woman explained, "Sometimes I got feeling; he got more feeling." This seems generally true that the women's interest in sexual relations and coitus decreased after they had performed their role of producing heirs or having their children. A number explained that the presence of growing children curtailed their interest. Others simply felt they could do without it. Among the postmenopausal women, a common response: "Sometimes the husband wants it... well it's just too bad;" or "We're old. Why do we want to bother — we don't feel nothing."

Women were asked whether they experienced orgasm when they engaged in coitus as a service to win the husband's favor. "What is that?" asked one of the older women. However, most, twenty-two (75.9%) of the premenopausal women did regularly experience orgasm as against only five (18.5%) of the women in the older category referring to their younger years. A few women experienced pain during intercourse, but one of the younger women said it was true "only when trying out some funny tricks."

Changes in desire for and frequency in sexual intercourse is directly related to age. About half the premenopausal women said that they had lost interest; could do without it; or could certainly live without it. The postmenopausal women frequently placed a marker on their decline of interest; namely, change of life. One explained, "I stopped feeling for it when I started having change of life." Others quit at age forty-six or fifty or fifty-three due to menopause. When asked whether they noticed a change in their sexual desire associated with menopause, only six (24.0%) said no. With others the change in desire or interest comes earlier in the marriage. Mrs. Habib, a school teacher, gave vent to her feelings. "Since I was twenty-three I was fed up with it — could have done completely without it having had my two children. I was fed up with going to bed earlier. But the husband decides, and if you don't he goes to other women. It was such an effort for me. My husband would wake me up two to three times during the night. I finally said, 'No, this is enough!'"

In most cases in the older category, the husband decided about having intercourse. Two of these women responded differently, one saying, "I just take my pillow and go to sleep in my daughter's room — then the day passes." Another (with a slight twinkle in her eye) explained, "When I go to cover him up he catches me..." Most of the younger women said that both the husband and wife can decide about intercourse. One offered an elaboration. "Both, but the husband must decide — he can have it when he wants it and I'm always available."

There are cases where women initiate matters, frequently in what we have called a "service act." A number of younger women had comments: "If I notice my husband is depressed, perhaps due to the business, I feel I should cheer him up." Said another, "If I'm in the mood, especially if he's very tense, I feel it'll help him." And a third, "When you find your husband is in a shit mood, try to get him off it and please him." Perhaps the best expression was given by a bright and lively young woman who explained, "When I'm completely relaxed and in a good mood, I don't mind giving the old boy a treat." But Mrs. Habib saw the value of service to a husband who was not a teacher or intellectual: "When my husband is unhappy or cross with me, I ask whether I can rub his back — he knows that means sex. Then afterwards I get up to go to the study to do my schoolwork or grade papers. My colleagues all say the same." But many Indian South African women do not take the initiative. "I'm too shy," said one. "It's not a wife's role," said another — both in the younger age group. Postmenopausal women explained: "In our culture we are shy." Another said. "We have respect." And a third, "That is a man's role." It is, they explained, the man who initiates and the wife who submits. This submission, we would venture, occurs more during the first years of marriage while the wife is young and insecure. As she establishes herself in a household and especially once there are children, she has a firmer base on which to stand and to insist on some compromise. The service element is still there, but a certain reciprocity now enters into it.

If women are not always satisfied or happy and if men sometimes are away on business or family trips, do these women ever experience sexual fantasies? Do they have thoughts and feelings of a sexual nature? Furthermore, do they ever act on these sexual feelings? Nineteen (70.4%) of the younger and seven (26.9%) of the older women admitted to having such fantasies. "There is no woman who can deny it!" was the sweeping answer of one young woman. Another said that it was natural. But two women who had had quite trying experiences saw such fantasies as luxuries of the leisurely. One older woman said, "I had to raise sixteen siblings, then enter an arranged marriage to a man who didn't care for me; I did not have fantasies." Another told us, "After my husband died, I had to work as a dispatcher all day. I had no time to dream — I'd hit the pillow and sleep." But those with a more normal routine indicated that reading, daydreaming, and visual stimuli in movies were most frequent. One young woman said she "daydreamed about the night before, perhaps listening to romantic music;" another looked at "a girly magazine before going to bed." Most fantasies were created by visual stimulation while watching videos or movies; but equally important is the private world of the daydream. One young woman said if she and her husband had argued, she always pictured sleeping with "imaginary men." Another explained, "Maybe we'd been watching a video or T.V. When I'm with my husband, I fantasize about other men. I fantasize about whom I'm in bed with — will not reach orgasm if I just thought about my husband — I must think about other men."

The women did not apparently give expression to their dreams and daydreams unless these involved the husband entering their fantasy world. In such cases, the fantasy was discussed with the husband, and this inevitably led to renewed sexual intercourse. For those who had such fantasies but did nothing about them, there was the logical explanation of one older woman: " ... we have that shyness!"

Menstruation

There were four or five of the younger women with a good deal of education, especially in nursing and biological sciences, who were informed about menstruation. They know that in anticipation of ovulation the endomitrium of the uterus builds up and prepares to receive a fertilized egg. They know that when conception has not taken place, the woman's body is "cleaned out" as this lining is shed and along with "other impurities" is carried out of the body by blood. The general information concerning menstruation is present. Although the facts might be more or less empirical, there are no fantasies about what is taking place. This cannot be said for the majority of Indian women in both age categories.

Beliefs and Expectations

The first question obviously is why women menstruate. It is something unique to women (in contrast to men) yet common (all healthy women menstruate) so people must think about it. Responses fall into two categories, irrespective of age: a religious explanation or an attempted physiological explanation. "Eve, she ate the apple — now we're paying for it." The majority gave more or less vague biological answers suggesting, "The body must clean out refuse, like urine and stool cleans out the body — it gets rid of excretions." Or "The system must work out the impurities to clean the body so she won't be sickly."

Menstruation stops with pregnancy — most of them know that, but the relationship is not always clear. Women menstruate "to remove impurities from the body and after it to fertilize the egg," one of the older women explained. "Fertilize" was used her in the sense of fertilizer in the garden, i.e., to make it grow. Related to this is that the "blood clods and forms a baby;" or that the "blood is utilized to build a baby." Others do recognize the change which occurs as the woman reaches middle age and stops menstruating. This is because "her eggs dry up;" or "when you don't ovulate, the blood in the body decreases;" or due to the fact that "old women make less blood" and thus "become more like men who always made less blood;" when women are old "the blood gets finished." However, a Tamil woman explained that "after forty the womb becomes very small, then closes and she can't have periods nor feel for a man." This woman, one of those in the older category, recognized the permanent cessation of flow. A number of others addressed this condition.

In certain ways the most logical answer was that "God made it that way because old women shouldn't have children;" or "the Koran says: 'God doesn't want you to become pregnant so you do not ovulate any more.'" Old women are supposed to be grandmothers; they have a special role and should not have to care for any more babies. Why? Because "if she doesn't [stop having children] the world would soon be too full of people."

Much of this discussion contrasted younger and older women. The decrease in circulating estrogen is one of the major endocrinological changes which accompany the slowdown of the ovary and the secretion of ovarian hormones. Do these women recognize the presence of some substance in the body which influence how younger women look in contrast to older women? One of the younger women suggested that older women's "bodies are drier." Another noticed that "glow in your body" as expressed in the skin, eyes, and hair fades as you age. Two women saw specific causal factors. Mrs. Desai said, "Some look old because of hardship in life, especially in-law problems." Mrs. Alli pointed out, "When she goes through 'that phase,' she stops being a woman." The older women, however, said that it was "strength not a substance;" that it is "all in the mind;" and that it "depends on how she keeps herself." One of these wise older women even had practical prescriptions: "A cow gives milk — she's like a mother. Keep the body clean; keep the bowels clean; eat vegetables only four times per week; eat fish or chicken three days a week." But there is a problem, one suggested, regarding this "substance" we have been discussing because when a woman "stops having periods she retains the substance."

So what causes the signs of aging we all recognize? Is it due to this "substance," or to the fact that women no longer menstruate? Only sixteen (55.2%) in the premenopausal category related aging to the cessation of flow; eighteen (66.7%) of the older women did. We return to the familiar explanation, surplus blood and impurities which are no longer lost with flow.

"One who has regular sex life will age slowly because her full womanly nature is expressed." This statement suggests a relationship between heterosexual coitus and those acts associated with it and aging. That the expected relationship as represented in the responses of the younger, sexually active women is a positive one does not hold for those who have reached menopause and in many cases ceased sexual activity. When asked whether sexual intercourse affects how a woman ages, eighteen (62.1%) of the younger, and twenty-three (85.2%) of the older women stated that there definitely was a relationship. The younger women recognized this relationship as positive, but most of the older women were quite clear about the negative relationship. These are the same women who advocate ceasing sexual intercourse after children start to grow up and who talk about separate beds or separate rooms after menopause. Each category presents their arguments quite convincingly. One of the premenopausal women explained, "If you have a good relationship and feel needed and wanted, it will have a positive effect on aging." Another was more explicit, "If you have sexual intercourse regularly, you will remain fit. If you are strong enough for intercourse, you are strong enough for anything else." A third combined a number of positive aspects, "Satisfaction with life is what affects aging. Active, alert, eat nutritious foods, have a healthy outlook, and an active sex life is a form of exercise." But there are those who disagree. The "hot-natured look old faster," said one. "Sexual intercourse makes her older," stated another, adding that "children sure contribute to this." A third was convinced that "not having it" kept her young and healthy.

In the older category, much the same range of responses is present; but more of them saw a negative relationship. On the positive side was one older woman who recommended regular sexual intercourse "...she thinks she's still young; it stimulates the body; it's like nutrition for the body." Another felt that being wanted and loved was important to a woman and how she would age. In this regard, it was suggested that women who don't marry age faster than those who do. But the counter argument is equally strong. Said one "young" postmenopausal woman, "I left my husband's bed at age thirty-nine — that's why I'm so young." Others agreed for various reasons, "The amount of sex ages a woman;" "the married one is with the husband every night, it ages her;" "Sexual intercourse wears her out;" "The more sex the faster she ages;" "Being used will cause her to look old sooner;" and finally as regards herself and her age cohorts: "When she's menopausal, intercourse makes her body sag and messes her up."

Menarche

This discussion will deal first with a general overview of menarcheal studies and will then return to treat the data pertaining to the Indian South African women.

Sexual maturity. The status of sexual maturity is conferred on a woman almost universally when she experiences her first menstruation. Whether the menarche is marked by a ritual or some other public notice does not influence the fact that having a flow of blood (whether it occurs regularly every twenty-eight days as in modern societies or irregularly as in preindustrial societies) will result in certain acts and degrees of avoidance. Widely separated societies share the practice of setting women apart while they are menstruating. We shall subsequently return to this point from two different angles; menstrual taboos and practices, and the status and role of women in their reproductive years. Our emphasis here is on the reproductive years rather than on the biological fact of menstruating.

The attainment of physical maturity is marked in widely separated societies by either an individual or group initiation ritual; by some form of physical mutilation; or by some other status marker. That menstruation during the first few months or years may be anovulatory is not necessarily recognized by preindustrial societies. The possibility of pregnancy calls for certain behavioral and interpersonal changes between women and men. It also qualifies the pubescent woman for marriage, or at least for assuming the role of wife if a childhood marriage has been contracted. Being a wife elevates a woman to a status in contrast to that of nonwives; and being a mother frequently contrasts her with nonmothers. Achieving the status of wife and mother evidently raises the woman to the highest status attainable in many societies.

Menarche marks a particular culmination of hormonal and biological relationships during the process of female maturation. Henceforth, given certain physiological and metabolic requirements and the proper balance of hormones, a woman will regularly experience the different phases of the menstrual cycle as ovulation occurs and the uterus reacts to fertilization or nonfertilization. This reaction is also tied to conditions of health, nutrition, exercise, lactation and related but interacting factors.

On the sociocultural level, this marker of maturation is usually met in traditional societies with some ritual or ceremonial activity. It is useful to differentiate between menarche ceremonies, which have a biological basis and are always individual, and initiation ceremonies, which have a sociological-chronological basis and are at the group level. All societies have some recognition of menarche, but not all follow this with an initiation ritual. (In the case of males, puberty initiation is normally at the group rather than individual level.) Both menarche rituals and initiation rituals involve isolation;

and in many societies, this periodic isolation is carried over into a woman's adult life, frequently accompanied by such institutions as the menstrual lodge or women's house and associated taboos.

Through the years a large number of studies have been conducted on the topic of menarche. Many of these aimed at establishing the average age for menarche; others at establishing a trend in this average age, and still others at discovering factors which influence the age of menarche.

Reviewing data pertaining to Western Europe between 1830 and 1960, Tanner has suggested that the average age of menarche has been getting earlier by some four months per decade (1962:152). This would suggest that at the earliest date he uses, menarche occurred at seventeen years of age. Currently it is about thirteen. But this secular trend could obviously not have continued from the past, nor can it continue in the future. If we look at analyses of classical data, we must accept that the average age of menarche in Greece and Rome was between thirteen and fourteen. In the "eyes of the law all females were considered to be pubescent after completion of their twelfth year of life." (Amundsen and Diers 1969:131). Accepting these data creates a dilemma: how could women in Greece and Rome experience menarche at thirteen to fifteen years of age, Norwegian girls in 1840 experience it at seventeen, and their countrywomen, a century and a half later, experience menarche at thirteen years? What caused the rise in menarcheal age? Is there a universal secular trend? What factors are responsible for this decrease in the age of menarche?

Some of the early studies suggested that climate was a major influence. Mills points out that some of the early researchers saw a positive relationship between tropical conditions and early menarche. He maintains that, in fact, the tropics and the northern climes, such as Finland, Scotland, and Russia, have a later menarcheal age. Mills states that "in both animals and men growth and bodily development proceed most rapidly in regions of greatest climatic stimulation.... Sexual maturity in tropical countries comes fully two years later than in the most stimulating temperate regions" (1937:53). It is, however, not the mere temperature which is important but the ease or difficulty of heat loss from the body. Thus he concludes that "adequacy of diet cannot overcome the physical retardation that comes with difficulty of body heat loss" (1937:56). Wilson and Sutherland (1953) also use the tropics as criterion for menarcheal age in comparing girls from Nigeria, India, and Ceylon. Recognizing that climatic effects are perhaps not the most important,

Phyllis Eveleth (1966) nevertheless recognizes its potential as causing a delay in the onset of menses (see also Ellis 1950).

Most researchers have shied away from unicausal explanations. Thus Bojlen and Bentzon (1968) have given emphasis to dietary factors as mediating the effects of climate. Lee et al. (1963), Kennedy (1933), and Israel (1959) employ socioeconomic factors as mediating influences. Though Kennedy did not use the sophisticated terminology, the causal factors he discussed were quite clear. He explains: "In agricultural districts one finds the people live a more open life and are exposed to greater extremes of weather, the girls work harder and usually begin to help about the farm while still at school, diet is simpler and less stimulating, and hot baths are a scarcer luxury. All these influences can readily be understood to act in the direction of retardation" (1933:799).

Employing related criteria, designated as urban versus rural living conditions, Wilson and Sutherland (1950) compared two samples of Ceylonese girls and also a sample of southern England girls compared to a rural sample of Nigerians (used originally by Ellis). In both cases urban girls reached menarche at an earlier age. Using Indian data from Kerala and Madras, Madhaven (1965) also found earlier maturation among urban girls. Refining somewhat the socioeconomic measures, Foll compared climatic conditions and socioeconomic factors concluding that the latter are clearly more important in establishing age of menarche and that "nutrition is probably the most important of the many causes" (1961:304). A similar emphasis appears in Backman (1948) and Tanner (1966). While these writers have suggested diet to be a major factor in influencing the early onset of menarche, Kralj-Cercek is more specific in her findings that "girls who ate predominantly proteinous food had their menarche sooner than girls who ate mixed, whereas those who ate carbohydratic food menstruated last" (1956:399). Others who have touched on the interpretation include Burrell, Healy and Tanner (1961), and Leary 1969).

Altitude is a related factor that might be involved. This was mentioned by Tanner (1966). Zacharias and Wurtman discuss a study by Valsik and co-researchers which suggests that menarcheal age might be delayed by as much as three months for every hundred meters above sea level. "As the authors pointed out, the economic and nutritional conditions at high altitudes are poorer, and the caloric requirements for existence may be greater" (1969:869). Though not dealing specifically with menarche, researchers have found that factors such as high altitude hypoxia as well as malnutrition and caloric deficiencies may slow or prolong growth (Friscancho and Baker 1970:290). It is also known that among Bundi and Lumi girls menarche does not occur before age 18 (Malcolm 1970). Once again, this slow development measured both in body growth and maturation is due to protein deficiency among these New Guinea villagers (Malcolm 1976:70) and related factors of altitude.

Other partial explanations or causally related factors include the season of the year (Valsik 1965) and heredity. The latter implies genetic factors which may be within the same family such as mother-daughter (Kantero and Widholm 1971), or sibling (Maresh 1972) or even twins (Tanner 1962). Genetic factors may also imply patterning due to membership of the same breeding population or ethnic group (Weir et al. 1971). However, studies in this context such as a comparison of Nigerian and English girls (Ellis 1950), or Negro and Caucasian girls in the United States (Weir et al. 1971) may have been recognizing socioeconomic dietary factors. When the socioeconomic factors were held constant there was no appreciable difference in menarcheal age (Michelson 1944). Sohar and Rieber (1960), who compared Ashkenazi, Oriental, Sephardic and Yemenite settlers who had been both in Israel or abroad, also found no significant differences in age of maturation.

An interesting counterargument suggests that there "is a uniform, relatively early prototype for the menarcheal age which applies to the whole human race and which becomes delayed as the result of adverse external circumstances" (Fluhmann 1958:54). One of these sets of circumstances would be malnutrition, which slows down development and growth; another may be disease. Brown (1966:12) suggests that during the nineteenth century due to diseases such as tuberculosis and nutritional deficiencies, there may have been a delayed onset of menstruation. Other factors which affect menarche are diabetes before puberty (White 1960); body weight (Frisch and McArthur 1974); and strenuous exercise resulting in low weight for height ratio (Frisch et al. 1980).

We now turn to a discussion of menarche among Indian South Africans. In the case of both the pre- and the postmenopausal groups information will, of course, be based on recall. Damon et al. (1969: 173) state that their sample checked against longitudinal data for the mean age of actual and recalled menarche were within two months. It is common for people to remember critical events because they were usually recalled as relevant to other events or within a matrix of experiences.

Menarche. Without exception, the women who were interviewed in the current study of Indian South Africans could recall the details of their menarche. They could thus establish their ages at the time of this event. Table 25 lists the menarcheal age for the two categories. The average age of the premenopausal category was 13.31 years. These average ages compare well and are slightly lower than those given by Israel (1959) for a group of women in India and their mothers, for whom she established menarcheal ages of 13.42 and 13.59, respectively. In a study of Indian South African girls, Kark (1953) found a mean age at menarche of 13.56. She goes on to make an association we discussed earlier: "It thus appears that school-leaving is related to the occurrence of the menarche and that a number of Indian girls leave school at this time due to the attitude of the family, the community and the individual girl herself, that a girl, having approached the menarche is grown-up and ready for marriage and should therefore leave school and remain at home" (1953:32). In a subsequent analysis of these same data, Kark divided the sample, based on the occupation of the father, into five socio-economic classes. She found that when these girls were "considered in terms of social class there is a progressive trend toward later menarcheal age from class one to class five, the menarche occurring 5.3 months earlier in girls of the upper than in those of the lowest social class" (1956:87).

We would suggest that in most cases the same factors as those involved in social class differentiation are operative in intergenerational differences. Progressively, even as a (political) minority group

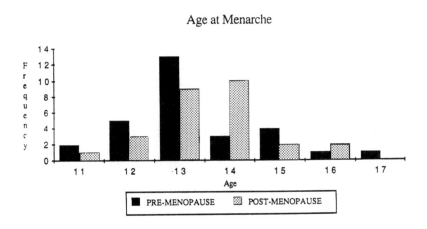

Age at Menarche

TABLE 25

Age at Menarche of Indian South African Women

	Premenopausal		Postmenopausal	
Age	Number	Percent	Number	Percent
11	2	6.9	1	3.7
12	5	17.2	3	11.1
13	13	44.8	9	33.3
14	3	10.3	10	37.0
15	4	13.8	2	7.4
16	1	3.4	2	7.4
17	1	3.4	–	–

in South Africa, living conditions for most Indians have improved. Measured in terms of hygiene, housing, and nutrition as well as health and clinical services, the younger women have it easier than did their mothers; and girls today have better living conditions than did their mothers. We were, unfortunately, dissuaded from doing a study of menarche among schoolgirls as we were told the men of the community would express strong opposition. The point is that Kark's social class differences in menarcheal age might be seen as suggestive of the intergenerational differences reported in this study. For a comparative study dealing with menarche among black South African schoolgirls, see du Toit (1987).

The experience. The first and most important point to be made is that Indian mothers did not, as a rule, prepare their daughters for this dramatic and potentially shocking experience. In numerous variations, we were told that women never spoke of babies, pregnancy, and similar matters in front of their daughters — babies "came from the mountains." Indian women had "respect;" they had "that shyness." What a girl did know at the time of her first flow she learned form older sisters or age mates who had themselves stumbled into the experience. A number of cases will clarify the dilemma of the menarcheal girl. One of the older women related, "We were playing outside when I saw blood. I came inside to tell mother. She called my brother's wife's sister, an adult, to explain what had happened. She said, 'Don't let a boy touch you or you'll die.' I had to use a flannel cloth and wash it regularly. At the end of the period I was to have a bath and wash my hair." One of her age cohorts was just 13 years old and playing with friends in the yard when she noticed blood. "I went to the toilet outhouse. I was shocked. I had a fright. In those days our parents didn't tell us anything. I went in and out, washing every time. In the middle of the night I woke my brother's wife and told her...I used rags, then washed them and hung them up to dry and then used them again." Yet a third older woman said that she was twelve and had had some warning from talking to friends. So when she had the first flow, she did not pray or touch the Koran. "Mother asked why but I did not answer and so she knew. I had to stay home all the time in my room and read *Kanya Bursa* (a book in Gujerati) which explained about menstruation. Friends advised me what to do. We did not have pads yet and used clean rags, pillow slips, or old sheets." But this reticence is not restricted to the older women. The mothers of younger women also did not prepare their daughters. One young woman said, "I was at home — very early in the morning — when it happened. I was not warned (did not know), but had a vague idea from talks at school. I walked to my elder sister, who explained what I should do, but nothing more. Even then, mother did not mention it. I had to read up for myself what it was all about. In standard nine and ten (i.e., ages sixteen and seventeen), I really was able to find out what it was all about." Another of the younger women had an "auntie in hospital with very heavy bleeding at menopause. I thought I had the same sickness as auntie. I didn't tell mother. We had that 'respect' — you know." One was at home. "I told mother something was wrong. She told me to go across the street to a lady her age. She told me to be careful, let nobody see it, be clean. She said, 'Be careful of boys. Don't let them touch you or you'll have a baby and your father will kill you.' Mother and I never talked about it. She was ashamed and had 'respect'."

Quite a number of women remarked on the shock they experienced when first noticing blood. One was chopping wood — "I thought I had ruptured myself internally...." Another was riding a bicycle and told her mother that she had hurt herself. One was at school. "My clothes were soiled. I was so self-conscious; I ran home. I didn't ever go back to school." Another said she "just didn't know what to think. I thought I was going to die — I was so scared — I knew nothing of it."

Most of the women could clearly remember their age at the time of menarche. In fact, they could pinpoint it by specific events associated with the first flow. Thus, women responded to questions about their age at the time in the following ways: "I was eleven, it was three months before my twelfth birthday;" "I was seventeen (my mother also menstruated late) but I had had rheumatic fever and had been waiting for it...."; "I was fifteen years and nine months. Mother was worried and had taken me for a checkup;" and from a premenopausal woman, "I was twelve years and seven months. Mother remarked on my early menstruation."

The event was accompanied in some cases with physical discomfort. Most the those who reported on it remember pain or cramps in the abdominal region, possibly uterine, as well as lower back pain. Some also had headache and most experienced added, initial stress due to uncertainty about what was happening to them. Some felt good — especially if they had some information, even if it was gleaned from schoolmates. One woman said, "I felt good; at last I also had something to talk about at school. Some friends had menstruated two or three years before."

Kin support. We have already remarked that Indian mothers did not as a rule discuss matters concerning biological aspects of maturation and reproduction with their own daughters. Many families resided in the extended family household, and there usually was a married sibling or sibling in-law or an extended-kin member available. The knowledge shared was limited, but the critical fact is that it was reassuring. It said to this scared little thirteen-year-old not to worry — that what she was experiencing was normal and women all had such experiences.

The person who was usually in the home and available was the mother, and this also is the most natural support person for a young girl. In fact seventeen (58.6%) of the pre- and sixteen (59.3%) of the postmenopausal women first turned to their mothers. The next most common was an elder female sibling or another close relative.

Irrespective of whom the young girl turned to, the response was fairly uniform, consisting of an explanation that what had just happened was normal for women; that it would recur henceforth every month; and that a woman would be ritually unclean. She should not go into the kitchen or eat from the same dishes as others did. She also should not participate in religious observances while she experienced flow. She was told to wash herself regularly and have a ritual bath and washing of her hair at the end of the period.

Women who menstruate are not allowed into the kitchen, they certainly may not help at pickling time, and, according to Gujerati-speakers, must avoid children who have chickenpox. "If a menstruating woman goes near a child with chickenpox she might give off an aura (reflection) to the child." A woman may also "feel dirty —

she becomes antisocial — maybe people smell it" (see du Toit and Suggs 1983). Menstruating women are not allowed to slaughter animals, "especially a chicken, which is normally done by a house-wife." Equally important, however, is the moral warning given every girl — not moral 'instruction' but clearly 'warning': "You are a young girl now, beware of men." To save her name, that of her family, and her chances at a good marriage, she should avoid close male contact and real or implied sexual relations. This injunction was given over and over again: "You're a young girl now. If men call you, don't go;" "If a boy just holds your hand you'll have a baby;" "You're big now, don't go with boys." One young girl experienced flow while her mother was out and told her sister. "She told me a whole tale of stories and said mother would beat me because I must have been out with a boy. Mother put my mind at ease...."

Fathers were not supposed to react and to behave as if they did not know. In some cases, they did not know; in others, their wives informed them. A mother may make excuses for a girl's not joining in prayers at the family gathering the first time but after that the father became aware. In most families "fathers never spoke to daugh-ters in those years." But one young woman thought her father knew. "He never said anything, but after this he always told me to wear shoes." It is different for the Tamils, as we will see, and a father congratulates his daughter on her new status.

Rituals of puberty. Indians who are Muslims are taught early in life that a girl must be modest in her behavior and dress. There is no puberty ritual that has religious or sacred overtones. When a girl reaches menarche, she comes under Koranic proscriptions and legally is ready for marriage. It is recorded that the Prophet stated: "'If the woman reaches the age of puberty, no part of her body should be seen, but this,' and he pointed to his face and his hands" (Badawi nd:6). Since a girl of this age is ready for marriage, the clothing requirements which apply to women at marriage also apply here. These are spelled out in the Koran in sura XXIV:31.

And tell the believing women to lower their gaze and be modest, and to display of their adornment only that which is apparent, and to draw their veils over their bosoms, and not to reveal their adornment save to their own husbands or fathers or husbands' fathers, or their sons or their husbands' sons, or their brothers or their brothers' sons or sisters' sons, or their women, or their salve, or male attendants who lack vigor, or children who know naught of women's nakedness. And let them not stamp their feet so as to reveal what they hide of their adornment. And turn unto Allah together, O believers, in order that ye may succeed.

Hindus, particularly those whose ancestors derive from South India, and this includes the Tamils, used to mark the menarche with a fertility ritual. This culminates her growth toward womanhood and, thus, the potential assumption of her roles as provider and procreator. Although the puberty ritual is dying out, certain parts of it remain. Of the twenty-six Hindu women in this study, seventeen (65.4%) had been secluded and undergone certain parts of the ritual. However, this total contained almost twice as many post-menopausal women representing an earlier generation and indicated a decline in this practice.

The following description of the puberty/fertility ritual is compiled from the various statements of their experiences. Only eight women, all Tamilians, had experienced the whole ritual.

When a young girl first notices the onset of menstruation, she is confined to her own room or to a special room for nine or ten days. She must sleep on the floor and keep herself clean. She is warned that a bad wind will catch her if she is dirty. Her mother takes her for a bath every morning, or at least for the first three days of her isolation. Following this, her father's sister may come to bathe her and if there are a number of these aunties, each will get a turn. Following the bath she is treated with Indian herbal preparations and must drink a soup of roast ground herbs and masala to give her strength; she must also eat plenty of roasted garlic. She may leave her room to go and bathe or to go to the toilet (this usually was outside). Kuper states that "should she have to go outside she carries a pen knife and/or syringa leaves for protection against harmful spirits" (1960:160). My informants spoke of "the syringa ritual," but none of them volunteered the information Kuper presents. The young girl may be allowed to wander about the house but may never enter the kitchen. "Even today," a Hindi-speaker in the younger age category stated, "I do not go into the kitchen when I have my period but allow my mother-in-law or some old lady to do the cooking."

During this time, the young girl may not use the family plates but will receive her own plate and cup. She will also be denied meat and subsists on vegetables and rice. However, she gets plenty of good food, including fruit, nuts, and sweets. The fried food is done in butter only, "That's why I'm so strong today," explained a sprightly older woman. Every morning during her isolation, the girl must swallow a raw egg from the halved shell; the shell is then immediately used to give her an equal amount of plant oil or sweet oil "to prevent backache." This egg-and-oil consumption follows the morning bath. During this time, the girl wears a half sari which covers the breasts and the loin only, because "you are half a woman."

Following her last day of isolation, a priest will be approached to set an auspicious day for the coming-out ritual. This may be up to three months after the time of isolation but usually is much closer. The priest uses a book and calculations, based on when the girl first noticed flow. Usually it will not be before nine in the morning or after four in the afternoon because there are bad cross-drafts at this time. The priest now sets the day and the time for what some women called the "fertility ritual" and others called the "syringa."

On the morning of this special day, the girl will once again bathe. She will now be dressed in a full sari and blouse, both of which will be white, and have flowers in her hair. Kinsmen and close friends have been invited by her mother and they bring gifts. The whole gathering is, according to statements, "like a little small wedding." No men are present, and although her mother's brother must pay for the ritual, even he is not permitted to attend.

In preparation for the girl's emergence, the women gather in the courtyard and prepare an amount of mealie meal and turmeric. With this dry mixture they trace a *rangoli* either in the form of a circle on the ground or, more commonly, a square with numerous detailed designs inside the square. The Tamils call this a "ritual flower" or *theta*. A small bench is placed in the middle of the circle or design and covered with a white cloth.

The girl now emerges, frequently to the accompaniment of music, from the house in her new sari and blouse. She is decorated with flowers and receives a beautiful garland. Her father's sister or her mother's brother's wife now leads her to the bench and allows her to sit down in the middle of the design to absorb strength and purity. The ritual lamp is lit, and frequently camphor and incense are burned during the entire ceremony, though it may be started slightly later in the ritual. The women have brought a number of small brass or copper containers of religious significance that are used in family rituals. These are filled, according to some, with castor oil, sweet oil, and coconut oil; according to others, with sunflower oil, turmeric powder, and *sundano* (sandalwood powder).

These containers are passed around the girl's head three times, and her head is then anointed with the oil as the women one by one rub the oil into her hair. Frequently at this stage incense is added to a burning coal contained in a clay bowl The turmeric and sandalwood powder are mixed with rose water and made into a paste. This paste is smeared on the girl's forehead, cheeks, hands, and feet. Depending on the number of women present, this might be done by three, five, or seven women, all of whom must be fertile, i.e., premenopausal and mothers.

Some women described a more detailed ritual at this stage. Three small brass bowls are prepared. The first contains a small amount of rice covered by three marie-biscuits (a plain, round, thin cookie). The second is filled with water and turmeric powder with a little lime, which causes it to turn red. The third contains camphor powder in water. Each woman who is participating takes the first bowl and passes it around the head of the seated girl, then traces it down the length of her body to her feet. The last woman then leaves it on the ground at the girl's feet. At the same time, and immediately following the previous action, the woman will hold a grinding stone and piece of cloth and once again circle the girl's head three times before they are traced down the body and placed on the ground in front of her. Each woman does this three times with each of the three containers. When it is her turn to handle the container of camphor powder and water, each woman may place one or more small coins in it.

At the conclusion of this stage, the contents of these bowls, including the small coins, are thrown into the river and bad luck is washed away. In modern town settings, the water faucet is allowed to run throughout the ceremony to remove bad omens.

Since the girl is now grown up, one of the women, frequently her mother, will place the *kungum* on her forehead. The girl is given jewelry which is put on her "like a bride," a woman pointed out. "The function is said to be 'like a wedding,' and some informants said it was her 'first wedding' because in the past she was given at this ceremony to her maternal uncle or his son" (Kuper 1960:160). The girl now gets up from the stool or bench where she has been seated throughout the preceding events, walks around the white circle or design three times, and then goes indoors to take off her sari and have a bath. "You must not wear that sari and blouse again but give it to somebody else — you must not wear it again." The girl must also prepare a *dano*, (a tray filled with dahl, rice, tamarind, and raw vegetables) and give it to a poor person. At this stage her mother informs her of her maturity. "Now you are a young woman."

It is obvious that this ritual contains all the elements of what Arnold van Gennep called *rites de passage*. We recognize here the isolation or separation, the seclusion or marge, and the glorious reincarnation, not of a girl but of a young woman. The description is replete with the ritual number three, symbolism of productivity (in the sense of provider and household manager) and fertility, acts of charity, and symbolic washing away of negative forces. The period of marge is used for instruction, and Kuper points out that even in

> ...homes where no ceremony is practised, there is still emphasis on special food, ritual ablutions, and specific avoidance. The girl is also given advice by her mother and other older female relatives on how to comport herself in the future; she must not go about alone but in the company of respectable women and girls; the only men with whom she may appear in public are her father and brothers; she must not talk loosely or behave indecorously; she must pay careful attention to her appearance and be strict in her personal hygiene (1960:160).

Premenstrual Syndrome

In years past physicians used to speak of premenstrual tension, but since the symptoms of this condition have been studied and form such a core, it has become customary to designate this a syndrome. However, there is no internationally accepted scheme for defining, classifying, and grading this condition (Abraham 1982:2). PMT or PMS as it is abbreviated may also be referred to as secondary dysmenorrhea to distinguish it from menstrual cramps or painful periods.

Abraham (1980:11) lists the most frequent symptoms. There are about 150, but some of these have specific cultural contexts or are very limited and specialized. The most common complaints are found cross-culturally but at different frequencies. They include nervous tension, irritability, fatigue, breast tenderness, abdominal bloating, depression, and crying. In some cases, the tension and associated actions have been recognized as beyond the woman's control. The syndrome turned up in court twice in 1982 in Britain, where a scullery girl had killed a barmaid and blamed it on PMS —

the judge was sympathetic and placed her on probation. In the second case, a woman who killed her lover was found guilty of manslaughter rather than murder because she suffered PMS (*Newsweek* November 8, 1982).

Among the women in our study sample, twenty-two (75.9%) of the pre- and fourteen (51.9%) of the postmenopausal category stated that they do or did suffer from PMS. The lower percentage among the older women may be due to selective amnesia — women not remembering the unpleasant. According to Mukherjee (1954:82), in a study of premenstrual tension in a sample of Indian women, headache was the most frequent symptom of which they complained. The women in our study had quite a wide range of symptoms and headache was not a primary complaint.

The most frequently mentioned symptoms were: irritability (17), stomach cramps or abdominal pains (15), lower back pain (12), tenseness (6), depression (4), water retention (4), headache (4), and breast tenderness (2). These symptoms usually manifest themselves about two weeks to ten days before flow. One young woman was quite clear on how she felt. "Two weeks before I get my period I feel tense, discomfort. I eat a lot, and I'd like to murder my husband." Another remarked on the fact that she felt as if she could "go off the deep end." Abraham (1982) discusses four major types of PMS and the association of feelings of violence or tendencies to suicide. Another young woman gave expression to the interrelationship of symptoms. "About ten days before I start menstruating I start having terrible stomach pains which make me get cross and irritable." The latter complaint, irritability, said a Muslim, is the reason "the Koran does not allow women a prominent position." A Hindu woman suffered from stomach and backache until she went to a priest. "He blessed me and I started using blessed water during my periods." Other complaints were more varied. Pain in the ovaries; womb sensitivity; pain in the thighs; pimples on the face; and limp hair are some of these complaints. Two women had discomforts which are not common. One said, "A couple of hours before flow, I get a deep cutting pain in my uterus;" another had what we would call postmenstrual tension since she suffered the worst pain for about three days after the period ended.

Two of the younger women stated that they had some symptoms into their early twenties but they seem to have outgrown them. Mrs. Gani, on the other hand did not feel sorry for herself. She explained that when she was at school "our P.E. teacher said, 'Half the world menstruates, get on with your sports!'"

Experience

There is, conceptually at least, a clear distinction between pre-menstrual syndrome (also referred to as secondary dysmenorrhea) and pain and cramps experienced during the menstrual period. When not due to obvious lesions of the female organs, these painful period are referred to as primary dysmenorrhea. To many of the women, they seem to be related.

The experience of menstruation has two major responses: one refers to physical discomfort; the second to relief.

There are two patterns of flow. In the first, a majority of women experienced flow in more or less the same intensity. These women seemed to have less pain and, therefore, had a more positive feeling about the experience. A second, smaller group of women experienced heavy flow for the first part of the menstrual period and then a slight decrease both in flow and in the pain and feeling of discomfort. They explained that bleeding was heavy for the first day or the first two days and was associated with backache. A number of women had felt so uncomfortable that they remained in bed for a few days. One said she has severe pain and heavy bleeding and would lie down for two days. There were five more days of her period. Another explained that her mother had given her an old Dutch remedy, *lewensessens* (see Appendix) to take when she had her period, and she still used it...she has been postmenopausal for a number of years!

Physical discomfort includes simply feeling dull, rundown, or worn out. "I hate it; at the beginning there is a lot of pain — that changes but I hate it!" was one young woman's evaluation. Another explained, "The first day I feel very sick with pain — just plain miserable."

In the second category are those who meet the arrival of the monthly flow with "relief." They state that they are relaxed, and feel renewed, lighter or cleansed. These emotions mark the onset of the menstrual period and women state they are not conscious of their period the rest of the time.

The menstrual patterns of the two age groups in our study sample show a great deal of uniformity. In regard to the length of flow, Table 26 reports the experience of the premenopausal women and recalls that of the postmenopausal group. We see that in both the mode is five days, and the mean is 5.2.

The same uniformity is present when we look at the monthly cycle. The figures given in Table 27 present figures for the premeno-

TABLE 26

Duration of Menstrual Flow of Indian South African Women

Duration in Number of Days	Premenopausal		Postmenopausal	
	Number	Percent	Number	Percent
1	2	7.7	–	–
3	1	3.8	3	12.0
4	4	15.4	3	12.0
5	11	42.3	12	48.0
6	3	11.5	1	4.0
7	3	11.5	5	20.0
8	1	3.8	1	4.0
9	1	3.8	–	–
N.R.	3	–	2	–

pausal women which might be suspect. The span of sixteen or twenty days between periods might reflect perimenopausal status, but these figures were given in the interview in spite of the request to report the "normal" number of days between menstrual periods. (It is also possible that respondents might have calculated the days between the end of flow and the start of the following flow.) The mode in both cases is twenty-eight and the mean for the younger category is 27.3 and 28.3 for the older age category.

More than half, seventeen (58.6%) of the premenopausal women, state that they have experienced painful menstruation; only ten (37.0%) of the older ones recalled such discomfort. A great part of this discomfort was associated with the experience of primary dysmenorrhea. Some women recalled painful periods during their teenage years, and others noticed changes which were more recent in origin. One young woman explained that if she drank a lot of fluids before her period, it was more uncomfortable and painful — possibly due to the characteristic oedema. Another woman remarked on painful periods but justified them saying, "I may have been barefoot in the rain." A third said she sometimes experienced painful menstrual periods "when I have a rash on the vagina." Some women noticed greater discomfort in menstruation since reaching age forty and could be perimenopausal. It will be recalled that menarcheal girls in the Hindu tradition are given raw egg and some form of oil during their ten days of isolation. One Tamilian woman said her first day was always very painful, but she then started eat-

TABLE 27

Monthly Cycle of Menstrual Periods of Indian South African Women

Duration in Number of Days	Premenopausal		Postmenopausal	
	Number	Percent	Number	Percent
16	1	3.4	–	–
20	1	3.4	–	–
21	1	3.4	–	–
25	–	–	1	4.5
26	1	3.4	1	4.5
27	1	3.4	2	9.1
28	20	69.0	9	40.9
29	–	–	5	22.7
30	3	10.3	3	13.6
31	1	3.4	1	4.5
N.R.	3	–	5	–

ing a raw egg and a tablespoon of sweet oil before her period started and she discovered relief.

Brief mention needs to be made here of a small number of women who complain of severe headache or a variety of abdominal or back pains at the end of the period. If PMS is a reaction to hormonal changes in bringing on the menstrual flow as has been suggested, then such postmenstrual tension could be the same kind of reaction as hormone balances change again.

Relatively few women had experienced irregular or in-between bleeding. Most women recalled the on-again-off-again experience associated with their teenage years shortly after menarche. Others have associated such irregularity with stress, e.g., examination pressure at college or other tension of a personal nature. One of the younger women recalled three occasions when irregularity manifested itself: when she discovered her husband was being unfaithful; when they went overseas; and when her husband died. Others referred to bleeding twice a month. It needs to be stated that in selecting women for our research sample, clear criteria were employed to select postmenopausal women who had not menstruated for twelve months, and premenopausal women who menstruated regularly. During the one-year course of this study, it is quite possible that some of the women in the second category could have become perimenopausal.

Unusually heavy bleeding frequently is associated with post-partum conditions or the approach of the menopause. Just slightly less than half the women in this study, respectively 44.8% and 44.4% of the two age categories, indicated that they have in the past experienced unusually heavy bleeding. Those who have experienced relief credit performance of a dilation and curettage or injection of Depo Provera (DMPA). Theron states that irregular bleeding is one of the possible side effects of the injection of this contraceptive. Mild bleeding is treated with an estrogen-dominant combined pill. "Should the bleeding not have stopped by the 10th day of treatment a repeat injection of DMPA is given "(1987:84).

Indian South African women have a fairly uniform reaction to the experience of menstruation: it is mostly negative. On the other hand, permanent cessation of the monthly flow marks the onset of old age. There was a range of additional physical complaints identified with menstruation. These include: colds or flu; "cold in the vagina or womb because the womb is open;" being anaemic and having a low resistance. In fact, seventeen (58.6%) of the pre- and seventeen (63.0%) of the postmenopausal women thought that a woman was more susceptible to illness while she was menstruating. One older woman explained that she is "susceptible to germs because the body's resistance is down due to blood loss." MacPhail and his co-workers comment on the presence of anaemia among 38% of a sample of women they studied. Although diet does affect this condition, the "important role played by the loss of iron via menstruation in the genesis of iron deficiency was clearly illustrated by the improvement in iron status that occurred after 45 years of age" (MacPhail et al. 1981:942; see also Theron 1983). Women during this period are "losing blood," are "weak," their bodies are "more vulnerable to common viruses" and they are subject to nervousness and migraine headaches. For further discussion of the menstrual experience and folk explanations regarding this event, see du Toit (1988).

There are, however, women who hold a positive view about menstruation. "It is healthy and gives resistance," said one. An older woman stated that since old blood is leaving and being replaced by fresh new blood it must be beneficial. Added another, "The body is renewed every month."

7

The Menopause

Introduction

As women progress in age through a life stage normally referred to as the climacteric, changes start to occur. There is a general decline in a woman's reproductive ability during her middle thirties. This is reflected in lower fertility and greater frequency of miscarriages (Schwartz 1982). During these years the pituitary gland continues to produce follicle-stimulating hormone (FSH) and luteinizing hormone (LH) and to deposit them in the bloodstream for transportation to the ovaries. However, the aging ovaries fail to respond. Follicles are no longer stimulated to mature and ovulation becomes erratic, finally ceasing. The slowdown of ovarian function also results in decreasing amounts of estrogen and progesterone and finally the near absence of progesterone. Small amounts of estrogen continue to be produced. The ovarian shutdown is relieved somewhat by the continued production of minute amounts of these hormones by the adrenal glands. Estrogen decreasing to almost nothing may contribute to the physical sensations referred to as "menopausal symptoms." Most women are perimenopausal between ages forty-five and fifty-five, experiencing the cessation of menstruation either as one final event, or more frequently, as a gradual or infrequent experience of flow. A woman is menopausal, or in our terminology, postmenopausal when she has not menstruated for twelve months.

In contrast to studies dealing with the onset of fertility, there have been relatively few studies which are not of a clinical nature that deal with the termination of fertility. Part of the reason is that life expectancy in traditional societies did not allow this status as a universal. Also, there is no ritual marking the end of the reproductive stage in the life cycle. Women did not advertise the fact that they had lost their status as potential mothers. Menopause brought losses and gains (see du Toit (1984)).

In the first chapter of this book, we reviewed contributions to the study of menopause and aging in general. The clear focus which emerged there was one which concentrated on aging rather than climacteric studies; clinical studies employing a biomedical model rather than field studies employing a socio-cultural model; case studies rather than a cross-cultural approach; and an involvement with Western societies rather than studies which scan the panorama of human adaptations and cultural expressions.

It is only recently that anthropologists have studied the menopausal experience in its social and cultural setting. Some notable examples are Dona Lee Davis's (1983) study of a Newfoundland fishing community; Yewoubdar Beyene's (1984) comparative study of Maya and Greek women; David Suggs's (1986) discussion of the climacteric among Tswana women; and Margaret Lock's (1986(b)) analysis of the experience of Japanese women. In these cases the researchers spent a period of full-time residence among the people being studied. They conducted studies of qualitative depth, with case studies, life histories, and also quantitative analysis. Emphasis here is on the attempt to understand the experiences of climacteric women rather than to conduct only survey research. Much of the latter is valuable and offers a quantitative perspective that is much needed, but it does lack the feeling and understanding that is provided by an ethnographic approach. In the kitchen or yard with women, the ethnographer observes the transfer of information and behavior toward seniority and also discovers what people discuss. This frequently represents the transfer of information.

Information Concerning Menopause

Knowing what we do about menarche among Indian South Africans and the fact that girls are hardly ever prepared for the event, what is the case with the menopause? Is there some form of socialization as preparation for the event? Is there some anticipation for a woman approaching her late forties? These two questions of anticipatory socialization and timeliness of the event are important in the overall experience of menopause.

If there is little socialization of an anticipatory nature to prepare women for the slowdown in production of ovarian hormones and finally the stopping of their menstrual periods, how do women learn about it? How do they react to this change which in their past indicated pathogenesis or pregnancy? The overwhelming majority said that when it happens women wonder about it, ask an acquaintance or kinswoman, or less frequently, consult a physician.

Acquisition of Knowledge

Younger women now discuss it openly and middle-aged women would not be reluctant to discuss it in the company of women who have had early menopause. A woman in her mid-thirties has, in most cases, completed the reproductive phase of her life. However, there is no standard preparation of women and little expectation. "I listened here and there — like the birds and the bees," said one middle-aged woman, "and when I realized I no longer menstruated, I figured it out." Sometimes close friends (age mates) or relatives might discuss the subject. They might talk about another woman experiencing hot flashes or related symptoms or compare notes. Some of the younger ones even joked about it, like warning somebody "don't get a change-of-life baby!" Younger women are also more likely to have visited the family planning clinic or the antenatal clinic. In these settings as well as through the community health program, women now receive information which helps to prepare them for the change. Quite a number indicated that they learned about it from books and magazines.

These changes, however, are recent. "In our time nobody knew" is a common response from the older women. It was a taboo subject in the traditional society and even the family wouldn't know about it. In those cases where women were informed, it came from friends or relatives and the three most frequently mentioned are sisters, brothers' wives and husbands' sisters. Such women were all of the same generation but might be a few years older or may simply have experienced menopause at a slightly younger age. If women were not specifically told, they learned from hearing others talk about it. The mother seldom talked about it, as one of the older women explained. "Mother never told me, but during Ramadan I noticed she wasn't fasting." Others were conscious that their mothers were experiencing very heavy bleeding which then either stopped or resulted in a visit to a physician. There may be little transfer of information between generations, but there is enough intragenerational knowledge to interpret events taking place.

Anticipatory Socialization

In a study dealing with menstrual taboos, Young and Bacdayan (1965) suggested that menstrual taboos and male solidarity are aspects of an overall structural characteristic which they call rigidity. "If social rigidity is defined as the relative lack of intercommunication among the parts of the system, then a group wherein men and women are sharply separated, as measured either by male solidarity or by menstrual taboos, is clearly rigid" (Young and Bacdayan 1965:230–31). Although the Indian South African society has a degree of male solidarity and some menstrual taboos, a much more important characteristic is the relative lack of intercommunication between parts of the racial system. This applies to gender categories as well as age categories. It is almost as if we were dealing with information restricted to women, and specifically to relative age categories within this gender.

We have seen that young girls are not prepared for the event of menarche. They are not prepared for what to expect on their wedding night and traumatic experiences are numerous. Once a young woman is pregnant, anticipation of an heir did allow for some sharing of information by the in-laws; but women who lived alone with their husbands did not know what to expect. Menopause was something that occurred unannounced, with the fear of an unwanted pregnancy or a visit to a physician as possibilities. There simply was no openness. A great deal of mystique surrounded changes in the stages of the life cycle. Misinformation was perpetuated because communication was always horizontal (with members of a woman's own relative age group), rather than vertical, to learn and to pass on information.

Anticipatory socialization would have permitted intercommunication not only within bit especially between different age groups. This would prepare a person for experiences still to come; it would also allow women in different generations to share the same stereotype (Johnson and Snow 1979); in general, it would facilitate the maturational and aging process.

Indian South Africans are now in a stage where rigidity is breaking down. Those taboos which restricted the movements of a woman during menstruation are disappearing, though a conservative woman still won't enter the kitchen. Restrictions of sexual intercourse during menstruation are still recognized, but some of the young women based the justification on "being messy" rather than a taboo. Increasingly, men are becoming more companionable with their wives and communication does occur. Now older women are also starting to talk to and with younger women and girls. All of this is part and parcel of secularization and the spread of education. "Thus we should expect social control in rigid societies to be tight, religion to be strong and orthodox, leadership authoritarian and restricted to a few, boundaries relatively impermeable...." (Young and Bacdayan 1965:231). As education increases and secularization spreads, orthodoxy is breaking down; authoritarianism disappearing; boundaries becoming more permeable; and overall rigidity decreasing.

Knowledge Sharing

Some women stated that they would be willing to discuss menopausal changes with younger women (51.7% of the younger and 33.3% of the older women indicated this willingness). There is a difference, however, between talking to younger women and talking in the company of younger women. A number of the latter have learned about menopause because they, being over thirty, were in the company of older women when information was shared. Many younger women admitted that they did not know anything about the change of life. As one expressed it, "...I've never heard it told." Some of the older women were traditional and reserved and some were more progressive. Among the former are women whose excuses for not divulging information might involve traditional conservatism ("It is a shame for us to talk to younger women on this subject") — the same reason that young girls arrived at menarche with no preparatory socialization. Excuses may also involve shifting the responsibility of transferring knowledge to the young women themselves. ("Young people are clever, they can read about it.") As another suggested, "they must learn for themselves. Get a book and have a better idea than we had. Now you can even get a book about having a baby." The more progressive women, though fewer, are best represented by one who explained, "In those days older women did not talk to young ones. Today they do. We were ignorant. I want to assure that my daughter and granddaughter know what to expect."

Most women expressed a willingness to discuss menopause within their age group and some were willing to talk about it with younger women; but only five (17.2%) of the younger women and one (3.7%) older woman said they would broach the subject in the company of men. This might occur if close friends are discussing their wives or symptoms they are experiencing or if the topic arose in some other way. Most of the women stated that to do so would not be proper in the Indian community or that there were personal and religious reasons for not dealing with this topic in mixed company. Quite a few, however, were convinced that men just wouldn't understand. About three out of every four women in both age categories, again slightly more in the younger category, would discuss menopause and their experiences with their husbands. These women felt that there was enough openness and confidentiality that this could and should occur. Those who would not are divided between women who state that this should not occur in the Indian community and those (mostly older) women who said, "No, he's too stupid." This term was used quite frequently to describe themselves and others. The implication in nearly every case was ignorance and the lack of a frame of reference. Stupidity merely meant that they would not understand and did not have basic knowledge to serve as a basis for integration of such information.

As might be expected, there is a near universal willingness to discuss menstrual changes and menopausal symptoms with a physician. But not any physician. Table 28 indicates the preferences of the pre- and postmenopausal women. Most favored was a white female doctor. Those who would choose a white doctor or a "white-black" combination far outnumber those who stated a preference for an Indian doctor. The reason for this is that whites are outside the social field of Indians, and any confidential information would, therefore, be safe. If an Indian doctor were consulted, it was explained that she should not be a close friend. Bear in mind that the Indian

Table 28

Ethnicity and Gender of Physicians Preferred
by Indian South African Women

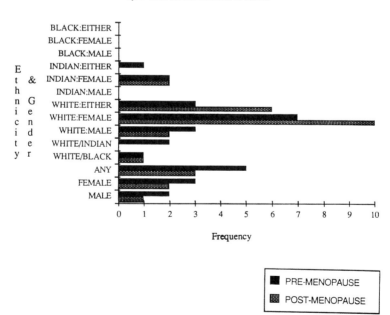

community is relatively small and geographically concentrated. Social networks, which are likely to transcend linguistic and religious boundaries, might overlap. Indian women are home-centered and quite private; and the Hippocratic oath not withstanding, they would not entrust confidentialities to someone who might divulge them.

Expectations Concerning Menopause

When entering upon a discussion of expectations, we are of course allowing for a plethora of explanations, some based on actual experiences, others on hearsay, and still others on psychosomatic causes. But there is a further implication here — that such explanations enter the personal culture of women. The result is that expectations based neither on empirical knowledge nor on actual experiences become the expectations of the next generation and so are perpetuated. In the absence of education, there emerges in time a wealth of old wives' tales. For the United States, Loudell Snow and her associates (Snow and Johnson 1977(a); 1977(b); and Snow, Johnson, and Mayhew 1978) have discussed those pertaining to menstruation and by extension the cessation of menstruation. Referring specifically to the menopause, de Senarclens points out: "It is a fact that the menopausal woman's image of her body is not only the result of her reflection in the mirror, or even her physical discomfort; it depends above all on how far she has managed to preserve a sense of wholeness. One sometimes shudders to think of all the women who have had hysterectomies just because they were in pain and who then have to face this additional castration alongside the normal biological deprivation of the age" (1979:80). Reflections in the mirror conjure up images created in the mind, and these images are based on accounts received and information imparted by others who may or may not have more factual knowledge. The result is that expectations will vary and will variously be adjusted as expectation turns to experience. This was succinctly stated by one of the older women who said, "They told me more than I experienced!"

General

One of the first and basic questions is whether all women experience menopause? There were, in fact, three (10.3%) of the pre- and one (3.7%) of the postmenopausal women who thought that sexual activity and childbearing ultimately resulted in menopause. The beliefs and superstitions were quite diverse.

The one postmenopausal woman who thought that not all women reached menopause stated, "Women who were never married and who never had sex and never had children, do not have menopause." The argument, if it were logical would then maintain that the fewer the number of children (or the lower the incidence of sexual activity), the later menopause. Others also believed this. "If a woman has no children, the menopause comes later. The more children the earlier the menopause." The reason for this is the belief that the uterus is exhausted by multiple births. Those who "get it very late are very strong."

Being "strong" applies both to the condition of the uterus and a woman's general health, factors also believed to influence how the perimenopause is experienced. For some, flow decreased gradually over time, becoming irregular and skipping months before disappearing completely; for others, flow "stopped only once." Is ease of menopause also associated with number of children? There are women who believe this. One of the older women explained, "Some have less and less every month; some have very heavy bleeding and then it stops. I stopped all at once because I didn't have many children; I think my womb was still strong." This is confirmed by another who said, "Unhealthy people have irregular stopping. I'm healthy and I had one time stop." The matter of health or the lack thereof in many cases returns to the concept of blood and pollution already discussed. It will be recalled that flow cleans out the body; and when menopause is reached, the old blood remains in the system. Well, the passing of the placenta and membranes with the blood has a purifying affect. "If you get a lot of children all pollution leaves the body with the afterbirth and you have an easy menopause" was one explanation. Another is that the body finally runs out of surplus blood. "Maybe there is not enough blood in your body when all has been cleaned and washed out...then comes menopause," explained an older woman.

We discussed the timeliness of an event and how if girls expect menarche, they can better cope when it occurs. The same is true about menopause. When participants in this study were asked when women normally experienced menopause, we received responses like "most are grandmothers" or "when a body can't bear children a woman has menopause." Pressed for a little more specificity in age, one young woman said, "Some at thirty-eight, others are fifty-five." This turned out to be almost exactly the range of answers. Table 29 presents the ages at which women are believed to or in fact did experience the onset of menopause. The first missing

TABLE 29

Age at Which Menopause Starts
According to Indian South African Women

	Premenopausal		Postmenopausal	
Age	Number	Percent	Number	Percent
Below 39	1	3.4	2	7.4
40–44	9	31.0	2	7.4
45–49	10	34.4	14	51.8
50–54	7	24.1	7	25.9
55 and above	2	6.8	2	7.4
Average Age	45.4		46.7	

of the menstrual period frequently raises the logical question of pregnancy; after all, that happened before. One of the older women explained, "I was forty-five when my periods stopped. I expected it on the fifteenth but it never came and I thought I was pregnant like my sisters. Nine months later they gave birth; I was still waiting. No sickness or problems.... "

Physiological Changes

This last statement suggests that some women might expect "sickness" or "problems." Once again, since we are dealing with expectations, these beliefs are based on information transfer; information, moreover, which has been influenced by verbal transmission. It is significant that although twelve (44.4%) of the older women had not discussed the menopause before they experienced it and for that reason did not expect anything specific, only five (17.2%) of the premenopausal women did not know what to expect.

Physiological changes they had been told to expect included, in order of frequency mentioned: hot flashes (associated in some cases with night sweating and/or cold shivers); weight gain; bloating of the stomach; headache; lack of sexual interest; dizzy spells; an energy drop; and constipation.

In terms of anticipation, a number of conditions emerged as to how they thought they'd feel and the reasons for this. A number of women pointed out that menopause coincided with aging. The symptoms they experienced were "simply due to the fact that as one ages you have less strength and energy." Those who had been active would remain active and vice versa; but at that age people do tire more easily. This is due to a loss of energy and a general decline in activity.

Grandmothers "think they must sit," or "because they are mothers-in-law they tend to retire." We have two role models: the first looks after her grandchildren and turns to religion; the second expects a daughter-in-law to do most of the work and cooking while she supervises. This was particularly true in the big house and extended family. Women who become noninvolved "don't have the same kind of thinking [as younger women] — they just think of themselves and their monotonous life."

A large number of women remarked on the loss of childbearing ability. It will be recalled that the Indian South African woman, at least those in the previous generation found their full expression as mothers. The loss of this potential is important and was expressed variously: "Some feel they're not all woman;" "Quite a few go into depression — feeling inadequate;" "Most women feel they now are a shell of a woman;" "Depressed, they feel themselves more or less like a man and they don't have the feelings of a real woman;" "I'll feel relieved, but yet I'm not a complete woman anymore."

Not every woman expects such negative feelings. Quite a number said they expected a sense of relief. There would no longer be the danger of pregnancy, and they would also be free of the monthly premenstrual tension and of the "bother" or "hassle" of periods. They also knew that this condition will allow them full participation in religious matters. A physician's wife went on hadj while we were in the field and received pills from her husband to prevent her from menstruating while in Mecca as this would have made her impure. (She complained that he would not supply the same for their teenage daughters who accompanied her.)

Emotional Changes

Here we have a fertile field for old wives' tales and superstitions based on rumor. People tend to remember selectively and to remember outstanding experiences rather than humdrum routine. The result is that frequently a dramatic event or a unique experience of an acquaintance might become the major part of what a woman expects. Estelle Fuchs (1978) wrote one chapter entitled; "You don't go crazy at menopause" in her study, *The Second Season*; Pauline Bart (1972) deals with depression in middle-aged women; others have used terms like "empty-nest syndrome" and "forty-year-old jitters;" and Pat Kaufert (1982) rebuts the myth created, in part, by the medical profession.

As we expected, Indian South African women have their own set of myths. We suggest that the number of myths about an event such as menopause is in direct relation to the degree of openness with which the subject is discussed. When the subject is not taboo, being discussed by women even in the company of men, the openness will result in correction of individual misconceptions. When the subject is discussed only in certain circles, be this among women only or among men only, there will be a degree of misconception and misinformation. When the subject is not discussed at all or only by age mates, one can expect the restricted exposure to result in misinformation and mythbuilding. In our study sample, twenty-two (75.9%) of the premenopausal women expected emotional changes to occur at menopause. Only seven (25.9%) of the postmenopausal women said they expected such changes, but we might be dealing with ex post facto reasoning, i.e., their perspective has been changed by hindsight. But at the time, more might have expected such changes.

The most frequently mentioned anticipated change involves womanhood and their roles of mother and wife. This was perhaps best expressed by one young woman who lamented the loss of the childbearing ability. She said, "You *can't* bear children, even if you don't want to." Here again is the loss of potential: the loss of an ability achieved and celebrated at menarche; confirmed by a proposal, and solemnized at her wedding. It found expression in the birth of her children — providing an heir and earning acceptance by the in-laws, and gaining the dedication, support, and sometimes love, of her husband. Others expressed this sense of loss in much the same way. Japanese women experience feelings of relief tempered with concern about aging and sadness at the loss of their sex appeal (Lock 1986(b):32).

When a woman "doesn't bleed anymore, she feels lost and uncertain." She feels she has "come to the end of the line — depression — end of life is close." "Some worry or expect emotional changes, they say: 'Where is the dirty blood going?'" Others become "moody because blood doesn't work." The loss of menstruation causes "the blood to go to her head, she becomes more hot-headed...." It also makes her "irritable, short tempered, (have) memory loss," and finally, "noises irritate her because there is less blood in the system" since she can't menstruate.

The simple fact of no longer menstruating is seen by some women as a major adjustment. "They think it's an abnormal thing happening to them — only during the transition — they don't accept it." More to the point, one woman explained, "You've had periods for so many decades you look forward to them and got into a routine." In a more philosophical mood, one woman suggested, "You'll get your off days, like getting your periods." But a woman soon gets used to the new routine. Having an understanding husband certainly uncomplicates matters for a woman who is experiencing these changes.

All these changes cause concern and worry because women realize they are getting old. Some worry about death, others are depressed at not being young any longer. Others worry about being sickly. With a twinkle in her eye, one woman said, "My elder sister says its a good excuse for being irritable."

Some of the women saw a correlation between the amount of knowledge and the degree of worry. On the one hand are those for whom ignorance is bliss. "If you know a lot, you worry because you know too much — I knew nothing and wasn't worried," explained on older woman. On the other hand are those who feel that "women don't know what is happening to them; they are uninformed and scared." It may also be a product of sensitivity. "If you are sensitive it will bother you; but if you accept it in your stride, it will not bother you."

Looking back on the change of life, women will be able to comment on how they experienced it. They will also be able to debunk some of the misconceptions and myths.

Experiencing the Menopause

During the climacteric years, hormonal balances are being altered and changes occur in the body. Clearest and most striking is the cessation of flow, but this is usually accompanied, during the perimenopause, by experiences which are frequently referred to as symptoms.

General

In their study of the climacteric among Indian women in Varanasi, Sharma and Saxena deal with symptoms but also with the sociopsychological context of menopause. They point out that menopause is a taboo subject for Indian women; because of this "it is somewhat mystical and surrounded by misinformation;" and because of their stoic attitudes, women "tend to ignore the menopause and its related problems to an even greater degree than other health issues" (1981:12). Their data was collected, as was the material for the current study, by means of personal interviews. Their research also involved first gaining the subject's confidence before delving into what might be considered the more private aspects of her life. "This was necessitated by the fact that most middle-aged women in India are ill-informed about the menopause and are too shy and hesitant to consult a general practitioner or a gynecologist" (Sharma and Saxena 1981:17). Unfortunately, Marcha Flint does not discuss menopausal symptoms other than bleeding abnormalities, but she concludes that "few women had any problems associated with menopause" (1974:125). Sharma and Saxena, however, have a comparative table listing the pre-, peri- and postmenopausal occurrence of certain symptoms, and they conclude that overall the perimenopausal women suffer most from these symptoms (1981:16). The association will be discussed below within the symptom context.

Amundsen and Diers (1973) have reviewed classical and medieval sources and conclude that menopause occurred at about age fifty. This figure has not changed much, and most studies today suggest an average age of fifty for the menopause with a range from about thirty-five to about sixty. Figures pertaining to India suggest a somewhat earlier menopause. Wyon et al. (1966:328) reported an average age of forty-four for Punjabi women. Marcha Flint (1974) compared Rajput women living at two different altitudes. Employing the recall method, those at middle altitude had an average menopausal age of 46.5. The age was 47.3 when she employed probit analysis to do the calculation. Our sample is too small to do probit analysis, but we did do two surveys, one concerning when women think menopause occurs and the second, employing recall, recording when each postmenopausal woman concluded her last period. The average age at which women thought menopause occurred was 46.7; the actual age when the twenty-seven postmenopausal women in the study experienced menopause averaged out to 47.3. This is based on figures presented in Table 30.

Physiological Changes Experienced

In an attempt to establish those symptoms which are associated with the menopausal experience, a list based on the original research of Neugarten and Kraines (1965) was presented to the Indian women. They were asked to confirm or deny having experienced these symptoms. Because some of the women in our younger age category might be perimenopausal and because symptoms might be associated with premenopausal women as well, this list was administered to all the women in the study.

TABLE 30

Expected and Actual Ages at Menopause of Indian South African Women

Relative Age Category	35	36	37	38	39	40	41	42	43	44	45	46	47	48	49	50	51	52	53	54	55	56
Expected:																						
Premenopausal				1		9					8			1	1	7					1	1
Postmenopausal	1			1		2					10			3	1	5		1	1		1	2
Actual Experience:																						
Postmenopausal	1			1		1	1				5	2	1	2	3	3	3	1	2			1

Mean Average:
  Expected:
    Premenopausal–45.4
    Postmenopausal–46.7
  Actual:
    Postmenopausal–47.3

Hot flashes. Sharma and Saxena divided their research sample into three groups: pre-, peri, and postmenopausal and found that approximately the same percentage of women in each group were currently experiencing hot flashes. This led them to conclude that this symptom is experienced by most women over a considerable time spread (1981:14). In their three analysis groups, they found that respectively 59%, 61%, and 61% were experiencing hot flashes.

In our study, five (17.2%) of the premenopausal women said they had experienced hot flashes and flushing accompanied by cold sweats; but in only two cases was this an ongoing condition. Of the older women, eight (29.6%) had experienced hot flashes, but in at least two cases these had ceased. Our research in this area was guided by Ann Voda's work. We included in each survey interview schedule a copy of her diagram (1981:82 and 1982) on which we recorded location and spread of hot flashes. Most of the women who experienced hot flashes had them in the facial area first; a second group felt the flush in the neck and between the breasts, from where it spread upwards and sometimes down. Two statements will suffice. "It starts in my face. I perspire all over, then suddenly I feel cold again. Then the rest of my head and ears are hot and then the rest of my body feels uncomfortable." Another stated, "It starts in my neck and above my breasts and spreads up into my face and forehead — only in front. Then down the front to my knees...." All but one of the women who experienced these vasomotor changes stated that they were uncomfortable; the majority were very uncomfortable. The women who reported hot flashes were equally divided between those who experienced them nearly every day, once of twice a week, and those who have not experienced them in the last two weeks. The latter were all postmenopausal women.

Ten of the women who reported experiencing hot flashes (and this includes both the premenopausal women) stated that they noticed changes in skin temperature during such perceived temperature change. One explained, "My skin gets hot from the inside — cheeks hot." Another stated more emphatically, "I could even feel my face and neck were hot." Others, however, were less certain of this. "I feel cool but I am wet and must dry myself with a towel," said one, and another "sweated but I didn't actually feel my skin" or "...but I could not feel the skin temperature change."

Flushing was experienced by exactly half of those who got hot flashes, i.e., one of the pre- and six of the postmenopausal women.

They remark on "red cheeks and forehead," or "feeling red" and "people remark on skin change." Another older woman complains that her skin "gets darker — can't put makeup on." Another said, "During the day I become flushed, I look like a tomato."

Hot flashes are also associated with cold sweats. Women explain that this often occurs at night when they wake up wet with perspiration, discarding blankets and opening windows only to close them an hour later and search for a cover. One woman related that she got uncomfortably hot followed by getting very cold. "I try to fan myself and then go put on a jersey," she said.

Table 31 lists those symptoms which were reported most frequently. Symptoms marked with an asterisk appear on the Sharma and Saxena (1981:16) list where perimenopausal women in their study predominated over pre- and postmenopausal women. Those symptoms include backache, numbness/tingling in hands and feet, dizziness, tiredness, headache, sleeplessness, and irritability. All of

TABLE 31

Percentage of Indian South African Women
Currently Reporting Menopausal Symptoms

Symptom/Complaint	Premenopausal		Postmenopausal	
	Number	Percent	Number	Percent
Somatic				
1. Hot flushes	5	17.2	8	29.6
2. Constipation	6	20.7	10	37.0
3. Backaches*	13	44.8	10	37.0
4. Numbness/tingling*	11	37.9	9	33.3
Psychosomatic				
5. Dizziness*	18	62.1	10	37.0
6. Feelings of tiredness*	22	75.9	17	63.0
7. Headaches*	19	65.5	13	48.1
8. Palpitations*	11	37.9	6	22.2
Psychological				
9. Sleeplessness*	11	37.9	12	44.4
10. Nervous tension	16	55.2	13	48.1
11. Difficulty concentrating	14	48.3	15	55.6
12. Feeling blue/depressed	20	69.0	16	59.3
13. Irritable*	22	75.9	17	63.0
14. Forgetfulness	20	69.0	20	74.1

them are also among the symptoms most frequently mentioned by the women in our study. That figures for pre- and postmenopausal women rate certain symptoms highly would confirm that they are indeed climacteric symptoms. It is interesting that the premeno- pausal women reported a higher experience incidence in all the psychosomatic symptoms, while somatic and psychological symp- toms were mixed. One further physical symptom, vaginal atrophy, was reported by only one premenopausal and four (14.8%) of the postmenopausal women. Most state that they did not notice any change but one old woman said there "certainly is no increase in sensitivity;" another complained that the "vaginal area becomes dry and less feeling for sex."

Discussing changes and symptoms which they recognized during the menopause added some experiential data to the simple listing of symptoms. Without listing specific symptoms, one of the older women said, "At age forty a woman feels old age is creeping up — menopause simply confirms it." Others complained of loss of appetite, weight gain with decreasing breast size, and the loss of sexual feelings. "I don't feel like having sex — just don't have the energy — all due to increase in blood supply." Others also blamed the heavy feeling on "too much blood inside." One older woman explained: "At menopause you lose energy and slow down. Dirty blood is running in your body. When you have your babies you get cleaned out but later the dirty blood slows you down. You're not so smart either."

Quite a number of older women, however, had positive com- ments. Most were glad to be "free of the botheration (sic)" of periods month after month. Some are healthy and strong and very active, but most women are *"kaput."* One woman was very proud. "I can carry big pots and pans and do any work even gardening. Young girls can't do this."

In reviewing some of the cross-cultural studies reporting on climacteric symptoms, Margaret Lock points at results that seem contradictory. In a number of cases there is a near absence or absence of somatic symptoms e.g., the Rajput (Flint 1974); the Maya (Beyene 1984); North Africans residing in Israel (Walfish et al. 1984); and the Japanese (Lock 1986(b)). In other cases, especially those pertaining to North America and Europe but also Zimbabwe and India, much higher somatic symptoms are reported. The latter ref- erence is to the study of Sharma and Saxena (1981), whose record- ing of symptoms are certainly higher than those we report. Lock concludes: "It remains to be seen whether these findings represent real differences or if they are simply an artifact of research design and administration. My belief if that there are some genuine differences, probably both biological and socio-cultural, but also that some of the reported variation is indeed due to poor research methods" (1986(a):3). We concur with Lock on this last point. It might be useful for researchers to confer and to compare not only their results, but more important, their tools and research methods.

Emotional Changes Experienced

Becking and Vida (1979:214–16) discuss factors which contribute to the psychological and emotional condition of the menopausal woman. They include loss of predictability and assurances which marked her earlier years; children leaving home (analogous to Bart's (1971) discussion of the empty-nest syndrome); loss of energy, which places a limit on what a woman can do; and changes in her relationship to her partner. They ask whether the menopause causes changes in this relationship or whether these changes already existed at the time menopause was reached. "If the change is accompanied by feelings of doubt, uncertainty, loss of identity, and decrease in libido, then it certainly will have an effect on the relationship" (1979: 216, du Toit translation).

Hot flashes and flushes are emotionally upsetting, women state. One explained, "You think you are going to die." This is particularly true when they occur at night when it is dark and when a woman is alone and uncomfortable. Asked whether hot flashes upset them emotionally, all eight of the postmenopausal women stated affirmatively — most of them were very upset. For some there was the fear of blood pressure, from the common belief that blood which does not leave the body by flow, remains inside. All of these things also affect mood, especially during the change of life. When asked about their general disposition and mood in the morning and again in the evening, the older women — those no longer perimenopausal — had a more positive feeling. Of them, 74.1% felt good and positive at the end of the day in contrast to only 34.5% of the younger pre- and perimenopausal women.

In Table 31 we noticed that feelings of depression, irritability and forgetfulness are among the most frequently experienced symptoms of these Indian South African women. However, it is essential that we recognize that symptoms do not originate *de novo*, nor do they exist independent of each other. That a woman feels more run down or experiences lapses in concentration or memory causes concern and irritability or depression. Some women state that they had anticipated more than they experienced. "Some said I'd become very sick, others said you'll die if flow doesn't come . . . nothing happened." Or again, "I expected attitude and personality changes . . . nothing happened."

It is important, though, to recognize that the uneducated Indian women are most affected by the termination of their womanly roles as childbearer and sexual partner. This is why many feel that old age is upon them, that they have experienced a loss, that they are not fully women any longer. This is not so for the younger women who see their careers as a future, something to tide them over the change of life when it comes. To paraphrase Becker (1963), Indian South African women created menopausal depression among themselves by not seeing to it that women in their forties had more than a domestic role as justification for their lives. They created this depression because they are subjects of a system that lacks anticipatory socialization. As the rigidity of the society is replaced by openness and information flow within and across age categories, uncertainty and fear will end. Along with this generally negative view, there is an acceptance of the inevitable.

Menopause usually comes after women have passed the reproductive and sexually active stage. Menopause gives them justification to sleep in separate beds or rooms.

Cognition

This discussion pertains to ways in which women view menopause. One would expect that the better informed women are, the greater will be the uniformity of their responses. It could be hypothesized that in societies where there is a clear rigidity and where women lack anticipatory socialization, there would be a greater fear or negative attitude among younger women concerning menopause. As education and anticipatory socialization increase, and consequently, as rigidity decreases, there would be a more neutral view of the menopause.

General

In 1963 Bernice Neugarten and her associates published the results of a study in which they utilized an index of attitudes toward the menopause. They found that younger American women held a generally "negative and more undifferentiated attitude" when compared to older American women (1963:150). In an attempt to update these findings and to develop a tool to be used in our cross-cultural research project, we administered an expanded and revised version of the Neugarten index, part of which had also been used in other climacteric research (see Chapter I). This adapted attitude index was administered to two samples of women ranging in age from their early twenties to their mid-seventies. We concluded: "The results reported here indicate that women's attitudes toward the menopause have not changed significantly in the last twenty years. However, while the results of Neugarten et al. (1963) are not challenged by this research, their interpretation is questioned. Younger women are found to hold a neutral view of the menopause, while older women see it as an occurrence which is life-enhancing. It is suggested that

TABLE 32

Nonvarying Responses to Questions Concerning Menopause

Statement	Premenopausal		Postmenopausal	
	% Agree	% Disagree	% Agree	% Disagree
1. There are some good things about menopause.	93	7	100	0
2. Postmenopausal women can participate more fully in society than premenopausal women.	97	3	100	0
3. Thinking about menopause does not bother me at all.	83	17	100	0
4. I have never worried about menopause.	90	10	100	0
5. Since menopause is inevitable there is no point worrying about it.	97	3	100	0
6. Thinking about menopause disturbs me.	10	90	7	93
7. The only difference between a woman who has not been through the menopause and one who has, is that one menstruates and the other doesn't.	93	7	100	0
8. Menopause may not be a bad experience.	100	0	96	4

this is probably an age-yielding response to cognitive dissonance" (Suggs and du Toit 1983:49).

Attitude Index

For the present study, we used essentially the same forty-item schedule, constructed in typical Likert scale format in which the four possible responses range from "strongly agree" to "strongly disagree." For obvious reasons of maximum comparability, we did not include a "don't know" category. Items were scrambled and no logical sequence was present in the order of questions.

Eight of the questions presented in Table 32 resulted in responses showing little if any variation. This suggests a generally positive attitude toward menopause. The seven postmenopausal women who agreed with item six and the four who disagreed with item eight might have experienced some problems which influenced their decision. In all the other cases, the postmenopausal women responded unanimously. It is important to keep in mind that by the time menopause occurs, Indian women have long passed their reproductive years and are most likely grandmothers. They have already assumed elder status and started their roles as adviser and household administrators. These are the positive elements indirectly associated with menopause, but they are actually associated with completing the reproductive phase of life and of assuming the status of elder. These changes are not brought on by menopause. Thus, negative aspects are also not brought on by menopause but by old age, and menopause is only one step towards it and one more reminder that it is imminent. It is interesting that both categories of women responded somewhat similarly to these eight items.

In contrast to the former items and responses, Table 33 represents those items for which there is the greatest range of difference between the two subsamples. In none of these items is there a range of difference below twenty. Those which are furthest apart are: item four and item five which are identical. The younger women are not pleased by the thought of menopause, nor do they think that postmenopausal women are happier than they are. The first six items all allow a retrospective view of menopause. Since it has already happened, a woman can state that she looked forward to it; that women who have gone through menopause are lucky; that it may be the best thing that ever happened to them; that there is pleasure and happiness in the experience; and that knowing what they now know versus the perimenopausal experiences of heavy bleeding and related problems, they really wish it had come earlier

TABLE 33

Questions in Which There Is the Greatest Range of Difference
Between the Two Subsamples

Statement	Premenopausal		Postmenopausal	
	% Agree	% Disagree	% Agree	% Disagree
1. I look forward to experiencing menopause.	52	48	74	26
2. Women who have gone through menopause are lucky.	55	45	93	4
3. Many women think menopause is the best thing that ever happened to them.	55	45	89	11
4. The thought of going through menopause pleases me.	41	59	82	18
5. Postmenopausal women are happier than premenopausal women.	41	59	82	18
6. I wish menopause came earlier in life than it does.	17	83	44	56
7. Menopause results in emotional strains in women.	76	24	33	67

in life. It will be recalled that most women commented on menstruation as a bother. Postmenopausal experiences are liberating and allow greater freedom as well as religious and ritual involvement. Having gone through menopause, the older women look back with the knowledge that they do not have more emotional strains than their younger cohorts. The seven questions clearly underline the importance and absence of anticipatory socialization. They contrast expectation with experience, superstition with knowledge.

Almost in contrast to the previous table are the eight items listed in Table 34, where no more than seven points distinguish the responses of pre- and postmenopausal women. A number of these responses can be grouped together; others should be discussed separately. Most women disagree with the first item, but the fact that percentages are not higher represents the degree of acculturation and secularization that has already taken place. Indian brides

TABLE 34

Questions in Which the Response Variation is
Essentially Identical for Both Subsamples

	Premenopausal		Postmenopausal	
Statement	% Agree	% Disagree	% Agree	% Disagree
1. Postmenopausal women are more likely to experience divorce than premenopausal women.	21	79	15	85
2. Menopause is just a part of growing older.	93	7	93	7
3. The thing that causes women all their trouble at menopause is something they can't control — changes inside their bodies.	90	10	85	15
4. Postmenopausal women are to be pitied.	21	79	22	78
5. A woman's body may change during menopause, but otherwise she doesn't change much.	90	10	93	7
6. The thought of going through menopause disgusts me.	14	86	15	85
7. Menopause creates new freedoms for women.	90	10	96	4
8. A woman who doesn't have to go through menopause is lucky.	45	55	52	48

were usually much younger than their husbands, and the chances that a postmenopausal woman would be widowed is, therefore, likely. This removes divorce as an alternative. It is also important that both the Hindu religion and Islam frown on divorce. It is easier for a man to divorce his wife, but a woman needs proven grounds of cruelty to prevail. Marriage guarantees some financial security and chances of remarriage after the age of reproduction has passed are extremely low. Thus, divorce is unthinkable unless initiated by the man. Items four and six are both negative responses; postmenopausal women are not pitied, nor is it disgusting to think of going through menopause — after all, it is only natural. We find items two, three, and five grouped together. Pre- and postmenopausal women agree that menopause is only a part of growing older which a woman can't control. It is only the body that changes, and in other ways she doesn't change much. One of the highest scores of agreement is on item seven: that the postmenopausal woman is relieved of many restrictions and taboos. She is free at all times to go about the house and kitchen; she has passed the limitations placed on her during menstruation such as lighting the Hindu lamp, handling the Koran, praying, and so forth; and she is free to assist in the temple or to lay out and dress a corpse in preparation for funerary rites. These changes are liberating and add to the activities of the older woman, who may also be a grandmother. We have, then, the coalescence of these three statuses: grandmother, old woman, and post-menopause, each with its own potentiating and empowering ability. In the end it is not clear which is most important.

For item eight, we find almost exactly the same neutral response by the two cohort groups. The normal response was:

TABLE 35

Other Statements Included in the Attitude Index

	Premenopausal		Postmenopausal	
Statement	% Agree	% Disagree	% Agree	% Disagree
1. The thought of going through menopause excites me.	31	69	48	52
2. If I could, I would choose not to go through menopause.	48	52	30	70
3. Postmenopausal women are healthier than premenopausal women.	41	59	67	33
4. In truth, just about every woman is depressed about the change in life.	38	62	30	70
5. Women worry about losing their minds during the menopause.	31	69	44	56

TABLE 35 *Continued*

Other Statements Included in the Attitude Index

	Premenopausal		Postmenopausal	
Statement	% Agree	% Disagree	% Agree	% Disagree
6. A postmenopausal woman is only half a woman.	21	79	30	70
7. The thought of going through menopause intrigues me.	31	69	52	48
8. Life is more interesting for a woman after the menopause.	62	38	82	18
9. After menopause women are less attractive.	24	76	37	63
10. A woman at menopause is apt to do crazy things she herself does not understand.	41	59	33	67
11. Postmenopausal women are less emotional than premenopausal women.	52	48	59	41
12. If the truth were really known, most women would like to have themselves a fling at this time in their lives.	31	69	41	59
13. The thought of going through menopause frightens me.	21	79	11	89
14. Reaching menopause marks the beginning of the end of life.	79	21	52	48
15. Menopause marks the end of life.	21	79	37	63
16. A woman gets more confidence in herself after the change of life.	76	24	89	11
17. Women generally feel better after the menopause than they have for years.	62	38	82	18

"Lucky. Why? that's something nobody can escape;" or "Everybody must have it, it's natural!"

Table 35 lists the rest of the items on the attitude index. In general, the responses confirm what we have already seen. Indian South African women did not find the thought of the menopause exciting or intriguing but on the other hand they didn't find it depressing or frightening either. The superstition that women during the menopause are somehow emotionally or intellectually affected was also debunked because these women did not think menopausal women lose their minds or do crazy things. However, the younger women were much less convinced than the older women that postmenopausal women are less emotional than premenopausal women.

Neither category felt that after menopause a woman is only half a woman or that menopause marks the end of life, but most premenopausal women did think that reaching menopause marked the beginning of the end of life. A majority of these younger women also thought that postmenopausal women were not healthier than the younger women.

Asking whether women approaching menopause would like "a fling" produced a number of chuckles and some off-the-record remarks. However, more younger than older women said that women would not enjoy a fling and the consensus was expressed by an older woman who said, "Not in the Indian community. Women are so much in a groove, they never think of having a fling."

Behavioral

Aspects of behavior include action and reaction. Because people never live in isolation, they are continuously involved in behavior; some of this being derived from who they are, some from how they are treated. Who a person is involves status and role. Young women can, then, be expected to behave differently from women who consider themselves or are considered to be old.

Within the ritual context, postmenopausal women are considered neutral and may participate fully in religious ceremony. A Hindu temple is said to post a sign that "women are not allowed during certain days of the month." Once the menses has permanently been disrupted, older women are free to enter. They may serve as volunteers to help in the temple and may participate in prayer meetings and social work. They may go to the altar during functions; bring offerings to the altar; clean and light the lamps;

open doors, etc. The Muslim woman may participate fully in the hadj; may pray continuously; may touch the Koran; and may fast for all four weeks of Ramadan. The ritually neutral woman is no threat to ceremonial purity and her interaction with younger women and men in general will, therefore, change.

General

Harmonious interpersonal relationships are of primary importance for matters of health but also for everyday living. Kupal (1960: 255) points out that the "disturbance of harmony: nonfulfillment of a vow, the breach of a taboo, the neglect of family obligations, conflict between kinsmen" have long range implications for health, but they first of all may sour interpersonal relations.

Since Indian South African women are primarily domestic, it is with relationships within the home that we must first deal. In cases of the big house and extended family, domestic relations include sons and daughters-in-law. In all cases (with the exception of widows), the first relationship is with the husband.

Women state that nature has taken its course and they no longer fear pregnancy. For some this leads to greater freedom and being more relaxed in connubial relationships. Many others point out that they withdraw from sexual relations, that they don't like being touched, or that Hindus sleep separately.

Whether the relationship becomes freer or more restrained, it does involve a change; and the husband is conscious of it. When women were asked how helpful their husbands would be or had been during the transitional stage of menopause, fourteen (48.3%) of the younger women thought their husbands would be very understanding and supportive. This may reflect on the younger, better educated generation or on the ideal and hope of these women. In the older category, only nine (33.3%) found their husbands to be so supportive; seven (25.9%) said their husbands had been no support to them — either they had not even noticed or had reacted negatively. "My husband doesn't like it because I'm not quite a woman anymore and my (sexual) feelings for him die," explained one older woman. Another pointed out that men don't like it when their wives reach menopause and "many start going out and running around with young girls." It is, of course, entirely possible — indeed likely — that the women saw themselves and were seen as old and that the presence or absence of menstruation was not an issue. More common was a reaction which reflects the lack of openness between the sexes and that among the older generation there was relatively little discussion of matters of this nature — even between wife and husband. With a smile one woman stated, "My husband didn't even notice." The mother of a large family chuckled, "He must have seen that the babies stopped coming; but we never discussed it."

Social Interaction

Menopause is never discussed with men, hardly ever with younger women, and seldom even with women of the same age. For this reason we can assume that people not intimately connected with a postmenopausal woman would be oblivious to her menopausal status. Changes in behavior are more likely to constitute a response to her status as grandmother or old woman. Some women felt that the postmenopausal woman's relations with younger women may be tinged with some jealousy, but on the whole, her behavior is more respectable, reserved, and proper.

Women may discuss the erratic or seemingly strange behavior of a friend and blame it on menopausal changes. This is always among women at the same stage of life. However, when a friend's behavior is unpredictable or if a friend is especially sensitive and irritable, the first thing that comes to mind is that she has problems at home or that she is emotionally upset — menopause is hardly ever mentioned as an explanation. Conflict with family members is the most usual occurrence disturbing the tranquility of middle age. Friends are not likely to be agents who support a woman going through menopause. Only seven (24.1%) of the younger and five (18.5%) of the older women indicated that friends would be very supportive and had helped them in the change.

Treatment

When asked whether postmenopausal women are treated differently by people in the family or in the community, the normal response was that nobody really knew the menstrual status of another. Thus, behavioral aspects were not predicated on menopausal status but on other factors.

Because a woman whose periods stopped was usually an older woman, frequently a grandmother, she was treated with the respect due one regarded as an elder. She would act as an elder, giving advice, speaking from experience, guiding, and generally presenting perspective. At a funeral, she will take the leadership role, preparing the corpse for embalming and funerary rituals. They would be out of place in the company of young women.

Children tend to take advantage of grandmother. She has more patience and is more tolerant than their own mothers. She is loving but tends to spoil her grandchildren. She behaves with tenderness and speaks in a soft voice, so children see how far they can go before her patience is exhausted.

Estelle Fuchs discusses the older woman in Jamaican and Greek society. Her conclusion to a great extent summarizes the position among Indian South African women. She explains: "They fear menopause, often denying it to themselves and their husbands. For many the end of menstruation means becoming old and dependent on sons and daughters. The discrepancy in age with their husbands, who are so often older, means that widowhood is not far off. Their lives, invested in children, their femininity tied in with traditional roles, seem to come to an end. It is at this time that many, like the Jamaican women, devote their energies now to the church, removing themselves from active participation in the world around them" (1978:171).

8

ello

Conclusion

This research project addressed in design the need, outlined by Greene and Cooke in 1980, to study a younger group of women simultaneously with an older group, permitting a comparison of pre- and postmenopausal experiences. We have shown how expectation and experience compare. We have shown, too, how women who are a generation apart differ in their perspective and in their encounter with life-changing events. I use the word *encounter* in this context because of the unfamiliarity and unexpected element in these experiences. Essentially, we have incorporated the life-cycle approach into the social structure of Indian women forming part of the South African population. The bare facts describe women of Indian extraction who are pre- or postmenopausal and who reside in Transvaal, South Africa. However, each is also a homemaker, wife, mother, grandmother, teacher, etc. Meyer Fortes has pointed out:

> What I am suggesting is that recognition and consideration of chronological age as opposed to maturation and generation depend on the differentiation between the politicojural and the domestic domains of social life. Strip the individual of kinship status — that is, let the identity of the person's parent or child or spouse or sibling be irrelevant to the granting of citizenship, with all its economic and other concomitants — and what remains to serve as a criterion for social classification other than sex, local association, and chronological age? (1984:115).

These latter criteria are the very ones which guided our selection of research subjects. These are the criteria contrasting our two cohort groups.

Age could have been a basis for selection. The advantage of age, especially when it is the basis of age sets which keep age-mates together, is that groups can be contrasted with each other relative to expected roles. However, age is relative and difficult to use as a marker. In societies not based on an age-set system, there still is a relative age stratification which contrasts role and achieved status of one group with another. These age cohorts might be premarital, postmarital, postreproductive, and so forth.

The reason for contrasting cohorts is that they constitute two stages of the life cycle. There are problems in reconstructing cohorts' experiences because of changed conditions: do women who are presently premenopausal see the change of life the same way as those who are a generation older? Riley et al. (1972:29–90, 583–618) raise some questions in this regard. Foner (1984:205) points out that there has not been any systematic analysis of the anthropological literature to generate theories concerning cohort differences, either due to or resulting in social change. The present study recognizes changes due in part to time but especially to social change in the Indian community.

Among the different criteria that can be employed to contrast cohorts, we have selected menopause. This status is not advertised but implied. When a woman refrains from certain activities or engages in others, it is assumed that she is postmenopausal, i.e., not polluted by the monthly flow. It is this assumption by others which contrasts her with other women in the eyes of community members. What we contrasted were women at different stages in the climacteric process — women who represented a point where certain roles have been assumed and others discontinued. The way in which each cohort dealt with such transitions simultaneously reflected social, religious, or economic conditions and influenced those conditions for the next cohort. This is particularly true when the community under analysis forms an ethnic enclave in a wider society.

A major characteristic of these women was that although menopause was seen as a procreative marker, it was so only in theory. Women had completed their reproductive careers years before biological change and had overtly recognized this by altering their sleeping arrangements. Those in the younger cohort might have been less emphatic than the older women, but it was a status change recognized by almost every woman. The reason for generational differences in this context relates to differences in attitudes about sex. For the older cohort, sexual intercourse was essentially instrumental in reproduction; for the younger women, there was a recognition of their own sexuality and a reciprocity in the experience.

The second major difference observed in this study was the way the younger cohorts viewed the menopause and aging in general. For the older category, the role of old woman is accompanied by mature children, grandchildren to spoil, and preparation for death. Age fifty to sixty was seen as old, and women became sedentary. Among the younger cohort, age is relative. Better education and jobs outside the home have expanded their vision and given them a new perspective on women's status, opportunities, and roles. According to them, women who have completed their reproductive years are not old, nor are they through with living. While they would not go so far as to endorse the statement that "life begins at fifty," they would claim that "life continues beyond fifty."

Two of the major characteristics of the female life cycle among Indian South African women relate to the absence of anticipatory socialization and its relationship to the rigidity of the society. Without preparation or education, each generation successively "discovers" menarche and, less sharply, menopause — only then to be informed that this is a natural occurrence. The breakdown of rigidity should lead to better information, greater openness, and a decrease in the vagueness of information. More open communication should result in the correction of myths about menopause. This is evident from various studies of literacy as well as the findings of Kaufert and Snow specifically regarding the climacteric. In regard to medical myths which are somewhat set apart because of their frame of reference, Lock and Martin have demonstrated greater tenacity.

An interesting theme emerging quite early is that of the Indian girl and woman as lonely, somewhat ignored persons. It was particularly true a generation ago when girls were kept home, strictly chaperoned, sent off in an arranged marriage, and spent the greater part of their lives in a world dominated by men. These men were not the most caring, empathetic creatures. The result was being dominated and punished as a child, physically abused as a bride, and frequently ignored as an adult homemaker. In numerous interviews, there was a clear feeling of resentment. It is only in the post-reproductive stage of her life that a woman, usually by now secure in her own home and soon to achieve the enviable statuses of mother-in-law and grandmother, comes into her own. It is almost as if she now finds that the husband, usually older and frequently in ill-health, needs her and that the tables have turned. Unfortunately, the cultural prototype was for her to sit back and await old age and death. "Ayas used to look old early;" they also used to act old as they retired into the role of grandmother. In part this was caused by the fact that grandmothers, irrespective of age (or menopausal status) were expected to perform similar roles. Status and role expectation conflicted with relative age. Being "granny" fills a clearly defined niche and is simultaneously a marker of old age. There is nothing beyond it except death. Although it did assure a certain degree of role continuity and continued integration with the family, women in this status awaited the end of life. The generational contrast between the older postmenopausal and the younger premenopausal women is clear. For the younger ones, there is something to life besides their families; and there will be something when the children have left home. This "something" may be a profession, a wider interest generated by a better education, or hobbies and reading. The whole definition of being a woman is expanded. As rigidity decreases and information flow increases (in part through education and the media), women will have a better idea of what to expect and when to expect it. Knowing what to expect allows a woman to know that she is "on time." Menopause and other transitional changes will not be crises and thus not stress-producing.

When we look at role, we see the usefulness of Shirley Angrist's suggestion that, to paraphrase her, roles come in bunches. A woman is never just a woman but at the same time occupies a number of other statuses. Role conflict is certainly possible, but these Indian South African women have clearly differentiated notions of which role is more important and how these roles must be performed. The Indian woman, both in terms of the ideal woman and in terms of role selection, is a homemaker-wife-mother. This is the context for which she was socialized and it is the context in which she finds expression and satisfaction.

A major product of Indian social structure is that most Indian mothers are "Jewish mothers." An Indian woman is socialized to the role of motherhood; she satisfies husband and in-laws by achieving motherhood; and she finds her fulfillment and future insurance in practicing motherhood. It is in the family that she lives and finds expression. Women in the older cohort used to lose daughters and gain daughters-in-law. The joint family gave some continuity. For younger women, the empty nest was both threat and reality because children marry at an older age and become distanced from the parental home by education, secularization, employment, and residential arrangements. Related to the actual experiences of families are their expectations. Discussing the generation gap on the American scene, Bengston et al. (1976:255) point out that parents who were reared in an Old World culture frequently have Americanized offspring. This same problem pertains to Indians reared in India or by parents from India who have children socialized to the opportunities and challenges of modern South Africa. The one advantage for women is that role continuity exists. In contrast to their husbands, women change from mothers into grandmothers and continue much the same role. Since the older cohorts were sedentary and essentially housebound, they performed useful roles for their children. The younger ones expected and preferred what Baum and Baum (1980:165) call intimacy at a distance — living close to their children but not with them.

A further very interesting difference between the two cohorts relates to the older women's acceptance of domesticity. Their younger counterparts sought or were involved in activities outside the house, competing in some cases with men. Some of them derived pleasure in doing so. There was in this community a latent resentment toward, perhaps even frustration with, males. It may have been caused by fathers, authority figures who withdrew girls from school and dominated their wives and families. Or a man may have constantly used the threat of his extended family, his mother, and the possibility (among Muslims at least) of divorce or a second wife. This resentment may also have been due to the way in which women were kept in the home. The older women were uneducated, or at least undereducated, and socialized in strict traditional roles. The younger women were not only more secular, they were better educated and qualified and socialized to a wider society. When men treated them as women were treated a generation ago, they resented it and expressed their resentment unequivocally.

There has been a change in roles at the early end of the life cycle that we can expect to continue throughout the lives of Indian South African women. Girls are no longer isolated upon reaching menarche; they are no longer given in marriage as soon as possible; and they no longer automatically become homemakers. Better education, job opportunities, a longer life expectancy, and a change in attitude provide older women with new roles and new expectations. This involves careers, competition with men, and a life expectancy which assures health and strength into the middle and later years. Menopause was not of great importance to the older generation because it did not coincide with the termination of their reproductive careers. It was, however, associated with old age and with the slowdown in physical activity. Among the younger women, one can expect that menopause will continue to be of little importance because sexuality continues, professions and jobs are uninterrupted, and new roles open up that are not affected by biological conditions.

Menstruation is and will continue to be little more than "a monthly bother" to Indian South African women. Menopause will lose most of its mystique as women feel free to discuss it with other women, both older and younger than themselves. In this process menopause will be seen in its true meaning — the end of the reproductive phase of life and the end of menstruation. It will no longer be seen as the end of normal activities and the beginning of old age.

Appendix

EVERYBODY TRUSTS THE STRENGTH OF LENNON DUTCH MEDICINES

Dutch Medicines, Their Prescriptions, Dosage and Use

Description and Dosage of Each Product (Selected)

Borsdruppels. This excellent remedy has won a deservedly high reputation as an effective preparation for most common chest complaints. It loosens and breaks the phlegm, clears the chest and relieves the spasms of coughs, croup and bronchitis in both adults and children.

Adults should take half to one teaspoonful and children fifteen to twenty drops three times daily with water, tea, or honey.

Duiwelsdrek. In cases of nervousness, hysteria, and sleeplessness, this preparation will be found to soothe and calm the nerves. It can also be recommended for flatulence and stomach pains.

Sufficient to cover the point of a penknife should be taken mixed with milk or honey, three times a day.

Haarlemensis. This old and established remedy, discovered and founded in Haarlem in the year 1672, has proved to be very effective for minor kidney and bladder complaints and difficulty in passing urine.

Fifteen drops should be taken in milk at bed-time.

Jamaikagemmer. An excellent remedy for the relief of colic, flatulence, pains in the stomach and indigestion.

The adult dose is five to ten drops in water.

Lewensessens. A famous stomach tonic. For further details consult the literature enclosed with every bottle.

Staaldruppels. For enriching and restoring the blood, especially when there has been a blood loss, and for promoting health and vigour, these drops can be fully recommended. They are excellent for iron-deficiency, which is very common in women, and which is sometimes responsible for that feeling of ill-health and lassitude.

The dose is ten to fifteen drops in a wineglassful of water, three times a day.

Turlington. This old and approved preparation has won a high reputation for the treatment of coughs and other chest complaints.

As it does not mix well with liquids, it should be taken on sugar or mixed with egg-yolk.

The dose is half to one teaspoonful twice or three times a day.

Turlington is also very useful for applying to cuts and minor wounds and sores as it relieves inflammation and promotes healing.

Versterkdruppels. This is an excellent tonic preparation which promotes a feeling of well-being, rectifies digestive upsets, and stimulates the appetite.

Half to one teaspoonful should be taken in a wineglassful of water or wine, three times a day.

Witdulsies. This is a most useful medicine for checking colds and chills and for reducing the temperature in feverish conditions. It will be found beneficial in mild attacks of asthma and fainting conditions.

For colds and chills take half a teaspoonful in a wineglassful of water three times a day.

For asthma and fainting, take one teaspoonful in a wineglassful of water.

References

Abraham, G.E. 1980. Premenstrual tension. *Current Problems in Obstetrics and Gynecology* 3:5–39.

_____. 1982. *How to overcome premenstrual tension*. Torrance, CA: Optimax Corp.

Abrahams, R.G. 1967. *The peoples of Greater Unyamwezi, Tanzania*. Part XVII. London: International African Institute.

Abrahamson, J.H. et al. 1960. Age at Menopause of Urban Zulu Women. *Science* 132:356–57.

Achte, K. 1970. Menopause from the psychiatrists's point of view. *Acta Obstetrica et Gynecologica* 1 Supplement.

Ahmad, K. 1974. *Family life in Islam*. Leicester, U.K.: The Islamic Foundation.

Ammar, H. 1954. *Growing up in an Egyptian village*. London: Routledge and Kegan Ltd.

Amoss, P.T. 1981. Coast Salish elders. In *Other ways of growing old: anthropological perspectives*, P.T. Amoss and S. Harrell, eds., pp. 227–49, Stanford: Stanford University Press.

_____; Harrell, S. 1981. Introduction. In *Other ways of growing old: anthropological perspectives*, P.T. Amoss and S. Harrell, eds. pp. 1–24, Stanford: Stanford University Press.

Amundsen, D.W., and Diers, C.J. 1969. The age of menarche in classical Greece and Rome. *Human Biology* 41:125–31.

_____. 1973. The age of menopause in medieval Europe. *Human Biology* 41:605–12.

Angrist, S. 1972. The study of sex roles. In *Readings on the psychology of women*, J.M. Bardwick, ed. pp. 101–07, New York: Harper and Row, Publishers.

Ashton, H. 1967. *The Basuto*. 2d ed. London: Oxford University Press.

August, H.E. 1956. Psychological aspects of personal adjustment. In *Potentialities of women in the middle years*, I.F. Gross, ed., East Lansing, Michigan: State University Press.

Backman, G. 1948. Die beschleunigte entwicklung der jugend. *Achta Anatomica* 4:421–80.

Badawi, Jamal A. n.d. *The Muslim Woman's dress according to the Qur'an and Sunnah.* London: Ta-Ha Publishers Ltd.

———. 1979. *At-Taharah purity and state of undefilement.* London: FOSIS.

Ballinger, C.B. 1975. Psychiatric Morbidity and the Menopause. *British Medical Journal* 2.

Barnacle, C.H. 1949. Psychiatric implications of the climacteric. *American Practitioner* 4:154–7.

Barr, W. 1975. Problems related to postmenopausal women. *South African Medical Journal* 49:437–39.

Bart, Pauline. 1969. Why women's status changes in middle age: The turns of the social ferris wheel. *Sociological Symposium* (Fall).

———. 1970. Mother Portnoy's complaint. *Transactions* 8.

———. 1972. Depression in middle-aged women. In *Readings on the psychology of women*, J.M. Bardwick, ed. pp. 134–42. New York: Harper and Row, Publishers.

———. 1976. Portnoy's mother's complaint: Depression in middle-aged women. In *The Jewish woman: new perspectives*, E. Koltun. ed. New York: Schocken Books.

———. 1977. The loneliness of the long-distance mother. In *The family*, P.J. Stein, J. Richman, and N. Hannon, eds., pp. 28189. London: Addison-Wesley Publishing Co.

Baum, Martha, and Baum, Rainer C. 1980. *Growing old.* Englewood Cliffs: Prentice Hall.

Becker, Ernest. 1963. Social science and psychiatry. *Antioch Review* 23:353–65.

Becking, P.A.M., and Vida, S.L. 1979. Maatschappelijk werk en de vrouw in de oorgang. In *De Middelbare Leeftijd van de vrouw*, L.J.B. Jaszmann and A.A. Haspels, eds., pp. 211–17. Bunge: Wetenschappelijke Uitgeverij.

Bekker, Johann. 1977. Die Spreektaal van die Indier-Suid-Afrikaners. *Koers* 42:321–29.

Bengtson, Vern L. 1973. *The social psychology of aging.* New York: Bobbs-Merrill Co. Inc.

——— et al. 1975. Modernization, modernity and perceptions of aging. *Journal of Gerontology* 30:688–95.

Bengtson, Vern L., Olander, Edward B., and Haddad, A.A. 1976. The "generation gap" and aging family members: toward a conceptual model. In *Time, roles, and self in old age*, J.F. Gubrium, ed. pp. 237–63, New York: Human Sciences Press.

Benedek, T. 1950. Climacterium: a developmental phase. *Psychoanalytic Quarterly* 19:1–27.

Benet, Sula. 1951. *Song, dance and customs of peasant Poland*. London: Willmer Brothers and Co. Ltd.

_____. 1974. *Abkhasians: The living people of the Caucasus*. New York: Holt, Rinehart, Winston.

_____. 1976. *How to live to be 100: the life-style of the people of the Caucasus*. New York: Dial Press.

Beyene, Yewoubdar. 1984. An Ethnography of Menopause: Menopausal Experience of Mayan Women in a Yucatan Village. Unpublished Ph.D. dissertation. Case Western Reserve University, Cleveland, Ohio.

_____. 1986. Cultural significance and physiological manifestations of menopause: a biocultural analysis. *Culture, Medicine and Psychiatry* 10:47–71.

Beyene, Y. 1989. From Menarche to Menopause. Albany: State University of New York Press.

Bhattacharyya, S. 1953. Religious practices of the Hindus. In *The religion of the Hindus*, K.W. Morgan, ed. pp. 154–205. New York: The Ronald Press Co.

Binstock, R.H. and Shanas, E., eds. 1976. *Handbook of aging and the social sciences*. New York: Van Nostrand Reinhold Co.

Birren, James E. 1960. Principles of research on aging. In *Handbook of aging and the individual psychological and biological aspects*, J.E. Birren, ed. pp. 3–42. Chicago: University of Chicago Press.

_____; Schaie, K.W. 1977. *Handbook of the psychology of aging*. New York: Van Nostrand Reinhold Co.

Blanchard, W. 1958. *Thailand: its people, its society, its culture*. Connecticut: Human Relations Area Files, Inc.

Bojlen, K., and Bentzon, M.W. 1968. The influence of climate and nutrition on age at menarche: a historical review and a modern hypothesis. *Human Biology* 40:68–85.

Borland, D.C. 1978. Research on middle age: an assessment. *Gerontologist* 18:379–86.

Bourque, Susan C., and Warren, K. B. 1981. *Women of the Andes*. Ann Arbor: University of Michigan Press.

Briggs, J. L. 1977. *Symposium on the cultural phenomenology of adulthood and aging*. Cambridge: Harvard University.

Brijbhushan, Jamila. 1980. *Muslim women in Purdah and out of it*. Delhi: Vikas Publishing House.

Brochure. 1981. Golden Jubilee 1931–1981, Andhras in South Africa, Durban.

Brown, D. G. 1958. Sex role development in a changing society. *Psychological Bulletin* 55:232–42.

Brown, G. W. et al. 1975. Social class and psychiatric disturbance among women in an urban population. *Sociology* 9:225–54.

_____; Harris, T. 1978. *Social origins of depression: a study of psychiatric disorders in women*. London: Tavistock Publications.

Brown, Judith K. 1982. Cross-cultural perspectives on middle-aged women. *Current Anthropology* 23:143–48.

Brown, P. E. 1966. The age at menarche. *British Journal of Preventive Social Medicine* 20:15–21.

Brownmiller, S. 1984. *Femininity*. New York: Linden Press.

Buijs, Gina. 1986. Children of the sugar company. Tradition and Change in an Indian Community. In *Growing up in a divided society*, S. Burman and P. Reynolds, eds., pp. 226–47. Johannesburg: Ravan Press.

Burrell, R. J. W., Healy, M. J. R., and Tanner, J. M. 1961. Age at menarche in South African Bantu school girls living in the Transkei Reserve. *Human Biology* 33:250–61.

Chattopadhyaya, H. P. 1970. *Indians in Africa: a socio-economic study*. Calcutta: Bookland Private Ltd.

Chetty, Romila. 1980. The changing family: a study of the Indian family in South Africa. *South African Journal of Sociology* II:26–39.

Chinas, Beverly L. 1973. *The Isthmus Zapotecs: women's roles in cultural context*. New York: Holt, Rinehart and Winston.

Chiriboga, David A. 1982. An examination of life events as possible antecedents to change. *Journal of Gerontology* 37:595–601.

Chodorow, Nancy. 1974. Family structure and feminine personality. In *Women, culture and society*, M. Rosaldo and L. Lamphere, eds., pp. 45–56. Stanford: Stanford University Press.

Clark, M., and Anderson, B. 1967.*Culture and aging: an anthropological study of older Americans.* Springfield: Charles C. Thomas.

Clausen, J.A. 1972. The life course of individuals. In *Aging and society,* vol. 3, a sociology of age stratification, M.W. Riley, M. Johnson, and A. Foner, eds., pp. 457–514. New York: Russell Sage Foundation.

Cobb, S. 1976. Social support as a moderator of life stress. *Psychosomatic Medicine* 38.

Connell, Elizabeth. 1983. Contraceptive Needs for the Middle Years. Paper presented at Symposium Center for Climacteric Studies, University of Florida, March, 1983.

Cooke, D.J. and Greene, J.G. 1981. Types of life events in relation to symptoms at the climacterium. *Journal of Psychosomatic Research* 25:5–11.

Cosminsky, Sheila and Scrimshaw, Mary. 1982. Sex roles and subsistence: a comparative analysis of three Central American communities. In *Sex roles and social change in Native Lower Central American societies,* C. Loveland and F.O. Loveland, eds., pp. 44–69. Chicago: University of Illinois Press.

Counts, Dorothy Ayers. 1982. Comment on Judith K. Brown's cross-cultural perspectives on middle-aged women. *Current Anthropology* 23:149.

Cowgill, D. 1971. A theoretical framework for consideration of data on aging. Paper presented to the Society for Applied Anthropology, Miami.

Cowgill, D. and Holmes, L., eds. 1972. *Aging and modernization.* New York: Appleton-Century-Crofts.

Cox, F. and Mberia, N. 1977. *Aging in a changing village society.* Washington: International Federation on Aging.

Crapanzano, Vincent. 1980. *Tuhami: portrait of a Moroccan.* Chicago: Chicago University Press.

Cruz-Coke, R. 1967. Genetic characteristics of high altitude in Chile. Paper presented at the Meeting of Investigators on Population Biology of Altitude. Nov. 13–17, 1967, Washington, D.C.

Damon, A., Damon, J.T., Reed, R.B., and Valedion, I. 1969. Age at menarche of mothers and daughters, with a note on accuracy of recall. *Human Biology* 41:161–75.

Datan, N., Maoz, B., Antonovsky A. and Wijsenbeek H. 1970. Climacterium in three contexts. *Tropical and Geographical Medicine* 22.

Datan, N., Antonovsky, A., and Maoz, B. 1981. *A time to reap: the middle age of women in five Israeli subcultures.* Baltimore: Johns Hopkins University Press.

Davis, Donna Lee. 1982. Women's status and experience of the menopause in a Newfoundland fishing village. *Maturitas* 4:207-16.

_____. 1983. *Blood and Nerve: An Ethnographic Focus on Menopause.* Social Science Institute. Memorial University of Newfoundland, St. Johns.

de Kock, C. P. 1977*a*. Die waarde van permanensie in die huwelik by Blanke en Indiervroue. Research Findings No. S–N–83. Human Sciences Research Council, Pretoria.

_____. 1977*b*. Huweliksmaat-Seleksie by Indier-Suid-Afrikaners. S–N–82. Human Sciences Research Council, Pretoria.

Denig, Edwin Thompson. 1930. Indian tribes of the Upper Missouri. The Assininboin. J. N. B. Hewitt ed. *Annual Report of the Bureau of American Ethnology 1928-1929.* Washington: Smithsonian Institution.

Derrett, J. D. M. 1963. *Introduction to modern Hindu Law.* Bombay: Oxford University Press.

Desai, N. P. 1960. A history of the South African Hindu Maha Sabha. In *The Hindu heritage in South Africa*, R. S. Nowbath et al., ed. pp. 91-95. Durban: The Hindu Maha Sabha.

de Senarclens, Myriam. 1979. Pain and peri-menopause: some psychosomatic reflections. In *Psychosomatics in peri-menopause*, eds. A. A. Haspels and H. Musaph, pp. 75-82. Lancaster: M. T. P. Press.

de Young, John. 1955. *Village life in modern Thailand.* Berkeley: University of California Press.

Dorsey, J. Owen. Omaha sociology. *Third annual report of the Bureau of American Ethnology, 1881-1882.* Washington: Smithsonian Institution, 1884.

Dotson, Floyd, and Dotson, Lillian O. 1968. *The Indian minority of Zambia, Rhodesia, and Malawi.* New Haven: Yale University Press.

Dougherty, Molly C. 1978. An anthropological perspective on aging and women in the middle years. In *Anthropology of health*, E. E. Bauwens, ed. pp. 167-76. Saint Louis: C. V. Mosby Co.

Dougherty, Molly C. 1982. Comment on Judith K. Brown's cross-cultural perspectives on middle-aged women. *Current Anthropology* 23:149-150.

du Plessis, J. L. 1974. Attitudes toward fertility and family planning among Indians in the Transvaal. Research Finding No. S–N–33. Human Sciences Research Council, Pretoria.

du Toit, Brian M. 1974. *Akuna, a New Guinea village community.* Rotterdam: A.A. Balkema.

_____. 1979. Stress, crisis, and behavior — a South African case. *The Journal of Modern African Studies* 17:117–40.

_____. 1984. Menopause — a cross-cultural perspective. *Midlife Wellness* 1.

_____. 1986. The cultural climacteric in cross-cultural perspective. In*The climacteric in perspective,* M. Notelovitz and P. van Keep, eds., pp. 177–90. Lancaster: MTP Press Ltd.

_____. 1987. Menarche and sexuality among a sample of Black South African schoolgirls. *Social Science and Medicine* 24:561–71.

_____. 1988. Menstruation: Attitudes and experience of Indian South Africans. *Ethnology* XXVII:391–406.

_____. 1990. *Adolescent Drug Use.* Athens: Ohio University Press.

_____, and Suggs, D.N. 1983. Menopause: A sociocultural definition. *Florida Journal of Anthropology* 8:1–23.

Ebihara, May Mayko. 1968. Svay, a Kmer village in Cambodia. Ph.D. dissertation, Columbia University.

Eisdorfer, Carl and Wilke, Frances. 1977. Stress, disease, aging and behavior. In *Handbook of the psychology of aging,* J.E. Birren and K.W. Schaie, eds., pp. 251–75. New York: Van Nostrand, Reinhold Co.

Elam, Yitzchak. 1973. *The social and sexual roles of Homa women.* Manchester: Manchester University Press.

Ellis, Richard W.B. 1950. Age of puberty in the tropics. *British Medical Journal* 1:85–9.

Erasmus, Gerda. 1981. Users of the intra-uterine device in Daveyton. No. S–N–212. Human Sciences Research Council, Pretoria.

Esposito, John L. 1982. *Women in Muslim family law.* New Jersey: Syracuse University Press.

Evans-Pritchard, E.E. 1951. *Kinship and marriage among the Nuer.* London: Oxford University Press.

Eveleth, Phyllis B. 1966. Eruption of permanent dentition and menarche of American children living in the tropics. *Human Biology* 38:60–70.

Featherstone, Mike and Hepworth, Mike. 1985a. The male menopause: lifestyle and sexuality. *Maturitas* 7:235–46.

_____. 1985b. The history of the male menopause, 1848–1936. *Maturitas* 7:249–57.

Fessler, L. 1950. Psychopathology of climacteric depression. *Psychoanalytic Quarterly* 19:28–42.

Flint, Marcha P. 1974. Menarche and menopause of Rajput women. Ph.D. dissertation, City University of New York Graduate Center.

_____. 1975. The menopause: reward or punishment? *Psychosomatics* 16:161.

_____. 1976. Cross-cultural factors that affect age of menopause. In *Consensus in menopause research*, P.A. van Keep, R.B. Greenblatt, and M. Albeauz-Ferret, eds., pp. 73–83. Lancaster: M.T.P. Press.

_____. 1979. Sociology and anthropology of the menopause. In *Female and male climacteric*, P.A. van Keep et al., eds., pp. 1–8. Baltimore: University Park Press.

Fluhmann, D.G. 1958. Menstrual problems of adolescence. Pediatrics Clinics of North America. In *Symposia on gynecological problems*, C.D. Schauffler, ed. pp. 51–62. Philadelphia: Saunders.

Foll, C.V. 1961. The age at menarche in Assam and Burma. *Archives of Diseases in childhood* 36:302–04.

Foner, Nancy. 1984. Age and social change. In *Age and anthropological theory*, D.I. Kertzer and J. Keith, eds., pp. 195–216. Ithaca: Cornell University Press.

Fortes, Meyer. 1966. Introduction. In *The developmental cycle in domestic groups*, J. Goody, ed. pp. 1–14. Cambridge: University Press.

_____. 1984. Age, generation, and social structure. In *Age and anthropological theory*, D.I. Kertzer and J. Keith, eds., pp. 99–122. Ithaca: Cornell University Press.

Frazer, James G. 1954. *The golden bough: a study in magic and religion*. Abridged edition. London: MacMillan & Co. Ltd.

Friscancho, A. Roberto and Baker, Paul T. 1970. Altitude and growth: a study of the pattern of physical growth of a high altitude Peruvian Quechua population. *American Journal of Physical Anthropology* 32: 279–92.

Frisch, R., and McArthur, J. 1974. Menstrual cycles: fatness a determinant of minimum weight for height necessary for their maintenance or onset. *Science* 185:949–51.

_____, Wyshak, G. and Vincent, L. 1980. Delayed menarche and amenorrhea in ballet dancers. *New England Journal of Medicine* 303:17–19.

Fry, C. 1981. Anthropology and dimensions of aging. In *Dimension: aging, culture and health*, C. Fry et al., eds., pp. 1–11. New York: Praeger.

Fuchs, Estelle. 1978. *The second season: life, love and sex for women in the middle years*. Garden City, N.Y.: Anchor Press/Doubleday.

Gallin, Bernard. 1966. *Hsin Hsing, Taiwan: a Chinese village in change*. Berkeley: University of California Press.

Gamst, Frederick C. 1969. *The Qemant: a Pagan-Hebraic Peasantry of Ethiopia*. New York: Holt, Rinehart, and Winston.

Gillion, K.L. 1962. *Fiji's Indian migrants*. Melbourne: Oxford University Press.

Goody, Jack. 1976. Aging in non-industrial societies. In *Handbook of Aging and the social sciences*, R. Binstock and E. Shanas, eds., pp. 117–29. New York: Van Nostrand Reinhold Co.

Gough, Harrison G. 1952. Identifying psychological femininity. *Educational and Psychological Measurements* 12:427–39.

Greene, J.G. 1976. A factor-analytic study of climacteric symptoms. *Journal of Psychosomatic Research* 20.

_____. 1980. Stress at the climacterium: The assessment of symptomotology. In *Stress and anxiety*, I.G. Sarason and C.D. Spielberger, eds., pp. 127–37. New York: Wiley.

_____, and Cooke, D.J. 1980. Life stress and symptoms at the climacterium, *British Journal of Psychiatry* 136:486–91.

Grodin, J.M., Siiteri, P.K. and MacDonald, P.C. 1973. Source of estrogen production in postmenopausal women. *Journal of Clinical Endocrinology and Metabolism* 36:207.

Grunberger, Richard. 1971. *A social history of the third reich*. London: Cox and Wyman Ltd.

Gupta, Giri Raj. 1974. *Marriage, religion and society*. New York: John Wiley & Sons.

Gutmann, D. 1971. Navajo dependency and illness. In *Prediction of life span*, E. Palmore ed. Lexington: Heath.

_____. 1977. The cross-cultural perspective: notes toward a comparative psychology of aging. In *Handbook of the psychology of aging*, J. Birren and K.W. Schaie, eds., pp. 302–26. New York: Van Nostrand Reinhold Co.

————. 1980. Observations on culture and mental health in later life. In *Handbook of mental health and aging*, J. Birren and R. Bruce, eds., pp. 429–47. Englewood Cliffs, N.J.: Prentice Hall, Inc.

Halpern, Joel M. 1958. *A Servian village*. New York: Columbia University Press.

Hammel, Eugene. 1984. Age in the Fortesian coordinates. In *Age and anthropological theory*, D.I. Kertzer and J. Keith, eds., pp. 141–58. Ithaca: Cornell University Press.

Havighurst, R. et al. 1969. *Adjustment to retirement: a cross-national study.* Assen: Van Gorcum.

Held, G.J. 1957. *The Papuas of Waropen*. The Hague: Martinus Nijhoff.

Henderson, John et al. 1971. *Area Handbook for Burma*. Washington, D.C.: Foreign Area Studies Division, U.S. Government Printers.

Hiebert, Paul G. 1981. Old age in a south Indian village. In *Other ways of growing old: anthropological perspectives*, P.T. Amoss and S. Harrell, eds., pp. 211–26. Stanford: Stanford University Press.

Holmes, T.H. and Rahe, R.H. 1967. The social readjustment rating scale. *Journal of Psychosomatic Research* 2:213–18.

Hoyt, Danny R. et al. 1980. Life satisfaction and activity theory: A multidimensional approach. *Journal of Gerontology* 35:935–41.

————, and Creech, J.C. 1983. The life satisfaction index: a methodological and theoretical critique. *Journal of Gerontology* 38:111–16.

Huntingford, G.W.B. 1969. The Southern Nilo-Hamites. Part VIII. London: International African Institute.

Ishwaran, K. 1974. The interdependence of elementary and extended family. In *The family in India — a regional view*, G. Kurian, ed. pp. 163–77. The Hague: Mouton Publishers.

Israel, Sarah. 1959. The onset of menstruation in Indian women. *Journal of Obstetrics and Gynecology of the British Empire* 66:311–16.

Jackson, Linda A. and Cash, T.F. 1985. Components of gender stereotypes: their implications for inferences on stereotypic and nonstereotypic dimensions. *Personality and Social Psychology Bulletin* II:326–44.

Jardine, Andrea F. 1984. Endlovini: A Case Study of a South African Squatter Community. Master's Thesis, University of Florida.

Jaszmann, L. 1978. *De middelbare leeftijd van de man*. Deventer: Van Loghum Slaterus.

Jenks, Albert Ernest. 1905. *The Bontoc Igorot*. Manila: Bureau of Public Printing.

Jithoo, Sabita. 1970. Structure and developmental cycle of the Hindu joint family in Durban. Master's Thesis, University of Natal, Durban.

_____. 1978. Complex households and joint families amongst Indians in Durban. In *Social system and tradition in Southern Africa*, J. Argyle and E. Preston-Whyte, eds., pp. 86–100. Cape Town: Oxford University Press.

Johnson, Shirley M. and Snow, L. F. 1979. What women do not know about the menopause. *The Osteopathic Physician*. February.

Kamat, M., and Kamat, R. 1959. Diet and fecundity in India. Paper presented at the Sixth International Conference on Planned Parenthood, February 1959. New Delhi, India.

Kantero, R. L. and Widholm, O. 1971. The age of menarche in Finnish girls in 1969. *Acta Obstetricia et Gynecologia Scandanavia* vol. 14 Supplement.

Kapadia, K. M. 1966. *Marriage and family in India*. 3rd ed. London: Oxford University Press.

Kark, Emily. 1953. Puberty in South African girls: the menarche in Indian girls of Durban. *South African Journal Clinical Science* 4:23–35.

_____. 1956. Puberty in South African girls: social class in relation to the menarche. *South African Journal of Laboratory and Clinical Medicine* 2:84–88.

Karp, David A., and Yoels, William C. 1982. *Experiencing the life cycle*. Springfield: Charles C. Thomas.

Karsten, R. 1930. De Britsch-Indiers in Suriname. 's-Gravenhage: Martinus Nijhoff.

Kaufert, P. 1982. Anthropology and the menopause: the development of a theoretical framework. *Maturitas* 4:181–93.

_____. 1984. Women and their health in the middle years: a Manitoba project. *Social Science and Medicine* 18:279–81.

_____, and Gilbert, Penny. 1986. Women, menopause, and medicalization. *Culture, Medicine and Psychiatry* 10:7–21.

Keith, Jennie, and Kertzer, David I. 1984. Introduction. In *Age and anthropological theory*, D. I. Kertzer and J. Keith, eds., pp. 19–61. Ithaca: Cornell University Press.

Kennedy, W. 1933. The menarche and menstrual type: notes on 10,000 case records. *Journal of Obstetrics and Gynaecology of the British Empire* 40: 792–804.

Kerns, Virginia. 1983. *Women and the ancestors: Black Carib kinship and ritual.* London: University of Illinois Press.

Kertzer, D., and Madison, O. 1981. Women's age set systems in Africa: the Latuka of southern Sudan. In *Dimensions: aging, culture and health,* C. Fry et al., eds., pp. 109–30. New York: Praeger.

Kessler, Evelyn S. 1976. *Women: an anthropological view.* New York: Holt, Rinehart and Winston.

Kidd, Dudley. 1904. *The essential Kafir.* London: Adam and Charles Black.

Kisch, E.H. 1928. *The sexual life of women and the physiological and hygienic aspects.* New York: Allied Book Co.

Klass, Morton. 1961. *East Indians in Trinidad: a study of cultural persistence.* New York: Columbia University Press.

Kline, Chrysee. 1975. The socialization process in women. *The Gerontologist* 15:486–92.

Kolenda, P.M. 1968. Region, caste and family structure: A comparative study of the Indian 'joint' family. In *Structure and change in Indian society,* M. Singer and B.S. Cohen, eds. Chicago: Aldine Publishing Co.

Kolodny, R.C. 1971. Sexual dysfunction in diabetic females. *Diabetes* 20:557–59.

Kondapi, C. 1951. *Indians Overseas 1838–1949.* New Delhi: Indian Council of World Affairs.

Kralj-Cercek, Lea. 1956. The influence of food, body build, and social origin on the age at menarche. *Human Biology* 28:393–406.

Kuhlen, Raymond G. 1960. Aging and life adjustment. In *Handbook of Aging and the Individual: Psychological and Biological Aspects,* J.E. Birren, ed., pp. 852–97. Chicago: University of Chicago Press.

Kuper, Hilda. 1956a. An ethnographic description of a Hindustani marriage in Durban. *African Studies* 15:1–12.

_____. 1956b. An ethnographic description of a Tamil-Hindu marriage in Durban. *African Studies* 15:1–14.

_____. 1957. An interpretation of Hindu marriages in Durban. *African Studies* 16:221–36.

_____. 1960. *Indian people in Natal.* Durban: University of Natal Press.

Ladner, Joyce A. 1971. *Tomorrow's tomorrow. The Black Woman*. New York: Doubleday & Co. Inc.

La Guerre, John G., ed. 1974. *Calcutta to Caroni: the East Indians of Trinidad*. Port-of-Spain: Longmans Caribbean.

Lalla, B. D. 1960. A review of the work of the South African Hindu Maha Sabha. In *The Hindu Heritage in South Africa*, R. S. Nowbath et al., eds., pp. 107–11. Durban: The Hindu Maha Sabha.

Lauritzen, C., and van Keep, P. A., eds. 1978. Estrogen therapy, the benefits and risks. *Frontiers of Hormone Research* 5:1–25.

Lawrence, J. C. D. 1957. *The Iteso*. London: Oxford University Press.

Leary, P. M. 1969. Nutrition and the menarche. *South African Medical Journal* 5:324–25.

Lee, Marjorie M. C., Chang, K. S. F., and Chang, Mary M. C. 1963. Sexual maturation of Chinese girls in Hong Kong. *Pediatrics* 32:389–98.

Lemu, B. A., and Heeren, F. 1978. *Woman in Islam*. Chesterfield: Derbyshire Print.

Lennon, Mary Clare. 1982. The psychological consequences of menopause: the importance of timing of a life stage event. *Journal of Health and Social Behavior* 23:353–66.

Le Roux, M. M. 1971. Die aanwending van Maatskaplike groepwerk in n psigiatriese hospitaal. Unpublished Master's thesis, University of Pretoria.

Leslie, Charles. 1969. Modern India's ancient medicine. *Trans-action* 46–55, June.

Lewis, J. M. 1974. Patterns of protest among non-western women. In *Configurations*, R. Prince and D. Banner, eds. Toronto: C. D. Heath and Co.

Liang, J., and Warfel, B. 1983. Urbanism and life satisfaction among the aged. *Journal of Gerontology* 38:97–106.

Lock, Margaret. 1985. Models and practice in medicine: menopause as syndrome or life transition. In *Physicians of western medicine*, R. A. Hahn and A. D. Gaines, eds., pp. 115–39. Boston: D. Reidel Publishing Co.

_____. 1986a. Introduction. *Culture, Medicine and Psychiatry* 10:1–5.

_____. 1986b. Ambiguities of aging: Japanese experience and perceptions of menopause. *Culture, Medicine and Psychiatry* 10:23–46.

Lott, Bernice. 1981. A feminist critique of androgyny: toward the elimination of gender attributions for learned behavior. In *Gender and nonverbal behavior,* C. Mayo and N.M. Henley, eds., pp. 171–80. New York: Springer-Verlag.

Lotter, J.M. and van Tonder, J.L. 1975*a*. Infantiele mortaliteitstendense en oorsake van dood by Blankes, Kleurlinge en Asiers in Suid-Afrika-n Orientasie. Report no. S–N–46. Human Sciences Research Council, Pretoria.

―――. 1975*b*. Aspects of fertility of Indian South Africans. Report no. S–40. Human Sciences Research Council, Pretoria.

Lynn, D.B. 1966. The process of learning parental and sex-role identification. *Journal of Marriage and the Family* 23:446–70.

―――. 1969. *Parental and sex role identification: a theoretical formulation.* Berkeley: McCutchan.

―――. 1974. The Father: His Role in Child Development. Monterey: Wadsworth.

MacMahon, B., and Worcester, J. U.S. Department of Health Education, Welfare, 1966. *Age at Menopause, United States — 1960–1962.* Public Health Service, National Center for Health Statistics, Series 11, no. 19, Washington, D.C.: Government Printing Office.

MacPhaile, A.P. et al. 1981. Iron nutrition in Indian women at different ages. *South African Medical Journal* 59:939–42.

Maday, Bela C. et al. 1965. Area Handbook for Malaysia and Singapore. Washington, D.C.: Foreign Area Studies Division, Government Printing Office.

Maddox, G. and Wiley, J. 1976. Scope, concepts and methods in the study of aging. In *Handbook of aging and the social sciences,* R. Binstock and E. Shanas, eds., pp. 3–34. New York: Van Nostrand Reinhold Co.

Madhaven, Shanta. 1965. Age at menarche of South Indian girls belonging to the states of Madras and Kerala. *Indian Journal of Medical Research* 53:669–73.

Maher, Vanessa. 1978. Women and social change in Morocco. In *Women in the Muslim world,* L. Beck and M. Keddie, Eds., pp. 100–23. London: Harvard University Press.

Malcolm, L.A. 1970. *Growth and development in New Guinea: a study of the Bundi people of the Madang district.* Institute of Human Biology Madang, Monograph Series 1.

―――. 1976. Growth and development patterns and human differentiation in Papua New Guinea communities. In *Youth in a changing world,* E. Fuchs, ed., pp. 65–77. The Hague: Mouton Publishers.

Malleson, J. 1956. Climacteric stress: its empirical management. *Medical Journal* 2:1422.

Mandelbaum, D. G. 1974. Human fertility in India: Social Components and Policy Perspectives. Berkeley: University of California Press.

Maoz, B. 1973. The Perception of Menopause in Five Ethnic Groups in Israel. Master's Thesis, Leyden University.

_____. et al. 1978. The effect of outside work on the menopausal woman. *Maturitas* 1.

_____ and Durst, N. 1979. Psychology of the menopause. In *Female & male climacteric*, P. A. van Keep, D. M. Serr and R. B. Greenblatt, eds., Baltimore: University Park Press.

Maresh, M. M. 1972. A fifty-five year investigation of secular changes in physical maturation. *American Journal of Physical Anthropology* 36:103–10.

Martin, E. 1987. The woman in the body. Boston: Beacon Press.

Masters, William H., Johnson, Virginia E., and Kolodny, Robert C. 1988. *Human sexuality* 3rd ed. Boston: Scott, Foresman & Co.

Maududi, Abul A'la. 1974. *Birth control, its social, political, economic, moral and religious aspects*. Lahore: Islamic Publications Ltd.

Mayat, Zuleikha. 1981. *Nanima's chest*. Durban: Robprint Ltd.

Mayer, Adrian C. 1960. *Caste and kinship in Central India*. London: Routledge & Kegan Paul.

_____. 1961. *Peasants in the Pacific: a study of Fiji Indian rural society*. Berkeley: University of California Press.

McCarron, D. A. 1982. Low serum concentrations of ionized calcium in patients with hypertension. *New England Journal of Medicine* 307(226).

_____, et al. 1981. Dietary calcium profiles in normal and hypertensive humans. *Clinical Research* 29(267).

McCranie, E. J. 1974. Psychodynamics of the menopause. In *The menopausal syndrome*, R. B. Greenblatt, V. B. Mahesh, P. G. McDonough, eds., New York: Medcom Press.

McDonald, Gordon C. et al. 1973. Area Handbook for Yugoslavia. Washington, D. C.: Foreign Area Studies Division, Government Printing Office.

McElroy, Ann. 1975. Canadian Arctic modernization and change in female Inuit role identification. *American Ethnologist* 2:662–86.

McKinlay, Sonja and McKinlay, J. 1985. *Health status and health care utilization by menopausal women*. New York: Plenum Publishing Co.

McKinlay, Sonja, Jefferys, Margot, and Thompson, Barbara. 1972. An investigation of the age at menopause. *Journal of Biosocial Science* 4:161–73.

Mead, Margaret. 1935. *Sex and temperament in three primitive societies*. New York: Dell Publishing Co. Inc.

Meer, Fatima. 1969. *A portrait of Indian South Africans*. Durban: Premier Press.

———. 1976. *Race and suicide in South Africa*. London: Routledge and Kegan Paul.

Meer, Y. S., ed. 1980. *Documents of Indentured Labour. Natal 1851–1917*. Durban: Institute of Black Research.

Meyer, M. M. 1979. Die taak van die maatskaplike werk ten opsigte van geestesgesondheid. Unpublished Master's thesis, University of Orange Free State.

Michelson, N. 1944. Studies in physical development of Negroes. *American Journal of Physical Anthropology* 2:151–66.

Miller, P. and Ingham, J. G. 1976. Friends, confidants, and symptoms. *Social Psychiatry* 2.

Mills, C. A. 1937. Geographic and time variations in body growth and age at menarche. *Human Biology* 9:43–56.

Minai, Naila. 1981. *Women in Islam: tradition and transition in the Middle East*. New York: Seaview Books.

Mistry, S. D. 1965. Ethnic groups of Indians in South Africa. *South African Medical Journal* 39:691–94.

Moore, B. 1981. Climacteric symptoms in an African community. *Maturitas* 3:25–29.

Mostert, W. P. 1981. Fertiliteit van Asiers in Suid Afrika: n Demografiese ontleding. Report S–N–229. Human Sciences Research Council, Pretoria.

Mukherjee, C. 1954. Premenstrual tension: A critical study of the syndrome. *Journal of the Indian Medical Association* 24.

Murphy, Yolanda and Murphy, Robert F. 1974. *Women of the forest*. New York: Columbia University Press.

Myerhoff, Barbara. 1978. *Number our days*. New York: Simon and Schuster.

Naidoo, R. S. 1979. The Telugu language and literature. *Leader* (Durban) 12 January 1979.

Neugarten, B. L. 1970. Adaptation and the life cycle. *Journal of Geriatric Psychiatry* 4:71–100.

_____. 1977. Personality and aging. In *Handbook of the psychology of aging,* J. E. Birren and K. W. Schaie, eds., pp. 626–49. New York: Van Nostrand Reinhold Co.

_____. and Datan, N. 1973. Sociological perspectives on the life cycle. In *Life-Span Developmental Psychology: Personality and Socialization,* P. B. Baltes and K. W. Schaie, eds., pp. 53–69. New York: Academic Press.

_____. Havighurst, R. J., and Tobin, S. S. 1961. The measurement of life satisfaction. *Journal of Gerontology* 16:134–43.

_____. and Kraines, R. J. 1965. 'Menopausal symptoms' in women of various ages. *Psychosomatic Medicine* 27:266.

_____. et al. 1963. Women's attitude toward the menopause. *Vita Humana* 6:140–51.

Newcomer, N. W. 1973. A Study of Menarcheal and Menopausal Ages in a Micronesian Population. Unpublished Master's thesis, Pennsylvania State University.

Nukunya, J. K. 1969. *Kinship and marriage among the Anlo Ewe.* New York: Humanities Press, Inc.

Nydegger, Corinne N. 1981. Gerontology and anthropology: challenge and opportunity. In *Dimensions: aging, culture, and health,* C. Fry et al., eds., pp. 293–302. New York: Praeger.

Oosthuizen, G. C. 1975. *Pentecostal penetration into the Indian community in metropolitan Durban, South Africa.* Human Sciences Research Council, Series no. 52, Durban: Interprint.

Osako, M. 1979. Aging and family among Japanese Americans. *The Gerontologist* 19:448–55.

Osgood, Cornelius. 1951. *The Koreans and their culture.* New York: The Ronald Press Co.

Pachai, B. 1971. *The international aspects of the South African Indian question 1860–1971.* Cape Town: C. Struik Ltd.

Palanpuri, Muhammed. 1980. *Al-Hadiyyato Linnisa. Islamic laws regarding purity for women.* Johannesburg: Jet Printers.

Palmore, E. and Manton, K. 1974. Modernization and status of the aged: international correlations. *Journal of Gerontology* 29:205–10.

Pastner, Carroll McC. 1978. The status of women and property on a Baluchistan Oasis in Pakistan. In *Women in the Muslim world*, L. Beck and N. Kedie, eds., pp. 434–50. London: Harvard University Press.

Polit, D. and LaRocco, S. 1980. Social and psychological correlates of menopausal symptoms. *Psychosomatic Medicine* 42.

Potts, M. 1979. Discussion on sterilization and abortion in middle age. In *Fertility in middle age*, A. S. Parkes, M. A. Herbertson, and Jane Cole, eds., pp. 157–62. Supplement no. 6, *Journal of Biosocial Science*.

Rajah, D. S. 1980. An Analysis of the Family Status Dimension among the Indian Population of Durban, South Africa: An Experiment in Urban Factorial Ecology. Ph. D. dissertation, Clark University.

Ramasar, P. 1966. Emerging social problems among the Indian people of South Africa. The Indian South African. Papers presented at a conference held under the auspices of the South African Institute of Race Relations, Durban.

Rambiriteh, B. nd. A Hindi-Speaking Hindu Marriage. An Ethnographic Description. Manuscript in Documentation Centre University of Durban-Westville.

Reichel-Dolmatoff, G. and A. 1966. *The People of Aritama: the cultural personality of a Colombian Mestizo village.* Chicago: University of Chicago Press.

Report of the Director-General for Health and Welfare for the year 1984. Pretoria: Government Printer.

Riley, Matilda White. 1984. Foreword. In *Age and anthropological theory*, D. Kertzer and J. Keith, eds., pp. 7–10. Ithaca: Cornell University Press.

———; Johnson, M. and Foner, A., eds. 1972. *Aging and society*, vol. 3, A sociology of age stratification. New York: Russell Sage Foundation.

Roberts, D. F., Rozner, L. M. and Swan, A. V. 1971. Age at menarche, physique and environment in industrial northeast England. *Acta Paediatricia Scandinavia* 60:158–64.

Roberts, George W., and Sinclair, Sonja A. 1978. *Women in Jamaica.* Millwood, N. J.: K. T. O. Press.

Rogers, C. J. and Gallion, T. 1978. Characteristics of elderly Pueblo Indians in New Mexico. *The Gerontologist* 18:482–87.

Rosenmayr, L. 1968. Family relations of the elderly. *Journal of Marriage and the Family* 30:672–80.

Rosenthal, L. N. 1977. The definition of female sexuality and the status of women among the Gujerati-speaking Indians of Johannesburg. In *The anthropology of the body*, J. Blacking, ed., pp. 199–210. New York: Academic Press.

Ross, A. D. 1971. Changing aspirations and roles: middle and upper class Indian women enter the business world. In *Family and Social Change in Modern India*, G. R. Gupta, ed., pp. 103–32. Durham: Carolina Academic Press.

Ross, M. 1951. Psychosomatic approach to the climacterium. *California Medicine* 74:240–42.

Roy, Manisha. 1975. *Bengali women*. Chicago: University of Chicago Press.

Ryff, C. D. 1982. Successful aging: a developmental approach. *Gerontologist* 22:209–14.

Saunders, Margaret O. 1980. Women's role in a Muslim house town. (Mirria, Republic of Niger) In *A World of Women*, E. Bourguignon, ed. New York: Praeger Publishers.

Schalk, Adolph. 1971. *The Germans*. Englewood-Cliffs, N. J.: Prentice-Hall Inc.

Schapera, Isaac. 1941. *Married life in an African tribe*. Evanston: Northwestern University Press.

Schultz, J. et al. 1968. *Old people in three industrial societies*. New York: Atherton Press.

Schwartz, D. 1982. Female fecundity as a function of age. *New England Journal of Medicine* 306:404–06.

Shah, A. M. 1974. *The household dimension of the family in India*. Berkeley: University of California Press.

Shanas, Ethel et al. 1968. *Old People in Three Industrial Societies*. New York: Atherton Press.

Sharma, V. K. and Saxena, M. S. L. 1981. Climacteric symptoms: A study in the Indian context. *Maturitas* 3.

Shelton, A. 1965. Ibo aging and eldership. *Gerontologist* 5:20–23.

_____. 1968. Igbo child-raising, eldership and dependence. *Gerontologist* 8:236–41.

Sherman, B. M., J. H. West and S. G. Korenman. 1976. The menopausal transition: Analysis of LH, FSH, Estradiol and Progesterone concentrations during menstrual cycles of older women. *Journal of Clinical Endo-crinology and Metabolism.*

Silverman, Sydel F. 1975. The life crisis as a clue to social function: The case of Italy. In *Toward an anthropology of women*, R.R. Reiter, ed., pp. 309–21. New York: Monthly Review Press.

Simmons, L. 1945. *The role of the aged in primitive societies.* New Haven: Yale University Press.

Simon, A. 1968. Emotional problems of women: The mature years and beyond. *Psychosomatics* 9, Section 2.

Sinnott, J.D. 1977. Sex-role inconsistency, biology and successful aging. *Gerontologist* 17:459–63.

Skultans, Vieda. 1970. The symbolic significance of the menstruation and the menopause. *Man* New Series, 15:639–51.

Snow, Loudell F. and Johnson, Shirley M. 1977a. Modern day menstrual folklore. *Journal of the American Medical Association* 237:2736–39.

_____. 1977b. Myths about menstruation: victims of our own folklore. *International Journal of Women's Studies* 1:64–72.

_____, and Mayhew, Harry E. 1978. The behavioral implications of some old wives' tales. *Obstetrics and Gynecology* 51:727–32.

Soffan, Linda Usra. 1980. *The women of the United Arab Emirates.* London: Croom Helm.

Sohar, E., and Rieber, E. 1960. *The age of menarche in girls of the differnt Jewish communities in Israel. Harefuah* 59:303–05.

Stearns, Peter N. 1976. *Old age in European society.* New York: Holmes & Meier Publishers.

Stein, William W. 1961. *Hualcan: Life in the Highlands of Peru.* Ithaca: Cornell University Press.

Stenning, Derrick J. 1960. *Savannah nomads.* London: Oxford University Press.

Stern, K. and Prados, M. 1946. Personality studies in menopausal women. *American Journal of Psychiatry* 103:358.

Steward, Julian H., Manners, Robert A., et al. 1956. *The people of Puerto Rico.* Urbana: University of Illinois Press.

Stopes, M.C. 1936. *Change of life in men and women.* London: Putnam Publishers.

Suggs, David N. 1986. Climacteric among the "New" Women of Mochudi, Botswana. Unpublished Ph. D. dissertation, University of Florida.

_____. 1987. Female status and role transition in the Tswana life cycle. *Ethnology* 26:107–20.

_____, and du Toit, Brian M. 1983. Thinking about menopause: age, attitude and experience of American women. *Florida Journal of Anthropology* 8:37–49.

Tanner, J. M. 1962. *Growth at adolescence.* 2nd ed. Oxford: Blackwell Scientific Publications.

_____. 1966. The secular trend towards earlier menarche. *Tijdschrift voor Sociale Geneeskunde* 44:524–39.

Tapper, Nancy. 1978. The women's subsociety among the Shahsevan Nomads of Iran. In *Women in the Muslim world*, L. Beck and N. Keddie, eds., pp. 374–98. London: Harvard University Press.

Taylor, C. E. 1976. The place of indigenous medical practitioners in the modernization of health services. In *Asian medical systems*, C. Leslie, ed., pp. 285–99. Berkeley: University of California Press

The Lancet. Editoria "Research on the menopause". London, 17 July, 1982, p. 137.

Theron, E. S. 1983. Women's health clinics. *South African Medical Journal* 64:286.

Theron, F. 1987. *Contraception. Theory and practice.* Cape Town: Academica.

Tibbits, C. 1960. *Handbook of social gerontology: societal aspects of aging.* Chicago: University of Chicago Press.

Trigg, Elwood B. 1973. *Gypsy demons and divinities.* Secaucus, N. J.: Citadel Press.

Unger, Rhoda. 1979. *Female and male psychological perspectives.* New York: Harper & Row.

Usui, Wayne M. et al. 1983. Determinants of life satisfaction: a note on a race-interaction hypothesis. *Journal of Gerontology* 38:107–10.

Utian, Wulf H. 1980. *Menopause in modern perspective.* New York: Appleton-Century-Crofts.

Valsik, J. A. 1965. *The seasonal rhythm of menarche: A review. Human Biology* 37:75–90.

van Gennep, Arnold. 1960. *The rites of passage*. Translated by Monika B. Vizedom and Gabrielle L. Caffee. Chicago: University of Chicago Press.

van Keep, P. A. and Haspels, A. A. 1977. *Estrogen therapy during the climacteric and afterwards*. Amsterdam: Excerpta Medica.

_____. and Kellerhals, J. 1973. The aging women: aging and estrogens. *Frontiers of Hormone Research* 2:160–173.

_____. and Humphrey, M. 1976. Psycho-social aspects of the climacteric. In *Consensus on Menopause Research*, P. A. van Keep, R. B. Greenblatt, and M. Albeaur-Ferret, eds., pp. 5–8. Lancaster: M. T. P. Press Ltd.

Vermeulen, A. 1976. The hormonal activity of the post-menopausal ovary. *Journal of Clinical Endocrinology and Metabolism* 42:247.

Viljoen, Stephen. 1936. *The economics of primitive peoples*. London: P. S. King & Son.

Voda, Ann M. 1981. Climacteric hot flash. *Maturitas* 3:73–90.

_____. 1982. Menopausal hot flash. In *Changing perspectives on menopause*, A. M. Voda, M. Dinnerstein, and S. R. O'Donnell, eds., pp. 136–59. Austin: University of Texas Press.

Wagner, Gunter. 1960. The Abaluyia of Kavirondo (Kenya). *In African Worlds: Studies in the Cosmological Ideas and Social Values of African Peoples*, D. Forde, ed., pp. 27–54. Oxford: Oxford University Press.

Walfish, S., Antonovsky, A. and Maoz, B. 1984. Relationship between biological changes and symptoms and health behavior during the climacteric. *Maturitas* 6:9–17.

Walpole, Norman C. et al. 1965. U. S. Army Area Handbook for Algeria. Washington, D. C.: Foreign Area Studies Division, Government Printing Office.

Ware, Helen. 1979. Social influences on fertility at later ages of reproduction. In *Fertility in middle age*, A. S. Parkes, M. A. Herbertson, and J. Cole, eds., pp. 75–96. Supplement no. 6, Journal of Biosocial Science. London: Spottiswoode Ballantyne Ltd.

Warner, W. Lloyd. 1958. *A Black civilization*. New York: Harper and Bros.

Weir, M. A., Dunn, J. E., and Jones, E. G. 1971. Race and age at menarche. *American Journal of Obstetrics and Gynecology* 4:594–96.

Wentz, A. 1976. Psychiatric morbidity and the menopause. *Annal of Internal Medicine* 84.

White, Priscilla. 1960. Childhood diabetes — its course and influence on the second and third generations. *Diabetes* 9:345-55.

Wilson, Dagmar C. and Sutherland, Ian. 1950. Age at the menarche. *British Medical Journal* 1:1267.

_____. 1953. The age of the menarche in the tropics. *British Medical Journal* 2:607-08.

Winter, Edward H. n.d. *Bwamba*. Cambridge: W. Heffer and Sons Ltd.

Wyon, J.B., Finner, S.L., and Gordon, J.E. 1966. Differential age at menopause in the rural Punjab, India. *Population Index* 32.

Young, F.W., and Backdayan, A. 1965. Menstrual taboos and social rigidity. *Ethnology* 4:225-40.

Zacharias, Leona and Wurtman, Richard J. 1969. Age at Menarche. *The New England Journal of Medicine* 280:868-75.

Author Index

Subject Index

A

Abha, *see also* Punjabi dress

Abortion: Defined, 224; not allowed by Muslims, 165; not structured according to group membership, 166; possible reaction to unwanted pregnancy, 207; seen as sin by Muslims, 225; justification for, 226; received overseas, 226. *See also* Back street abortions

Abortion and Sterilization Act (Act 2 of 1975), 224

Achieved statuses, 145

Acquisition of knowledge, 261. *See also* Socialization; Education

Adoption: 93–94; does not produce natural bond, 108; possible action for unwanted pregnancy, 165

Adultery: legal grounds for annulment, 63

Aerobics: as exercise, 132

African societies: climacteric role expansion, 5

Afrikaans: use of derogatory term, 18; as home language, 21, 22

Age: acquiring new roles, 130

Age stratification: and roles and statuses, 85

Aging: sociological, 4; psychological, 4; as process, 10; cross-cultural, 11; generational, 84–85; produces fears, 96

Agwa, 59

Ajma, 214

Alcohol abuse: by husbands, 42, 161, 178, 188; by son, 95

Al-haiz, 206

Ama, 88

American Indians: and aging, 87

American women: climacteric role loss, 5

Anaemia: and menstruation, 258

Andhra Maha Sabha, 21

Andhra Pradesh, 49

An-nifas, 206

Anovulation: and climacteric, 88; and menarche, 241

Anticipated role changes, 269

Anticipatory socialization: and timeliness of the event, 260; and knowledge acquisition, 261–63; and menopause, 277; and absence of, 291. *See also* Socialization

Arabic: and vernacular school (Madressa), 60

Argumentative: husband, 195

Arranged marriage, 171

Arthritis: and middle-age, 94, 185; and postmenopausal women, 194; and men, 186

Aryan: as ethnic category in Indian subcontinent, 16

Ascribed statuses, 145

Asiatic Bazaar, 178

Asthma: family health problems, 190

Astrologer: and family planning, 192

Attitude index: administered in American city, 28; adapted for cross-cultural use, 28

Attraction: dress, decoration and behavior, 194

Attractive: ideal beauty, 115